Beyond the Teacup: 18th Century Sino-British Tea Trade and Design Cultural Exchange

Chi Zhang

Beyond the Teacup: 18th Century Sino-British Tea Trade and Design Cultural Exchange

palgrave
macmillan

Chi Zhang
School of Fashion Accessory
Beijing Institute of Fashion Technology
Beijing, China

ISBN 978-981-97-7690-0 ISBN 978-981-97-7691-7 (eBook)
https://doi.org/10.1007/978-981-97-7691-7

Jointly published with Shanghai People's Fine Arts Publishing House
Translation from the Chinese language edition: "茶杯里的想象：18世纪中英茶叶贸易与设计文化交流" by Chi Zhang, © Shanghai People's Fine Arts Publishing House 2022. Published by Shanghai People's Fine Arts Publishing House. All Rights Reserved.

This Palgrave Macmillan imprint is published by the registered company Springer Nature Singapore Pte Ltd.
The registered company address is: 152 Beach Road, #21-01/04 Gateway East, Singapore 189721, Singapore

This book is dedicated to my grandmother, aunt, and my mother.

Foreword

Historical Imagination and Writing

10 years ago, I met Zhang Chi in my office at the Central Academy of Fine Arts when she graduated from Kingston University. She was wearing a round black felt hat, black wide-framed glasses, a bright red velvet blouse, and a black velvet shawl: a typical London Oxford Street style. In my eyes her dresses represented a perfect example of Chinese culture reshaped by British fashion. Coming back to China, how would she bridge the gulf between these two cultures?

4 years after that, she submitted her doctoral thesis, *Tea Culture Infused into a Century of Design History between China and Britain*; in this year, she has upgraded her thesis into a book titled *Imagination in the Teacup: 18th Century Sino-British Tea Trade and Design Cultural Exchange*, which is going to be published by Shanghai People's Fine Arts Publishing House. I'm delighted to see the imagination in this title, and it opens up a new inter-discipline field of cultural history.

The proposition is extensive and has ample room for further research and development. While Zhang asked me to write a preface for her, I'm in fact an outsider to "tea affairs." So I would humbly offer this essay to express my congratulations, and to share some hopes for the future of design-specific research in Chinese historical contexts.

Zhang didn't write this book by accident. Early when she was at Kingston University, studying under Prof. Catherine Mcdermott, she had noticed that British scholars in design history paid great attention to the clues of the cultural interactions between china at the UK in their early trade. At the same time, Prof. Catherine Mcdermott strongly supported her in discovering relevant topics of early design exchanges between China and the UK. However, significant obstacles still remained in doing specialized research in design history.

Firstly, conventional literature searching in the UK did not provide sufficient research findings. The UK tops the world in the research of modern history, modern art history, and modern design history from any perspective; nevertheless, there are no research concerning the historical forms, processes, and structures of early Sino-British design exchanges. This is not surprising, as Britain transformed its "importing" civilization into "exporting" civilization in the eighteenth century, during the Industrial Revolution; with its technological, trade, and economic strength being pushed to the top of Europe and the globe, as exemplified by the saying, "Wherever the sun rises and sets, there is our nation's flag."[1] The Empire on which the sun never sets became the symbol of modern imperial system. Since then, the civilization of the British Empire has basically been synonymous with the export of industrial civilization, technological civilization, and political civilization. So it is rare to find the research materials, clues, and achievements related to the import of exotic civilizations, not to say Chinese tea culture and its design history. Under such a scarcity, a researcher has to face both external and internal obstacles. To some extent, the topic of "imagination in a teacup" is a way to construct an open research about design history across Atlantic, in the form of case study and all by herself. "Open" means that she needs to overcome at least two theoretical barriers: logical understanding and mindset understanding. The former refers to a series of epistemological dialectics regarding whether the design value of "tea affairs" exists: such as what creative activities can be considered as "design," "what is design subject," and "what historical forms can be listed as design history forms." And the latter is what supports the former: it is whether to include non-professional, folk, commercial, production, and consumption into the investigation of "design history." It takes a new form of objectivity to conduct such a historical thematic study, that's why I call it "open form of design history research." That is to say, by treating the object as a more general and collection-like historical materials, one can obtain more specific, real, and

[1] Li Yimin, *The Construction of the British Empire*, from Chen Duxiu - edited *Youth Magazine*, Volume 1, Issue 1, published February 1916; Shanghai Century Publishing Company, Ltd., 2011 publication of *New Youth*, issues 1 to 6, pages 1–644.

knowledge-oriented understanding of history. So that the scope of design history will expand and the book becomes more "secular" than average books of design history. Needless to say, it takes great courage to explore and sketch out this understanding from the vast history. In this regard, Zhang has taken a rather difficult but valuable step.

In the 1960s, American sociologist Wright Mills proposed the concept of "sociological imagination" while promoting his ideas of sociological transformation. He believed that sociology should focus on human diversity, which constitutes all human societies in the past, present, and future. In these societies, there are vast villages, children's organizations, and Navajo oil craftsman; there are metropolitan areas where the air force prepares for strikes within a hundred-mile radius; there are street police, intimate social circles, and strangers gathering in the same room; there are criminal groups; there are crowds swarming at crossroads in major cities at night; there are Hopi children and Arab slave traders; there are various political parties in Germany, social classes in Poland, and Mennonites (a Protestant sect originated from the Netherlands in the sixteenth century); there are mental disorders on plateaus and radio networks spreading around the world; various racial and ethnic groups mixing together while segregating in movie theaters; sweet but abhorrent marriages; and on business, industry, government, grassroots organizations, and all the countries, there are millions of divided fields, with millions of small but delicate trades occurring every day. Human diversity also includes individual diversity, which must be grasped and understood through imagination. In imagination, Brahmins stood together with Illinois pioneers in 1850; eighteenth-century British gentlemen stood side by side with Australian Aborigines; there are Chinese peasants from 100 years ago, contemporary Bolivian politicians, feudal French knights, English feminists on 1914 hunger strike, rising stars in Hollywood, and ancient-Roman nobleman.[2]

Mills advocates here for a more specific, in-depth, and comprehensive perspective on the social realities within the historical context, in order to understand history more diversely and return to the historical reality that may be obscured by rigid misunderstandings. To recognize human diversity, we need to maintain a long-term and close connection with the levels of historical reality and its meaning for individuals. Our goal is to

[2] C. Wright Mills. *The Sociological Imagination*[M]. Chen Qiang, Zhang Yongqiang, trans. Beijing: Life, Reading, New Knowledge Sanlian Bookstore, 2001: 146–147.

identify this reality and discern its meaning; only then can we sort through the issues of classical social science and discover the topics and concerns contained therein.[3]

The generation and development of design are deeply embedded in specific, complex, and diverse social life; but for the history of design, we are accustomed to cut it off from rich social life, such as daily market transactions, seafaring exchanges, and cultural plunder. As a result, design history became a surface history, stylistic history, and tool history that only has results without causes. Although this makes sense, it is a stylized interpretation that never enters real life. Mills's "social imagination" calls for legitimacy and inclusiveness, which incorporates the diversity of social life and the richness of individual experience into sociology. I believe this is also the freshness we expect from topics like "Imaginations in a Teacup." Although the topic of "Chinese and British Tea Affairs in a Hundred Years of Design History" is too large for such a limited research case, and it's too early to form a mature and complete understanding and explanatory framework, the formation of such a research outlook is worth expecting.

Finally, I would like to fix my post-reading impression on the "Oxford Street style" leftover ten years ago: round hat and black overcoat. I'm wondering, incorporating living experiences in the British Isles into Sino-British design culture history, is this what "social imagination" envisioned for this era?

School of Design
Central Academy of Fine Arts
Beijing, China

Ping Xu

[3] Same as footnote 2, p. 148.

Contents

List of Figures

CHAPTER 1

Introduction

This is a photo taken on a bustling street in downtown London, with the center storefront featuring the famous British tea shop Twinings Tea and the Twinings Tea Museum, with a history of over 300 years (Fig. 1.1). The front of this store is decorated with two statues of men in Qing Dynasty with long braids. For over 300 years, people have been walking on by, getting used, and turning a blind eye to them. Few would be interested in the history behind, not to say the relationship between the statues and the brand.

Tea has been flowing from China to the UK since the seventeenth century and is one of the earliest globalized commodities, as well as a key that led to social transformation in both the East and the West in modern times. Although a small leaf, tea has already been well-developed 1000 years ago as a traditional Chinese culture and consumer product. Drinking tea is not only about tasting the soup brewed, but also about enjoying a culture and experiencing an authentic, Chinese lifestyle, which cannot be separated from design. The process of tea being introduced from China to the UK is precisely the process of the typical Chinese lifestyle and Chinese design being introduced to the UK, impacting on the local culture and design of the later. At the same time, as tea entered the UK, a large number of exported tea sets came as well. In addition to typical ceramic tea sets, there were also a large amount of furniture and interior decorations.

C. Zhang, *Beyond the Teacup: 18th Century Sino-British Tea Trade and Design Cultural Exchange*,
https://doi.org/10.1007/978-981-97-7691-7_1

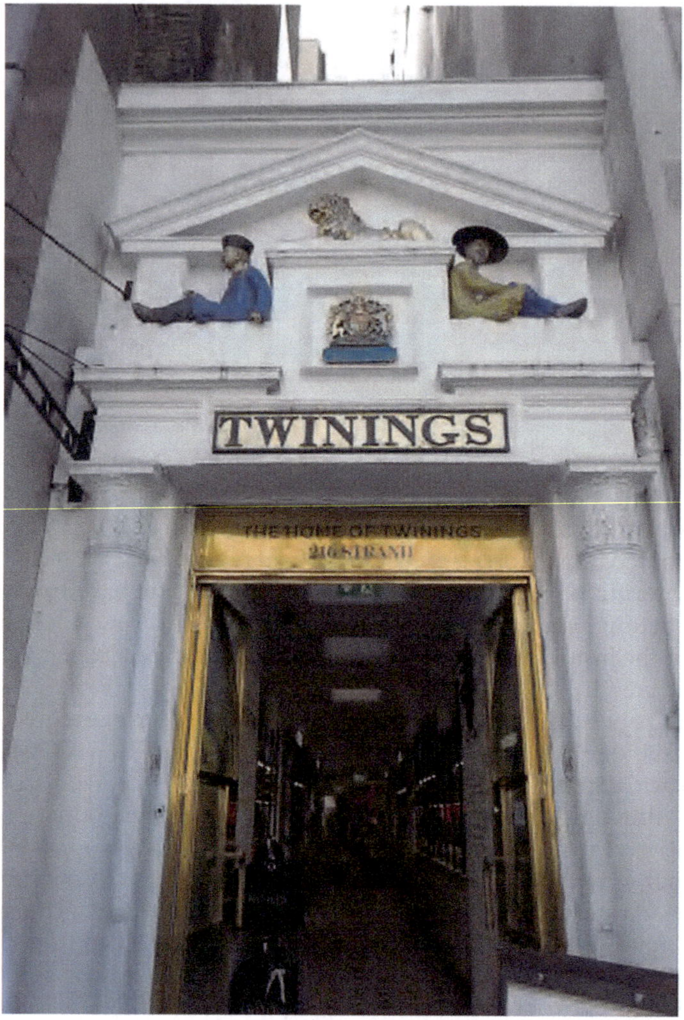

Fig. 1.1 The Twinings Tea Museum by the street in London, with a brand history of 300 years. (Photographed by Li leren)

The British regard tea drinking as a wise Eastern way of life, and they hope to enjoy tea in the most authentic way possible. This process has quietly changed the dietary habits, social habits, and aesthetic taste of the British, and also profoundly influenced related industries.

Against the backdrop of the British consumer revolution, Chinese tea and tea utensils entered the realm of popular culture from the aristocratic circles of Britain. Behind this process are mass production, large-scale processing, and the development of related industries. Firstly, in the face of the challenges of mass production, large scale, and "unique styles, no fixed sample" posed by the overseas market, the Chinese tea and porcelain industry has adopted strategies such as refining processing, constructing flexible and integrated production organization, and adjusting industrial layout. As a result, the Canton porcelain emerged with both Eastern and Western aesthetics. Secondly, when a large amount of Chinese tea entered the UK, the ceramic industry took it as an opportunity, imitating the patterns, shapes, and production organization of Chinese tea porcelain, and becoming an emerging industry in the first industrial revolution through mechanization and innovation. In addition to ceramic, there were also silver tea sets and tea furniture spreading Eastern aesthetics, which unconsciously infiltrated Chinese culture into British aesthetics, thereby comprehensively influencing the lives of British people.

For a long time, when it comes to the relationship between Chinese and British culture or the relationship between Chinese and British design, the academic community has usually focused more on how China could learn from Britain and how Chinese design is influenced by British design in the process of modern design development. Britain is a representative of strong Western culture, and its industrial and design culture continues to be exported to China, continuously exerting influence. However, we have overlooked that earlier and in a long period of time, it was actually China that influenced the West, including design. However, just like the two Qing Dynasty-shaped statues on the storefronts of Twinings, these details have been buried history and forgotten for a long time.

In fact, the development of design is a diverse and complex process with rich connotations and forms. The material and cultural exchange between countries through trade and travel includes communication, integration, and innovation in the field of design. Due to the long-standing dominance of Western centrism in design history, when it comes to the design exchange between China and the UK, the academic community usually focuses on the impact of modern British design. They would view the Industrial Revolution as the beginning of design history, and the research object as the design of industrialized products. However, if seen from a broader perspective, the exchange of design had already existed before Industrial Revolution, especially the export of Eastern design. This is not a one-way output, but interactive and circulating flow, playing an important role in shaping the mass consumption and daily life.

As argued by American cultural scholar Ralph Linton, there is no distinction between what is considered secular and elegant. Culture refers to all ways of life in any society, not just the elegant and delighting ones. Activities such as washing dishes and driving can be culture as well. That is to say, culture is anything that relates to human survival and living. Nevertheless, design is the creative activity that changes, enhances, updates, and develops existing things. It is the process of conceptualizing and solving problems, and involves all purposeful activities that create values.[1] The responsibility of design is to create and reflect meaning in the context of daily life.[2] It can be concluded that culture is a way of life, and design is the act and process of creating this way of life. So, design is closely related to not only life, but also the development of culture. The culture of design is in fact the culture of life, and, as the anthropologist Zhang Guangzhi believes, one of the shortest cut to the core of a culture is through people's stomach.

In February 2018, Teresa May visited China. President Xi and the First Lady Peng Liyuan served her tea in Diaoyutai State Guesthouse. This was an event of profound significance, for tea is one of the earliest media of contact between the two countries and a common language between the two nations.

Tracing back, there was no tea in Britain before the seventeenth century. Tea flowed to Britain in the seventeenth century, becoming one of the earliest globalized commodities, and a key factor leading to the social transformation in both the East and the West. Related to it were ceramics as tea sets. Behind the British lifestyle revolution triggered by tea there is a clue of design, with a long and far-reaching impact. Since tea was first introduced to Britain in the seventeenth century, this clue has been influencing the lives of both countries. It can be concluded that the influence and integration of cultures have never been one way or liner, but rather mutual.

Trade was the main communication between China and Britain before the Opium War, and tea was the largest commodity from the early

[1] Li Yanzu. 'The Cultural Identity of Design'[J]. *Journal of Nanjing Arts Institute*, 2007(3): 15.

[2] Penny Sparks. *An Introduction to Design and Culture* [M]. Qian Fenggen, et al., trans. Nanjing: Yilin Press, 2012: 11.

seventeenth century to 1833, dominated by the East India Company. Tea trade accumulated huge wealth for the company as well as British government, accounting for over 70% of total trade volume, peaking 80%~90% from the late eighteenth century to early nineteenth century. And the profit from tea trade with China accounted for about 10% of the total revenue of British treasure, which was almost the entire profit of the East India Company. Since the climate in the UK is not suitable for growing tea, the UK government sent a delegation to China, seeking free trade with China to ensure tea supply. However, China was an agricultural society that was cut off from the outside world, and didn't need any foreign trade. The delegation was refused, foreshadowing the later Opium War.

After that, Britain stole tea from China and successfully transplanted it into India, causing Chinese tea to be abandoned by British merchants. Seeing from the global perspective, the Sino-British tea trade in the eighteenth century revealed the quirkiness of history: while the influence of Chinese tea on Britain was largely positive, China itself was more of being robbed and invaded, falling behind the other parts of the world.

The transition of tea from a stranger to a national beverage of the UK can be regarded as cultural reshaping and reconstruction. Anthropologist Igor Kopytoff believes that biographies of things can bring to light the ambiguous. And cultural exchange can prove a point often emphasized by anthropologists: in the process of accepting foreign goods, what is important is not the process, but the way they are redefined and put into use in the new culture, just as accepting foreign ideas. From a cultural perspective, the global spread of Chinese tea since the mid-seventeenth century has not only been related to maritime trade, capital flow, and changes in daily habits in Europe (represented by Britain), but more importantly, in forming a global trade network, a local product leaves its home and is reshaped in another context to gain new cultural significance.

In this way, the introduction of tea to the UK actually reflects the introduction of Chinese lifestyle and design, and their integration with British culture. Brodell held that, to bring tea to Europe, there are four things that are indispensable: tea, teapot, porcelain teacup, and drinking hobby. Without any of them the innate charm of tea will fade.[3] When British tea culture began to form, people were basically imitating and being fascinated

[3] Fernand Braudel. *Material Civilization, Economics, and Capitalism from the 15th to the 18th Century*[M]. Gu Liang, Shi Kangqiang, trans. Beijing: Life, Reading, New Knowledge Sanlian Bookstore, 1996: 293–294.

by Chinese way of drinking, the use of tea utensils, and the arrangement of tea spaces. Along with tea, there were also a large amount of tea sets, furniture, and interior decorations. As a result, British ways of eating, socializing, and aesthetics were changed subconsciously, industries were boosted, and politics in both countries were changed as well.

Another angle is the changes in how British view China and Chinese culture. From the final result, the localization of tea in the UK and the sophistication of British tea culture synchronized with the expansion of the UK from a small island to an empire. At almost the same time, China, once accounted for one-third of world's GDP, degraded into a semi-feudal, semi-colonial society. Nevertheless, it is undeniable that Chinese culture has subtly influenced Britain in every aspect of life.

Nowadays, both countries boast tea as their national identity. Researchers are studying their respective tea cultures in various levels and angles. However, few scholars have touched upon issues including "What impact did tea have on the British lifestyle?", "How can design help tea enter British society and help build this new way of life?", and "What impact has the tea trade had on Chinese design as the production end?" These are exactly the objectives of this book. In short, this book aims to explore the role of design in cultural dissemination and formation, with tea as the medium.

CHAPTER 2

The Westward Transmission of Chinese Tea Culture Driven by Business Interest

1 The Image of Civilization

Tea originated in China. In the *Species Plantarum* published in 1753, Carl von linne, a Swedish scientist, set the scientific name of tea as Tea Sinesis, L.,[1] and later adjusted it to Camellia Sinesis l. The word "Sinesis" in this context precisely means "China" in Latin.[2]

The history of tea in China can be traced back to Zhou Dynasty, the earliest in the world. The tea sage Lu Yu recorded in *The Classic of Tea* that "tea originated from Shennong and gained popularity under Duke Zhou of Lu."[3] This indicates that tea appeared in China almost as early as agriculture. And in *Erya Shimu*, a chapter of *The Book of Songs*, there is a line that goes: "Cardamon, bitter tea." Tea was first discovered as a medicine. There was a story that goes: "when Shen Nong tasted hundreds of herbs, he encountered 72 poisons a day, and was de-toxicated by tea." Later in Western Han Dynasty, tea emerged as a daily beverage. In the book *Tong Yue* written by Wang Bao, there are historical materials such as "tea has been cooked and clean utensils have been ready," and "buying tea in Wuyang County." Wuyang here refers to Shuangjiang Town, Pengshan

[1] Gang Fu. *Tea Culture*[M]. Beijing: China Economic Publishing House, 1995: 3.

[2] Robert Finlay. *The Story of Blue and White Porcelain*[M]. Zheng Mingxuan, trans. Haikou: Hainan Publishing House, 2015: 143.

[3] Lu Yu, Lu Tingcan. *The Classic of Tea*. Beijing: China Friendship Publishing House, 2005: 28.

C. Zhang, *Beyond the Teacup: 18th Century Sino-British Tea Trade and Design Cultural Exchange*,
https://doi.org/10.1007/978-981-97-7691-7_2

County, in Sichuan Province. This indicates that was already a commodity on market. Then in Jin Dynasty, Sun Chu wrote in *Chuge*: "ginger, cinnamon, tea and coarse tea came from Bashu (two ancient cities in Sichuan)."[4] All these indicate that tea was originated in southwest China, Sichuan and Yunnan Province, and migrations caused by war have spread tea to other parts of the country. Gu Yanwu, a scholar in Qing Dynasty, recorded in his *Rizhi Lu* that "the practice of drinking tea was since the Qin Dynasty took Shu."[5] From Han to the Southern and Northern Dynasties, tea drinking spread to eastern China, south of the Yangtze River. But the way of drinking was still crude, tea brewing was basically cooking vegetable soup.

Then, in Wei and Jin Dynasties, tea was endowed with cultural and symbolic significance. Intellectuals and officials used tea to boast about frugality. According to the Book of *the Revival of the Jin Dynasty*, "at that time, General Xie An of Wei planned to Visit Lu Na, the prefecture chief in Wuxing as well as a famous tea practitioner. The nephew of Lu Na knew that he wasn't prepared but didn't dare to ask his uncle, so he prepared the meal for dozens of people. When Xie An came to Lu Na, Lu Na only served simple fruit tea, while the nephew hosted Xie An with a luxurious banquet. Later when Xie An left, Lu Na beat his nephew with a stick for 40 times and said: 'Since you can't benefit your uncle, how can you defile my frugality?'"

Guo Pu, a literary figure from the Lin Dynasties, explained in his annotation of *Erya* in *the Book of Songs*: the tree is small like a gardenia, which can be boiled and consumed as soup. Today, it is called "tea" in the morning and "Ming" in the evening; another name is "well," refers to a bitter tea in Sichuan.[6] In this age, tea drinking was described as "foam sinking and floating, shining like snow."[7] It gained favor from the upper class during the Southern and Northern Dynasties, forming a cultural trend with

[4] Sun Ji. *The Holy Fire of China - Some Issues in the Exchange of Ancient Chinese Cultural Relics with the East and the West*[M]. Shenyang: Liaoning Education Publishing House, 1996: 295.

[5] Same as 1, page 10.

[6] Same as 3, page 28.

[7] From Du Yu's "Chuan Fu" during the Jin Dynasty. "Chuan Fu" is the earliest tea poetry and prose work in China, using "沫沉华浮, 焕如积雪" to describe the artistic beauty of tea soup. It means that when the tea is just boiled, the foam sinks down while the delicate and light tea leaves float up, shining bright like glistening snow, magnificent and splendid like flourishing spring flowers.

certain influence. At the same time, tea utensils were differentiated from food utensils and became specialized. But tea was more popular in the south than in the north. When it moves to Tang Dynasty, Lu Yu wrote *the Classic of Tea*, consisting of three volumes and ten categories, with clear and detailed regulations on the production, processing, boiling, drinking, utensils, and the allusions and legends of tea. The book is seen as a milestone, marking the refinement of Chinese tea culture. As a result, Lu Yu is revered as the "tea saint." Just like the poem of Mei Yaochen in Song Dynasty, "Since Lu Yu was born, people have been devoted to learning to produce spring tea." This is how tea drinking became popular throughout the country.

Tea began to be exported during the Western Han Dynasty, and initially arrived in neighboring countries such as Japan and Southeast Asia. In 475, Turkish arrived at the Mongolian border to barter tea. In early Tang Dynasty, Chang'an was the cultural and economic center of the world, both the Central Plains and northwestern ethnic groups had the custom of drinking tea. Therefore, some believed that tea had already spread to Central, West, and Southwest Asia in the seventh century, but there's no firm written proof. Later in the Southern Song Dynasty, Arab, Jewish, Italian, Japanese, Indian, and other merchants engaged in trade with China. Quanzhou in Fujian Province, southeast China, became an overseas transportation hub, with tea from Fujian was exported in large quantities. During Ming Dynasty, the famous Zheng He's voyages to the West further promoted tea export. Chen Chuan believes that the import of tea into Southeast Asia is a prelude to China's tea trade with the West.[8]

European's earliest impression of tea came from the missionaries and merchants who traveled across the Eurasian continent. They got to know and drink tea in its original cultural context, and transmitted its knowledge back to their homeland through text. It can be said that their understandings of tea laid the foundation of European's, including British's understanding.

Among the currently known European literature, tea was first mentioned in 1559, in *Navigational et Viaggis* by Venetian Writer Giambattista Ramusio. Ramusio has had conversations with many famous travelers, and it is said that he has edited Marco Polo's travelogues. In the preface of the second volume of the book, he wrote that an Arab businessman named

[8] Chen Chuan. *A General History of Tea*[M]. Beijing: China Industry Press, 1982: 12.

Haji Monammad told him that there was a Chinese herb "Chiai Catai." Whether dried or in a fresh state, this mysterious herb can be brewed with hot water to relieve headaches and discomfort in stomach. And that this herb was a necessity in Chinese life, it was so valuable that Arab merchant were even willing to exchange a sack of Revend Cini for an ounce of tea. Mohammad believed that if Persian or European merchants had tasted tea, they would definitely give up rhubarb for tea. In the sixteenth century, Venice was a major transportation hub and commercial center between Asia and Europe. Marco Polo's experience in the East sparked the curiosity of scholars and merchants, and they would hold banquets for the explorers and businessmen from the East to know more and seek more trade opportunities. It was in the banquet that Ramusio first heard of tea.

Portuguese missionary Gasper da Gruz was the first Catholic missionary to come to China. He came to East in about 1540, spent 20 years in India, Malaysia, and China, and had been in Macao for several months. When he returned to Lisbon in 1560, he wrote the book *Tratado das cousas da China*. It was based on his own experience combined with the book *China Report* by Galeote Pereira, the first Portuguese that went to China in the sixteenth century.[9] In *Tratado das cousas da China* he detailed the lifestyle, customs, and natural environment of China, and mentioned that he often drank tea. He also introduced the social and medical uses of tea in Chinese background. The first English version was translated by Samuel Perchas; he emphasized one paragraph: "When decent people receive guests, the best porcelain cup at home is presented and a drink called teal is poured. This drink is slightly bitter with a dark red color, and it can cure diseases." According to his description, this should be oolong tea. The author also wrote about his own story: "Regardless of strangers or acquaintances, they will serve you a cup of tea as long as you're respected. I myself have been treated like this for many times."[10] In his description, China was an abundant country and "was extremely rich in food and all the necessities," leaving a deep impression on European readers.

[9] [British] Raymond Dawson. *Chameleon in the Dragon's Den: An Analysis of Europe's View of Chinese Civilization* [M]. Translated by Chang Shaomin and Mingyi. Beijing: Zhonghua Book Company, 2006: 35–36.

[10] [British] Markman Ellis, Richard Coulton, and Matthew Mogg. *Tea Empire: The Transformation of a World by a Blade of Grass* [M]. Translated by Gaoling Ya and Xu Bo. Beijing: China Youtong Book Company, 2020: 19.

Charles Ralph Boxer, the author of *South China in the Sixteen Century*, later commented that although most people believed that Jesuit writers were the first to bring China to Europe, it was Cruz that first observed Chinese' life and customs. *On Things in China*, along with *The Relationship of Fr. Martin De Rada* by another missionary, Fr. Martin de Eada became the basic material for Juan Gonsales deMendoza's *Historia de Gran Renio de la China*. This encyclopedia history book was published in 1585, providing a comprehensive introduction to China's natural environment, history, culture, customs, etiquette, religious beliefs, politics, and economy. It became a must read for the Europeans who want to know China, and Francis Bacon had read it as well. By the end of the sixteenth century, the book had been published in 30 versions, translated into all the major European languages.

Matteo Ricci, an Italian Jesuit missionary who lived in China for 28 years, translated Confucian classics and published them in Europe. He detailed in his book the tea-drinking habits in the cities he had been, the role tea played in family life, the price of tea, and the comparison of tea production between China and Japan.

There is a shrub whose leaves can be fried into a famous beverage called tea (cia) by Chinese, Japanese, and their neighbors. I guess Chinese haven't drunk it for too long because there are no ancient characters in their books that represent this beverage, while their calligraphic symbol can be very old. However, it is also possible that the same plants are found on our own land. They pick tea leaves in spring, dry them in a cool place, and brew them in hot water during meals or guests' visiting. In such occasions, hosts and guests would keep drinking as long as they are having conversations. Tea requires sipping instead of swigging, and is always consumed hot. It doesn't taste so nice but slightly bitter instead. It's considered healthy even when drunk in large amount.[11]

This book made a great impact when introduced in Europe and is the most important among the early tea literature. Although the author somehow misunderstood the history, production, and preservation of tea, he detailed the tea-drinking habits of Chinese at that time in a more in-depth way than the previous ones. This book has given European a glimpse of not only tea but also the reality in contemporary China. The articles in the books are mostly epistolary, translated and published in 1615 by Belgian

[11] [Italian] Matteo Ricci, Giacomo Ruggieri. *Matteo Ricci's Notes on China*[M]. Translated by He Gaoji, et al. Beijing: Zhonghua Book Company, 1983: 17.

Sinologist Nicolas Trigault, Named *De Christiana Expeditione apud Sinas*, it is a relatively complete work by European that describes China.

The knowledge of tea aroused the curiosity of local writers, whose re-editing and reprinting contributed to the wider dissemination of tea. Italian writer Giovanni Maffei's *Four Books of Selected Letters from India* was published in 1588 in Florence, reprinting records about tea. In 1589, Venetian pastor Giovanni Botero mentioned tea in *On the Causes Greatness in Cities*. He said that Chinese would extract juice from a herb as an alternative to alcohol, and it helps to maintain health, prevent diseases and the harm of alcohol. Later in 1610, the Portuguese book *An Account of the Kings of Persia and Ormus* introduced tea as a leaf from China. And the Italian book *The History of the Great and Renowned Empire of China* published in 1643 contained various narratives related to tea. Its English version was published in London in 1655, becoming one of the earliest guides for Britain to learn about tea and China.

In the UK, the earliest recorded literature on Tea was published in 1598, titled *lohn Huighen van Linschoten: His Discourse of Voyages into the East &West Indies*. Lohn Huighen van Linschoten was a Dutch businessman and explorer; he served as the secretary of the Archbishop of Portuguese Goa on the island of Gua in India from1583 to 1587. In this book, he introduced the customs, traditions, as well as various commodities in the Asian market in an all-round way, including tea and porcelain.

It can be said that these travel stories by folk merchants and missionaries have opened a window for Europe to understand China, and their understanding of China synchronized with their understanding of tea. Before the eighteenth century, China had been powerful and wealthy in European's mind, and tea, as a representative beverage, carried and presented Eastern culture. During Enlightenment period, tea was recognized by elites and rising middle class as an Eastern cultural image. Hugh Honour, a contemporary British Sinologist, believes that the Dutch East India Company may not have dared to buy tea without the seductive descriptions in those fascinating travelogues.[12] Although these may not be entirely authentic, or may only be simple fragments, they underpinned the popularity of tea after the seventeenth century.

[12] [British] Hugh Aung. *Chinese Style: The Lost Elements of China in the West for 800 Years* [M]. Translated by Liu Aiying, et al. Beijing: Peking University Press, 2017: 61.

2 The Contribution of Dutch

According to existing record, it was Portugal, the leader of the Age of Discovery in the fifteenth and sixteenth centuries, that first introduced tea to Europe. The Governor General of India appointed by the Portuguese monarch conquered Malacca in 1511 and arrived in Guangdong a few years later. In 1557, they were permitted by the Ming government to trade in Macau, turning the later into a trade base of Far East. Since then, Portuguese merchant ships sail to Europe via the perilous Maritime Silk Road with a dazzling array of goods. The goods include Europeans' beloved spices, a small amount of silk, porcelain, tea, and decorations. While they were the forerunner who brought tea to Europe, their contribution to tea was quite limited.

The real credit goes to the Netherlands, the maritime hegemon in the seventeenth century. At the beginning of the Age of Discovery, the hegemony of trade shifted between Portugal, Spain, and the Netherlands. In 1580, son of Emperor Charles V of the Holy Roman Empire, King Philip II of Spain, annexed Portugal. The trade between Spain and the East Indies was organized, managed, and supervised by the Council of the Indies, established in Seville in 1511. Lisbon, the capital of Portugal, was a major trading hub for Far Eastern goods in Europe at the time. Merchants from other European countries, including the Dutch, often stocked up here and then resold their goods in other countries. However, in 1579, the Dutch, led by King William I of the Orange dynasty, broke away from the rule of the Holy Roman Empire and founded the Dutch Republic.

Calvinism was welcomed in this new nation, but King Philip II of Spain was a devout Catholic who opposed Protestantism. In order to assert control and seek revenge, he decreed in 1594 to prohibit Dutch ships using Portuguese ports, which forced the Dutch and the British to seek alternative solutions. The following year, wealthy merchants from both Britain and the Netherlands joined forces, conspiring to find a way to trade directly with the places of origin. Ultimately, the British East India Company and the Dutch East India Company were, respectively, established in 1600 and 1602.

However, it was not going to be easy for everyone. The Portuguese had spent centuries building a relatively mature system for overseas trade. They had established their own posts and fort at key points along these trade routes to provide safe harbors for ships to dock, repair, and resupply. The East India Company of the UK and the Netherlands, on the other hand, had to drift at sea longer, and more likely to encounter risks. While it was unlikely to take the fortress of Portugal by force, it was possible to attack Portuguese's merchant ships to gain profit. In this way they effectively weakened Portugal's influence at sea, and they once again affirmed that the sea route to the East was the path to wealth. The money plundered from Portuguese's merchant ships helped the East India Company of both countries to accumulate capital to counter Portugal.

Although established slightly later than the British East India Company, the Dutch East India Company took control of the ocean in the seventeenth century. The fund it raised at its inception was ten times larger than that of British East India Company, and its organization was more advanced as well: they gathered about 6.5 million Dutch guilders and the company was managed as a limited liability system. The time horizon of the investment was fixed as ten years, and could only be withdrawn when the period ends. And new investors could only join during the general liquidation when the ten-year period ends. This system ensured the long-term stable operation of the company. They set up commercial centers and branches in East India, and sent permanent personnel, so that they could buy goods for storage when prices dropped, and ship them to Europe to maximize profit.[13] Such modernity of the company enabled Holland to lord it over on the sea during the entire seventeenth century. By 1699, the company had at least 150 merchant ships, 40 warships, and a permanent army of 10,000 under its name.

Thomas Short recorded the beginning of the Sino-Dutch tea trade in *A Dissertation upon Tea*: "When the Dutch made their second voyage to China, they brought along well-stored dried sedge to exchange for Chinese tea. The Chinese exchanged 3 pounds or 4 pounds of tea for 1 pound of sedge - they called it 'wonderful European grass'...Europeans could not export sedge in large quantities like they imported tea, so they purchased tea in China at a price of 8 pence per pound or 10 pence per pound."[14] (Note: 1 pound = 0.907 jin). William Milburn also confirms this view in his book *Oriental Commerce*, crediting the Dutch East India Company with being the first to add tea to their list of commodities.

[13] [Japanese] Asada Maru. *The East India Company: The Rise and Fall of a Colossal Business Capital*[M]. Translated by Gu Shanshan. Beijing: Social Sciences Literature Press, 2016: 12.

[14] Thomas Short, *A Dissertation Upon Tea: Explaining Its Nature and Properties by Many Experiments, and Demonstrating from Philosophical Principles, the Various Effects It Was on Different Constitutions, to Which Is Added the Natural History of Tea*, W. Bowyer, London, 1730, p. 12.

In 1619, the Netherlands occupied Batavia (now Jakarta, Indonesia), which became the trading and colonial center in Asia. Since Ming government wasn't interested in overseas trade, the Netherlands was unable to trade directly with China, but indirectly through the medium of Batavia. In 1637, the board of directors of the East India Company found an opportunity and wrote to Anthony van Diemen, the governor of the company in Jakarta, saying: "Since some of us have already had the habit of drinking tea, we hope that all returning ships can bring a few cans of Chinese and Japanese tea."[15] In less than 15 years, tea became a regular imported commodity with a certain sales volume, and began to retail in Paris, London, and cities in the Netherlands. However, the scale of tea trade was relatively small for a long period of time. In 1650, Dutch merchant ships only carried 30 pounds of tea; in fact, the amount of tea didn't grow much until 1677. Later in 1684, Qing government lifted the sea ban, facilitating the rapid growth of Sino-Dutch tea trade. In 1685, the board of directors of the Dutch East India Company requested the Dutch Governor General in India to provide 20,000 pounds of tea. As Milburn observed, from the beginning of tea trade to the end of the seventeenth century, Europe had been always bought tea from the Netherlands.

In the travel record of Dutch Jan Huygen van Linschoten, the author not only introduced the social conventions and customs of Asia in an all-round way, but also recorded the land and sea routes and precautions to Asia.[16] The following year after the publication of the book, the Dutch fleet bypassed the Cape of Good Hope and arrived in India, breaking Portugal's monopoly on marine trade with Asia. The rich profit contained in the trade with East stimulated the establishment of the Dutch East India Company in 1602. The Dutch set up a commercial center in Japan and brought back a small amount of tea in 1609; however, it was in February 1610 that tea first arrived in Amsterdam as commodity.[17] Swiss

[15] Same as footnote 10, p. 19.

[16] [French] Patrice Valfré. *Yixing Teapots Sold to Europe*[M]. Translated by Shi Yunqiao. Hangzhou: Xiling Seal Society Publishing House, 2015: 23.

[17] Another viewpoint is that as early as 1517, when the first Portuguese ship arrived in China, the Portuguese sailors on board brought Chinese tea back to their homeland (Wang Jingyu: "On the Foreign Trade of Tea and the Modernization of the Tea Industry in Modern China," "Modern History Research," Issue 6, 1987). In their ignorance of tea, the Portuguese referred to it as "hay water" (Hay Water) (Wang Jingyu: "On the Relationship between the Dutch East India Company and Independent Merchants and Other Issues of Chinese Modern Economic History Research", Chinese Modern Economic History

naturalist G. Bukin also believed that it was Dutch that first shipped tea from China and Japan to Europe in the early seventeenth century.[18]

As the European tea market gradually took shape, criticism about Dutch merchants began to spread. It was believed that French Jesuit missionary Alexandre de Rhodes was the first: he lived in Macau in 1630s and had been preaching in the Far East for 25 years. He published two books about his experience in the East. To make Dutch understand the benefits of learning and trading with China, he mentioned tea: "French learned about tea through Dutch agents. Unfortunately, most of this imported tea is aged tea that has lost its fragrance. It sells 30 francs per pound in Paris, while only bought at 8–10 sors (Peruvian currency) in China. Think how much money the Dutch has earned." He thought that French was "helping" Netherlands to become the most powerful country in the world by allowing them to trade with East India in France. Another French scholar Melchisedech Thevenot held the same point, believing Dutch was selling sage leaves as tea to make huge profit.[19]

Despite prejudices against the Dutch, Alexandre presented an early European experience in China, and the process of his getting to know about tea. "In China tea is so common…Someone even drinks 10 or 12 times a day; in other words, they're drinking all day long." He also described the production of tea, including picking, frying, and storage. He even summarized a tea purchasing guide: "To judge the quality of tea one needs to observe carefully: see if it's green and bitter enough, and dry enough to be crushed by fingers." He also detailed how Chinese prepared tea: "they boil water in a particularly clean container, and when large bubbles start to appear, they remove the water from the stove and put the leaves in. the amount of the leaves depends on the volume of water." From his experience we can also learn about the philosophical and religion connotation of tea: he believed that the refreshment of tea was a blessing for Jesuit missionaries, as they need to stay up late to listen to the repentance of those who visit at night.[20]

Research Materials (10), Shanghai Academy of Social Sciences Press, 1990). The Portuguese were not aware of the commercial value of tea, and there is no evidence to suggest that they engaged in tea trade.

[18] [British] *William Ukers. All About Tea*[M]. Translated by Nuo Jia, Liu Tao, Jiang Haidi. Shanghai: East Press, 2001: 25–26.

[19] Same as footnote 10, p. 24.

[20] Same as footnote 16, p. 24.

Another trace of Chinese tea spreading to Holland is the Dutch envoy. While Portugal was dominating in Eurasian relations, the Dutch East India Company's commercial routes to Guangzhou were restricted. So the Dutch decided to have an audience with Emperor Shunzhi for the right of free trade. In the 1650s, two Dutch ambassadors, Peter de Goyer and Jacob de Keyzer, set out from Guangzhou to Beijing, with a small team of attendants and interpreters. They finally made it to meet the Emperor on 3rd September, but only achieved limited results. The details of this visit were recorded by the manager Johan Nieuhof, and compiled into an Embassy sent by the East India Company of the United Provinces to the Grand Tartar Cham or Emperor of China (see Fig. 2.1). The book introduced at length the history, geography, scenery, architecture, customs, costumes, etiquette, and other aspects of Qing Empire in the seventeenth century, accompanied by prints. And Nihoff talked in depth about the role tea played in the highly hierarchical upper class. He wrote that the mission always started with drinking tea when communicating with the governors, all the way to Beijing. A print in the book depicts the scene of the envoy drinking tea in Chinese court. He wrote:

> The emperor's seat was about 30 paces away from the ambassadors, and his throne was inlaid with gold and gems, shining brilliantly: the ambassadors could barely see the emperor himself, perhaps only a glimpse of his face. Close to the emperor sat his ministers, princes, and other high court officials, all holding wooden cups and drinking hot tea, with the tea being continuously refilled... They added a handful of tea to clean water, then boiled it until a third of the water had evaporated, and then added milk, leaving about a quarter of the remaining water volume, along with a little salt, and drank it while hot.[21]

During their stay in China, missionaries like Alexandre became accustomed to the local way of drinking tea. When understanding its usage, they not only saw tea as an exotic beverage and Eastern medicine, but also incorporated it into their original lifestyles.

While tea was not a consumption in Europe yet (silk and spices were the largest commodities), missionaries and merchants had already begun the experimental consumption of tea, and transmitted the related information

[21] Same as footnote 10, p. 27.

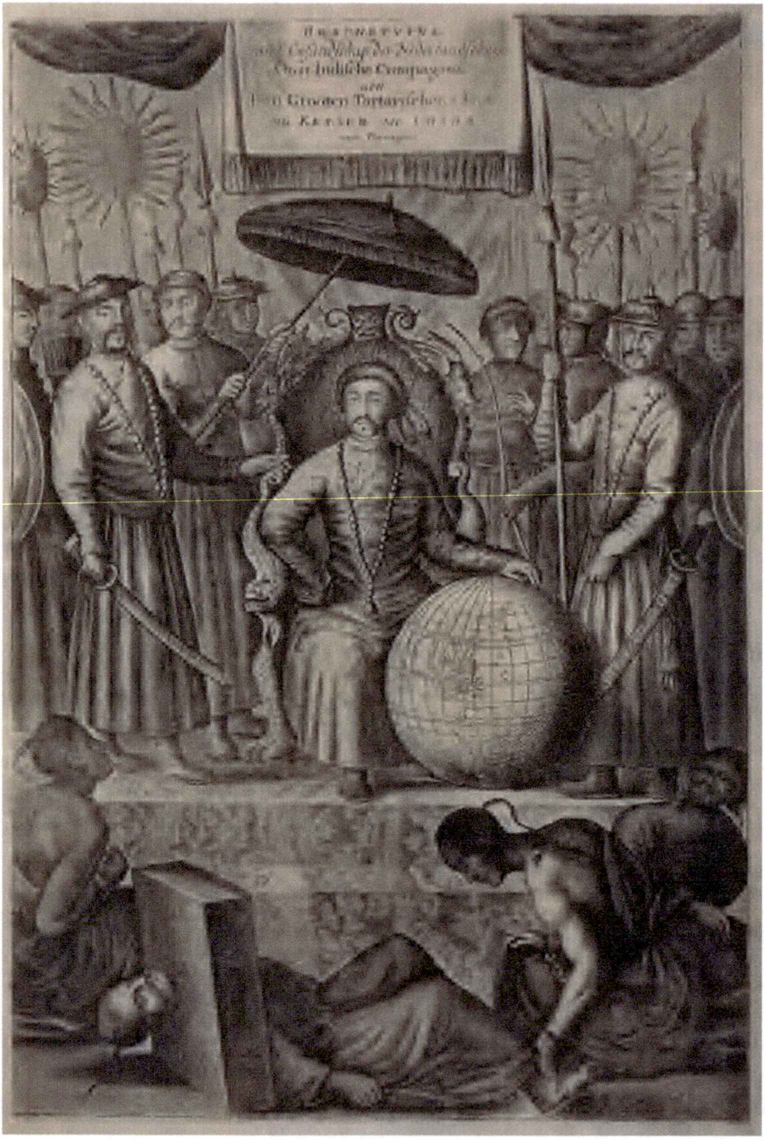

Fig. 2.1 An Embassy Sent by the East India Company of the United Provinces to the Grand Tartar Cham or Emperor of China by Johan Nieuhof

through books and letters. This laid the earliest foundation of tea spreading in Europe. To summarize, it was through missionaries, merchants, and the Dutch East India Company's staff who brought tea to the West.

3 British Catching Up from Behind

The first appearance of tea in England may have also come from the Netherlands. In *The Chronicles of the East India Company Trading to China*, 1635–1834, Masan Hesea Ballou Morse recorded, "The first recorded instance of England obtaining tea was in 1664, when the Directors of the Company purchased 2 pounds and 2 ounces (0.93 kg) of tea for £4 5s and presented it to the King. In 1616, they purchased 22 pounds and 12 ounces (about 10.27 kg) for £56 17s, which were probably obtained from the Dutch or possibly from their own ship employees."[22] Jane Pettigrew's *A Social History of Tea* also documents that in 1664, the East India Company bought tea from Dutch merchants to present to the King and Queen of England. These two instances further popularized tea in upper-class British society and elevated its status to one of prestige. "In 1664, the East India Company presented 2 pounds (approximately 0.9 kg) of black tea to the King of England, with a prize of 50 shillings per pound. Since then, English have been flocking to drink tea; this was reported on newspapers and spread to French."[23]

In 1668, the British government officially approved the East India Company to import tea. The following year, the company imported a large amount of tea: they indirectly bought 143 pounds and 10 ounces (approximately 65.15 kg) from Bandan.[24] But the import in this period wasn't stable. A few years later, Britain obtained the opportunity of direct trade with China through the Zheng family in Taiwan (the Zheng Chenggong family). In 1676, the Xiamen Commercial Building of the British East India Company was established. After that, tea began to be bought on a regular basis, becoming increasingly important. In 1684, Chinese tea was officially a major import item of the East India Company.

[22] [American] Massey. *The Chronicles of the East India Company Trading to China* [M]. Translated by Qiao Zonghua, Edited by Lin Shuhui. Guangzhou: Sun Yat-sen University Press, 1991: 10.

[23] Jane Pettigrew. *A Social History of Tea* [M]. London: National Trust, 2001:24.

[24] [British] George Leonard Staunton. *An Account of the Embassy to China*[M]. Translated by Ye Duyi. Beijing: Qunyan Publishing House, 2014: 26–27.

This can be proved by the documents by the company's directors: "Here, tea has become a commodity, and we sometimes have to present it to our friends who are in power. I ask you to send me 5 to 6 cans of the best and freshest tea every year. It can bring color to water, and the light green compounds dissolved are accepted with pleasure."[25] In 1685, the British East India Company saw the enormous hidden profit in the tea trade. The Madras headquarters received instructions:

> Tea is a promising commodity, a perfect gift for high-ranking officials in the palace. Hope I can send 5 to 6 cans of high-quality fresh tea every year. The most favored tea is the one with a bright and pure brown color after brewing.[26]

In 1702, the new East India Company was established and embarked on the reform to modern joint-stock company system, including limiting the power of major shareholders, and making sure that each shareholder had the right to vote and participate in shareholder meetings. In 1709, the company underwent restructuring and merger, renamed "The United Company of Merchant of England Trading to East India," "the British East India Company" for short.[27] At this point, the modern joint-stock company system had been refined, and shareholders had gained greater power. The board of directors and shareholders' meeting occupied the core position, and it was the 24 directors that were in charge of operation.

Morse believed that the restructured British East India Company laid great importance on tea trade: it explicitly requires ships to China to import tea. To ensure the sustainable development and reduce unnecessary losses, they worked out better packaging and storage method, which took into account the characteristics of tea and the potential damage to its

[25] Liu Zhangcai. "The Tea Trade between China and England in the 18th Century and Its Impact on British Society" [D]. Beijing: Capital Normal University, 2008: 20.

[26] Same as footnote 13, p. 134.

[27] The British East India Company underwent several reforms and reorganizations throughout its development. Scholars hold various views on when the company was actually established: the 1600 establishment theory, which refers to the granting of a charter by Queen Elizabeth I in 1600 and the subsequent trading activities conducted by the company; the 1702 establishment theory proposed by Marx, as the new East India Company established a democratic system of shareholders' meetings in that year; and some believe that the true sense of modern-characterized East India was established in 1709, and this system of joint-stock company continued until the nineteenth century.

quality caused by long-time transportation, bumps, and squeezing. In January 1694, a British merchant ship named Dorothy received an instruction, which included the detailed requirements for packaging and loading:

> We want a large amount of high-quality tea, wrapped in Chinese white copper foil, the tighter the better; and then load into a bucket. Make sure the tea is fresh and of good quality. Do not put tea in small jars or fragrant wooden boxes; be sure to use a container without any odor, especially the smell of welding oil.[28]

This indicates that they had already noticed the key issue of tea packaging: sealing, moisture-proof, and cross-flavor prevention. This latter became a common practice in world tea trade. In 1702, more detailed instruction was found on the ships named "Fleet" and "Union":

> In this country, everybody is drinking tea. So, as a commodity, tea must be carefully packaged to avoid damages to its taste and texture. You can never be too careful, for tea plays a vital role in the final profit. Therefore, do make sure that the tea is fresh and of high-quality. Recently, some people are trying to pack tea into boxes because they're bigger. We also found such boxes are better than buckets. We store it in the coolest part of the cabin, and open the hatch as often as possible for ventilation.[29]

From this passage we can see how important tea was to British East India Company. Besides packaging, there are also requirements for the placement.

Ma Shi commented on tea trade in 1717 that "tea has replaced silk as the main commodity." Afterward, tea import continued to soar. According to the data in *Chronicles of Sino-British Relations (3rd Century - 1760AD)* edited by Liu Jiantang and Zhang Li, tea import in 1690s amounted to 137,804 pounds (about 62,507 kg), the largest in the entire seventeenth century. In the next ten years, it jumped to 750,211 pounds (about 340,280 kg), but it was the smallest in the entire eighteenth century. The growth of the next two decades was astonishing: in the 1720s, annual average import was 880,000 pounds (399,761 kg), in the 1730s it raised

[28] Same as footnote 10, p. 67.
[29] Same as footnote 10, p. 70.

to 1.16 million pounds (526,167 kg), in the 1740s it ballooned to 2.02 million pounds (916,256 kg), and in the 1760s it reached 3.73 million pounds (1,691,899 kg). That is to say, compared to the first decade of the eighteenth century, tea import increased by 12 times in the following 40 years.[30] Therefore, British scholar Anthony Farrington referred to tea as a new miracle, greatly promoting the business of British East India Company with China.

Since the late 1720s, tea replaced silk as the first commodity in trade, and began to be transported with sago and porcelain: the three became a perfect match for that porcelain was heavy and not vulnerable to moisture, was placed in the bottom ballast, stabilizing the ship and avoiding tea getting damp. And sago was for filling the gaps between porcelains, which not only saved space, but also avoided the collision caused by turbulence. Tea was placed on the top, both avoiding moisture and lowering the center of gravity of the ship. And the loading of tea became more reasonable as well: the price varied among different types and qualities of tea, so cheaper tea was placed lower. This can further reduce damage during transportation and ensure profit.

Behind the soaring tea import in the UK was the establishment and development of trade relations between British East India Company and China. In 1673, with the support of the Zheng Family in Taiwan, the Company established the Macau Commercial Hall to trade with China directly. However, due to the unstable political status of Zheng and the severe corruption among local officials, the direct trade was limited. So the board of directors had been actively seeking for opportunities for relocating the Commercial Hall. Around 1690, the Chinese tea imported by the Company was mostly carried on Chinese ships to Batavia, Indonesia, which was the colony of the Netherlands. However, the trade channel of "China-Batavia-Britain" was not reliable yet, while the politics in China was quite stable under Emperor Kangxi, Qing Dynasty. In 1697, British ships first docked in Xiamen, marking the first time that Chinese tea was directly transported to England. In 1698, Emperor Kangxi issued an imperial edict to reduce the taxes and fees of Guangdong customs, loosening the trade limit in Guangdong. This sparkled the attention of the board of directors of the East India Company: they found that Guangzhou was

[30] Yang Jingping. "Chinese Tea in England in the 17th and 18th Centuries" [D]. Hangzhou: Zhejiang Normal University, 2006: 4.

better than Xiamen, and swiftly launched a plan to transfer their trade base. After obtaining the right to enter Guangzhou market for the first time in 1699, the Company transferred its trade center from Xiamen to Guangzhou in 1704, and made preliminary negotiations with the ports licensed. It was officially permitted to enter Guangdong in 1713, and established the Guangzhou Commercial Center in 1715. This signified that trade with China had finally matured and stabilized. Tea trade became regular since 1717.

Commodities changed as the Sino-British trade matured. Tea replaced silk and became the core commodity of the East India Company. In the second half of the eighteenth century, tea accounted for more than 80% of the entire trade volume, making Guangdong the trade center.[31] British scholar Anthony Farrington summarized in his book *Trading Places: The East India Company and Asia 1600–1834* that "Once the trade in Guangzhou became regular, it focused on 3 products: tea, silk and cheap porcelain."[32] This can be supported by the data in *Chronicle of the East India Company's Trade with China* by Ma Shi, and *Oriental Commerce* by William Milbum.

The late Ming Dynasty was the beginning of the large-scale sales of tea to Europe. Since Chinese drink tea with porcelain, the story of tea is also the story of porcelain to some degrees. Although porcelain entered England earlier, the export was very little compared to that after tea becoming popular. One of the biggest reasons was the difficulty to carry porcelain on camel on the land Silk Road, before the opening of the Maritime Silk Road. Even if you tried your best to stuff each piece with soil and beans, tie them into bundles with ropes, dampen them until the beans sprout and the root spread, tightening the entire packaging, very few pieces could reach Europe. Porcelain transported in this way to inner Europe was sold ten times its original price,[33] and was mostly decorated in noble families.

After the opening of the Maritime Silk Road, European's passion for tea further promoted the sales of porcelain. British people also believe that porcelain can enhance the beauty of tea as Chinese do: "a set of exquisite

[31] Same as footnote 13, pp. 139–140.

[32] Anthony Farrington, Trading Places: The East India Company and Asia 1600–1834, London: The British Library, 2002: 87.

[33] Same as footnote 2, p. 128.

porcelain can enrich the taste of tea."[34] It was the Dutch East India Company that first traded tea sets; but the British East India Company grew to the main player in the field after the eighteenth century. According to existing literature, the Dutch East India Company ordered a batch of tea bowls and 200 teapots in 1626. The Hatcher Cargo, which sank in the South China Sea in 1644, carried nearly 23,000 pieces of porcelain. After sorting and analyzing the relics of the sunken ship, it was found that there were 12 new types of tea sets, each with approximately 20 pieces, totaling 225 pieces. Later in 1680, it was recorded on the Dutch East India Company that the cargo ship Denardi, sailing toward Amsterdam, carried 1635 Chinese teapots.[35]

In 1717, two ships from the British East India Company, the Essex and Townshend, bought 610,000 pieces of porcelain for 44,000 pounds and sailed back to England. In 1722, the Company ordered 400,000 pieces. In 1735, ships named Grafton and Harrison departed from Xiamen and Guangzhou, respectively, transporting a total of 240,000 pieces. And in 1752, the Geldermalsen from the Dutch East India Company sank on its way from Guangzhou to the then Batavia, carrying a total of 162,000 pieces, including 27,531 tableware, 63,623 teacups and saucers, 578 teapots, 19,525 coffee cups and saucers, 821 large beer mugs, and 606 spit basins.[36] According to statistics by Alan McFarlane et al., from 1684 to 1791, 215 million porcelain pieces were transported to England.[37] Facing this, D. W. Davies lamented in his book *17th Century Dutch Overseas Trade: An Overview* that "The world need porcelain so much that in the end, Chinese cups and teapots are filled everywhere."[38] By the end of the eighteenth century, almost every British household had tea sets, which became an important daily necessity.

[34] Hou Tiejun. "The Other's Thing and the Self's Thing: A Study of Porcelain in 18th-Century British Literature" [D]. Wuhan: Wuhan University, 2015: 56.

[35] [American] Shirley Maloney Mueller. "Imagination and Diversity: The Teapot Trade in 17th-Century China" [J]. Translated by Wang Qian. *Beauty Formed Through Time*, 2016(4): 58–61.

[36] Same as footnote 2, pp. 26–27.

[37] Alan Macfarlane, Iris Macfarlane: The Empire of Tea: The Remarkable History of the Hant that Took Over the World. New York:Overlook Press, 2004: 91.

[38] Li Jinming. "The Spread and Impact of Chinese Ceramic Culture in the Ming and Qing Dynasties on the World" [J]. *Chinese Social and Economic History*, 1999(2): 45.

In short, tea was introduced to England from the mid to late seventeenth century through the Dutch East India Company. The volume of tea gradually increased as the British and the Dutch East India Company scrambling for the rights to trade in the East. As a result, tea volume became the largest in Sino-British trade. Tea utensils entered Britain at the same time, also in large quantities. As British writer Daniel Defoe observed, "The consumption of coffee, tea, and chocolate couldn't have spread so quickly without the increase in traded utensils. We can see that the most luxurious shops in the city are filled with expensive utensils for tea tables."[39] Indeed, at the same time when merchants brought tea to Europe, tea wares used in China had also arrived in this unfamiliar land and were widely popular.

[39] Ma Xiaoli. *A Multidimensional Perspective on the Study of British Tea Culture* [M]. Hangzhou: Zhejiang University Press, 2010: 30.

CHAPTER 3

Extravagance and Flaunt: The Consumption and Localization of English Tea

1 The Dowry of Portuguese Princess

On May 13, 1662, 14 British warships arrived at the Portsmouth Harbor after three weeks of storms. The esteemed passenger on the Royal Charles, Portuguese Princess Catherine of Braganza, the future queen, was welcomed by the coastal residents with salutes and fireworks. Six days later, King Charles II of England rushed to Portsmouth and held a secret Catholic wedding with her. Later that day, the couple arrived in London and went through another wedding, held by a Protestant bishop.

Royal marriages are often conspiracies of power and wealth, and this one is no exception. For King Charles II, the main motivation was probably her generous dowry. In addition to the 500,000 pounds in cash promised by the Portuguese royal family, this alliance also brought to Britain the African trade area of Tangier and Mumbai, as well as free trade with Brazil and the East Indies.[1] At that time, King Charles II probably did not realize what free trade, an exclusive previously to Portugal, meant for the UK. After that, Mumbai, part of the dowry, played a huge role when British realized the enormous profit in tea and decided to compete with the Dutch in East Indies.[2] This meant that the waterway to the only

[1] [English] Roy Moxham. Tea: A History of the World in a Cup[M]. Translated by Bi Xiaoping. Beijing: Life, Reading, New Knowledge Sanlian Bookstore, 2015: 18.

[2] Same as footnote 1, p. 20.

C. Zhang, *Beyond the Teacup: 18th Century Sino-British Tea Trade and Design Cultural Exchange*,
https://doi.org/10.1007/978-981-97-7691-7_3

origin of tea at that time—China—was opened, greatly accelerated the expansion of the British East India Company in East Indies.

Charles II, on the other hand, was more interested in the 500,000 pounds cash because he was urgent to repay his debt. Unfortunately, the dowry that came with the queen was only half of what the Portuguese promised, and this half was not even cash, but sugar, spices, and other sellable items instead. When he heard of this, he almost broke off the engagement; but in the end he gave up, still decided to marry her. Some of her dowry was her personal belongings, including a box of tea.[3] It is said that she took tea because she was worried that England may not agree with her, and she believed that tea was a miracle medicine that could cure all diseases.[4]

If we are to trace the history of Britain's addiction to tea, this Portuguese princess should never be neglected. She was bestowed the title of "Queen of Tea," and was related to countless tea stories. Although we cannot tell which is the historical fact and which is folk imagination and interpretation, she is the one who related tea drinking to elegance and civilization, not only within British aristocracy but also to European, thus developing it into a new court fashion (see Fig. 3.1). British courtier Edmund Waller once presented a birthday ode to her.

On Tea
Venus her myrtle, Phoebus has her bays;
Tea both excels, which she vouchsafes to praise.
The best of Queens, and best of herbs, we owe
To that bold nation, which the way did show
To the fair region where the sun doth rise,
Whose rich productions we so justly prize.
The Muse's friend, tea does our fancy aid,
Repress those vapors which the head invade,
And keep the palace of the soul serene,
Fit on her birthday to salute the Queen.[5]

[3] Same as footnote 1, p. 15.

[4] [Japanese] Kikuchi Takeo. A World History of a Cup of Black Tea[M]. Translated by Asagao. Shanghai: Oriental Publishing House, 2014: 11.

[5] [English] Markman Ellis, Richard Coulton, Matthew Mauger. Empire of Tea: The Asian Leaf that Conquered the World[M]. Translated by Gao Lingya and Xu Bo. Beijing: China Friendship Publishing Company, 2020: 44.

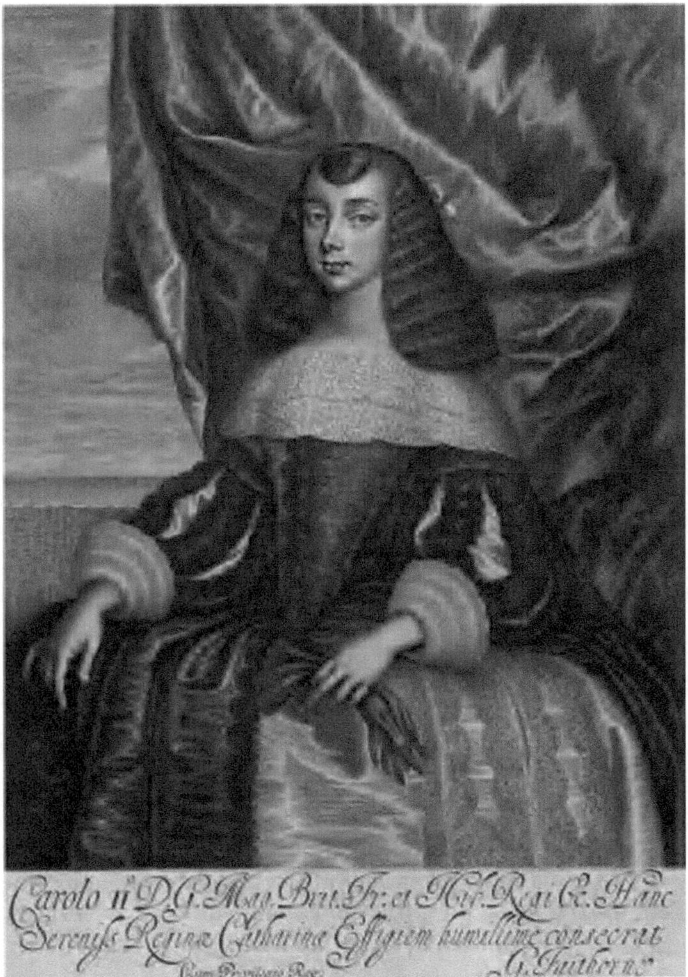

Fig. 3.1 Catherine of Braganza, the Queen of tea

It is easy to deduce from this poem that tea had been infiltrated into British culture, becoming an expression of scene and artistic conception. At the same time, we can also see the understanding of tea by some of the British, represented by Waller: "The best of Queens, and best of herbs" and "The Muse's friend, tea does our fancy aid," and their impression of

China: "the fair region where the sun doth rise," and "rich productions." After Catherine promoted tea in court, tea spread further to the upper society.

In the 1680s, tea had become an important part of the social and family life among aristocrats and upper class; with its cultural connotations and scarcity, it became an ideal beverage for royals and nobles to showcase their identity. From the existing household logs and accounting lists of the upper class, it can be seen that tea was indeed popular in the late seventeenth century. For example, in 1673, the records show that the attendants of Count Roo purchased boxes for storing tea. At the birthplace of afternoon tea, Woburn Abbey in Bedfordshire, southern England, the Duke of Bedford, William Russell, bought a tea set for his daughter Margaret Russell at 1 pound 14 shillings. Following this, the duke's attendants purchased a tea tray and a teapot in the years 1688, 1689, or 1690. In 1688, the inventory of Burghley House listed the Countess of Exeter as owning "a brown and white teapot, with gilded handles, a gilded spout top and bottom, a small pot body and top chain, and a white teapot with a cover, gilded pot, and chain."[6] According to the family documents of Woben Manor, we can also know that there were top servants who were specifically responsible for buying tea.

As mentioned earlier, with the technology in the seventeenth century, it took 18–24 months to ship tea from China to Europe. The high cost and risk in transportation led to high price and scarcity, making it impossible for tea to be sold in large quantities, and only the noble could afford it. According to *All About Tea* by William Ukers, in 1657, tea was sold at 6–10 pounds per pound in Britain,[7] while the annual income of a made was 3–4 pounds.[8] That means, she couldn't afford 1 pound of tea (approximately 0.45 kg) with all her salary of the year. Undoubtedly, tea was an ideal medium for the royals, aristocrats, and upper class to prove their identity.

Why should they prove their identity? Middle class sprang up with the further development of Eastern trade, and they began to expand and attempted to blend in the upper class, threatening the political, economic,

[6] [English] Jane Pettigrew. The Tea Book[M]. Translated by Shao Lirong. Jinan: Shandong Pictorial Publishing House, 2013: 20.

[7] [English]William Ukers. All About Tea [M]. Translated by Nong Jia, Liu Tao, Jiang Haidi. Shanghai: Oriental Press, 2011.

[8] Tania M. Buxton & Pascoe. A Taste of English Tea - The Cultural and Social Life of Tea in Visual Art [M]. Translated by Zhang Chi, et al. Beijing: Peking University Press, 2021: 37.

and cultural power of the later. The most obvious phenomenon was intimating the luxurious way of clothing and consumption of the noble. The upper class refused to surrender; to maintain the old order, they started "conspicuous consumption" to prove identity and distinguish their status.

The term "conspicuous consumption" was first coined by Canadian economist John Rae. He believed that vanity was a desire to own things that others have never owned. And Thorstein Bunde Veblen (1859–1929) thought that in societies with high mobility, consuming expensive goods is an important way to show wealth, and that conspicuous consumption is closely related to identity recognition. In his book *The Theory of the Leisure Class*, Buren proposed that for the leisure class always hope to highlight their wealth through the expenditures in daily life, thus showing their status and winning respect. In other words, every purchase was a fight for symbols, a fight to seek differentiation. The fight helps consumers to establish a sense of identity and uniqueness.

The upper class pursues not only rarity, but also their social perception. People who do conspicuous consumption believe that he will be watched, envied, and respected, so as to exclude the unmannerly upstarts who try to squeeze into the circle, but lack etiquettes. In this era, consumption is no longer only to meet basic material need, but a mental behavior that goes beyond material enjoyment, that interprets identity and improves status. As a result, tea, as a new and exotic beverage, carried cultural connotations beyond simple consumer good, and became a "gift to the civilized world." It represented a highly developed culture,[9] symbolizing wealth, fashion, and status. This symbolic significance made tea a tool for upper society to showcase their extraordinary taste.

As pointed out in *The Theory of the Leisure Class*, elegant demeanor, behavior, and lifestyle were effective proof of blue blood, and familiarity in etiquette is self-explained. For the upper class, their lives are built on red tapes. Unlike other goods, drinking tea is not only about tea, but also involves utensils, tea space, manners, and so on. It can be said that drinking tea is a systematic cultural activity. By the end of the seventeenth century, tea drinking became a regular social activity among the British prestigious. They developed a set of British manners of tea that matched their status, and tea sets were specially created for these manners to show elegance. French travel writer La Rochefoucault completed the book *A*

[9] Wu Guanzhong. The Origins of Modern Consumer Society - A Study of Consumer Issues in 17th and 18th Century England [D]. Nanjing: Nanjing University, 2014: 83.

Frenchman in England after traveling to England in 1784. He commented: "the trend of tea prevailed in England...Noble families brag about their wealth and status with teapots, cups and other utensils, because what they use are the most exquisite..."[10] When tea became a subject of conspicuous consumption, the tea, utensils, and places all naturally became props for upper class to express their ego.

2 The Pride in Ownership

Owning Chinese tea and utensils itself is a way to show wealth and status. So, the British nobility spared no effort to acquire Chinese specialties as much as possible for drinking tea and decorating tea spaces.

The tea set market emerged with the popularity of tea, and the British East India Company began to demand agents to purchase more porcelain tea bowls, teapots, and other goods. The prices of them in Europe were much higher than their cost. Since the profit would be too thin if they only levied transaction taxes based on costs, the Company adopted onshore auction, in which all ordered goods needed to be bid through auction. The auction hall was located in Greenwich Dock, where the company headquarters located and ships docked. This auction greatly boosted profit and aroused the enthusiasm of consumers.

When ships arrived, the tea sets would be sent to the auction house in boxes. This made it difficult for them to be sold in complete sets. So even wealthy families could not gather a set, but pieced them together instead. Nevertheless, this problem provided a new way of "conspicuous consumption": almost every family member had their own exclusive set, through this they defined themselves and showed their taste. Gladys Scott Thompson mentioned this in his book *Life in a Noble Household 1647–1770*: "Every time you buy a tea set, it's like buying a coffee set, each writes down the set they want and then put them together for pairing, forming a set of their own...Ceramic tea sets that came to Woburn with tea were much more expensive than the utensils for other beverage. Miss Margaret Russell received a tea set from her father, which was worth 1 pound and 14 shillings, for the following 3 years there were a set of 6, costing 20 shillings, and a tea plate worth 5 shillings."[11] Even porcelain

[10] Same as footnote 6, p. 41.

[11] Gladys Scott Thomson, Life in a Noble Household 1641–1770, Ann Arbor: University of Michigan Press, 1959: 168–170.

traders at that time could only combine tea sets themselves, and form the "best" combination according to their own understanding. Therefore, during this period, tea bowls and plate in mansions seldom appeared in matching forms.[12] Under this background, tea set became personal and expressive, representing the status and personality of the owner, as well as the trend.

Another way of conspicuous consumption was customization. As mentioned earlier, tea set wasn't within the official trade scope of the British East India Company, but rather as welfare for employees. With the navigation technology at that time, a voyage to China would take two to three years, and sailors had to suffer raging waves and stormy sea for very little salary. According to records, the annual salary of the British East India Company's crew was only 10 pounds in 1727, but if they engaged in private trade, they would earn an additional 2000 pounds. The British East India Company stipulated that crews could pay for a certain storage space on the ship, providing convenience for private trade. Therefore, it was usually employees including chief officer, and their families and friends who bought customized porcelain. They would first explain the requirement to the Company, hand over the order, which would be managed by chief officer. Upon arrival at the port, chief officer will immediately hand over the order with detailed drawing instruction to the local agent (i.e., comprador). Compradors would go to Jingdezhen to deliver them to kiln factories, ensuring that the products would be finished before the ships departed.

Buyers of customized porcelain usually had vested interest directly or indirectly related to the Company. Therefore, arm porcelain took up the most of customized porcelain. Arm first appeared in the twelfth century in England, initially carved on shields to distinguish enemies and allies. As time changed, its original function faded, and it gradually evolved into a symbol of family identity, and widely used as a visual symbol of the status and identity of its owner. Arm may appear in various eye-catching places, including the entrance of mansion, carriages, furniture, tableware, and even private letters.

The Portuguese royal family pioneered in customized porcelain. They had been ordering blue-and-white porcelain with their family customized porcelain since the first half of the sixteenth century. However, according to the statistics of ceramic historian David Howard, there are over "5000

[12] Same as footnote 6, p. 164.

types" of customized porcelain in Europe, "of which over 3000 are sold to Britain."[13] These are mainly arm porcelain ordered by royals, nobles, and companies, with family emblems or company logos on them.

Researchers of material culture believe that "objects have the capacity to do 'social work': that is to say, they can refer to subcultural associations, participate in professions, wealth, and limited activities, or from a certain aspect of social status to all aspects of social identity."[14] These nobles use porcelain to construct identities, distinguish and clarify hierarchical boundaries. On the one hand, these arm porcelain decorated with family badges and symbols externalize the identity and status of the owner in a tangible material form, thereby "reconciling the formation of self-identity and dignity." On the other hand, these arm porcelain virtually formed a material chain, "providing an ideal and new way to spread ideas such as social status and family ties."[15] They connected this family as well as other families that owned arm porcelain, distinguishing them from other social groups, and formed a material boundary.

Britain was the main market of arm porcelain. From the eighteenth century to the early nineteenth century, the number of arm porcelain customized to British market may reach up to 5000 sets. Followed by Dutch East India Company, which mainly flourished from 1730 to 1760, mainly consisting of family and company arm porcelain ordered by royals, nobles, and companies.

There are also some patterns that come from European prints, sketches, library tickets, game coins, and money coins, with detained instruction in their orders. In the *Canton Journal* of 1722, there is a record of a complete set of porcelain tea ware customized by a British East India Company captain, including 12 sets of cups, saucers, teapots, milk jugs, tea canisters, teapot stands, teaspoon racks, covered sugar dishes, and 6 hot chocolate cups. In 1740, the British East India Company designed a series of porcelain with tea-drinking patterns, including a polychrome plate named "Drinking Tea."[16] By looking at the porcelain order with the coat of arms of the Tovell family in England in 1728, we can see the painted design

[13] Rose Kerr, Luisa Mengoni. Chinese Export Ceramics, London: Victoria & Albert Museum, 2011: 39.

[14] Hou Tiejun. Research on porcelain in 18th century British literature: Things of Others and Self. [D], Wuhan University, 2015: 64.

[15] Same as footnote 14.

[16] Yu Chunming. China's Calling Card - Exploring the Origins and Collection of Export Ceramics in the Ming and Qing Dynasties [M]. Beijing: Sanlian Bookstore, 2011: 44, 56.

provided by the purchaser and the English instructions: "Six large bowls, with the coat of arms painted on the outside of the enamel porcelain; two sets of enamel tea ware, with the coat of arms painted on each side; lacquerware: two tea tables, an eight-foot high eight-folding screen; a dressing table; a square table," as well as the Chinese inscription noted by the purchasing agent: "eight folding screens, each eight feet high... two large tea trays, four small tea trays" (part of the content is missing, see Fig. 3.2).[17] In the Canton Journal of 1727, a captain's list of private trade goods is recorded, including 19 boxes, 26 small barrels, and 174 bundles of porcelain, of which 5 boxes are customized coat of arms porcelain for British noblemen, one of which is a coat of arms teapot customized for Peter King, the nephew of the famous British philosopher John Locke[18] (Figs. 3.3 and 3.4).

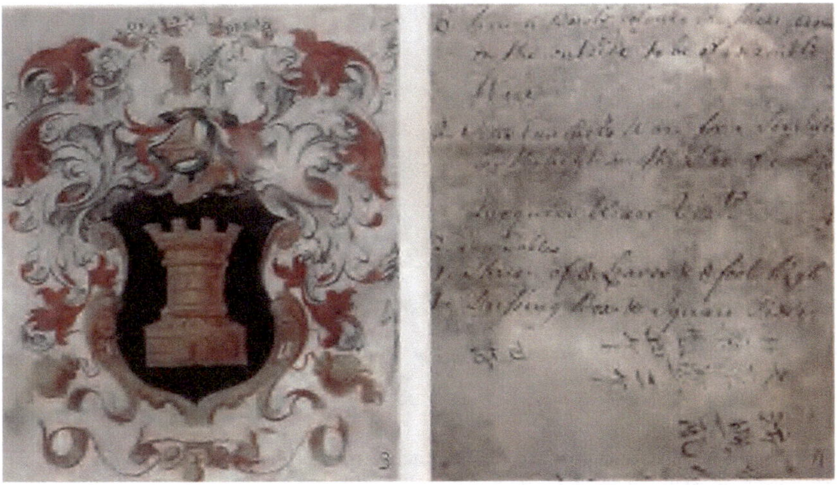

Fig. 3.2 An order by the Trowel family in 1728, with the painted picture provided by the customer, and an instruction in both English and Chinese

[17] Lv Zhangshen. The Charm of Porcelain - Selected Fine Collections of Chinese Export Ceramics at the British Museum and the Victoria and Albert Museum [M]. Beijing: Zhonghua Book Company, 2012: 18.

[18] Lai Qianye. Consumer Culture of English Aristocracy from the Perspective of Chinese Export Ceramics (1688–1730) [D]. Taipei: Political University of Taiwan, 2012: 31.

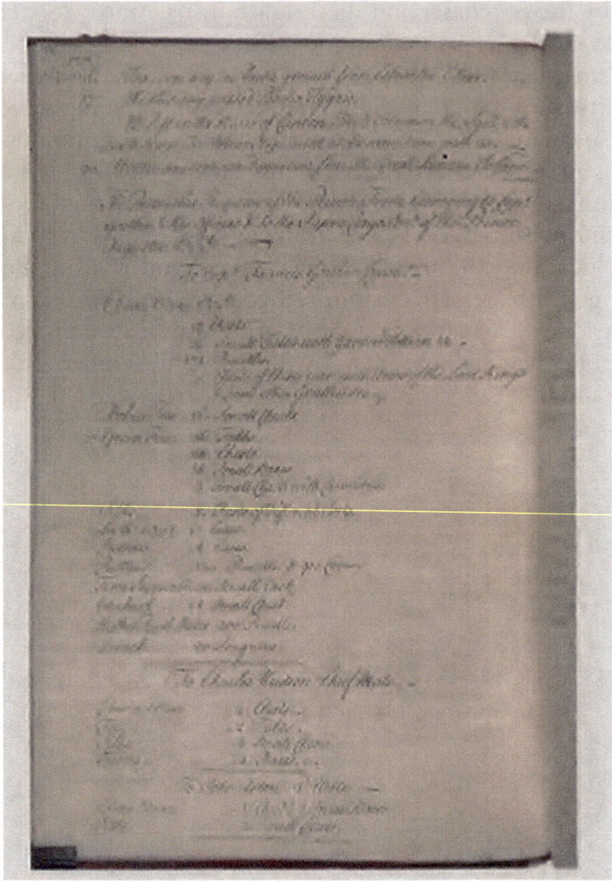

Fig. 3.3 A transaction record of the teacup ordered by Lord Peter King in 1727, the nephew of John Locke

Later, with the development of trade, other than arm porcelain, British also customized a large number of daily porcelain that fit their own life-style. For example, there are dishes like pantomime bowls, sauce bottles, double-necked oil and vinegar bottles, and mugs. Western scholars who specialize in studying customized porcelain have identified four types of

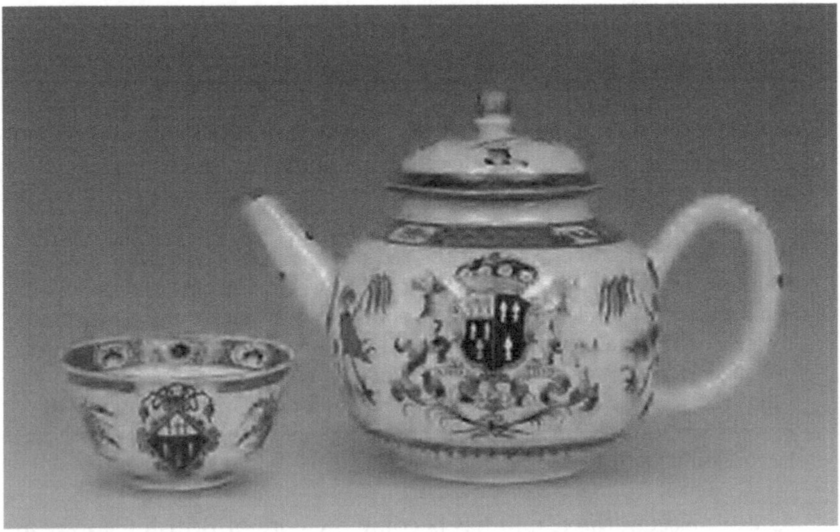

Fig. 3.4 The porcelain teapot and cup ordered by Lord Peter King in 1727, the nephew of John Locke

customized patterns, including: (1) European-style porcelain imitating European pottery, silver, and glass; (2) customized porcelain with European patterns decorated with Chinese elements; (3) white porcelain exported to Europe, decorated locally by European artists; and (4) decorated porcelain already made in China that is further decorated in Europe.

Of course, this is mainly based on European custom porcelain decorated in China.[19] Regarding this, *the Records of Pottery in Jingdezhen* records that "foreign goods are exclusively sold to foreigners, with many merchants from the eastern Guangdong region, selling them to foreign devils for market share." These market needs from Europe, which are "diverse in style and changeable over time," have put higher demands on China's ceramic industry and promoted related industries. This related content will be further discussed in Chap. 5.

[19] Margaret Jourdain, R. Soame Jenyns. Chinese Export Art in the Eighteenth Century. New York: Charles Scribner's Sons, 1950: 41.

3 Improve to Flaunt

A Teapot Equipped with a Golden Chain

When tea from China first spread among the upper class in the UK, how did British drink tea? Cornelis Bontekoe, a Dutch tea doctor in the seventeenth century, suggested:

> Prepare a teapot, either made of tin, red earth, or Delft porcelain. Rinse it with hot water, put some tea and pour in hot water, and cover the pot with its lid. Wait for a while, or steep the teapot into hot water, until the water in the teapot changes color. Then, pour a small amount of tea water into a porcelain cup. Of course, if there are many people to drink, each person should be served a cup. At this point, you could drink while it's hot. Gently blow it two to three times, sip it from the top, and continue until finished, leaving only the tea leaves.[20]

As can be seen, the teapot has become the core of British tea ware as a result of Chinese influence. As previously mentioned, in the early days, the tea ware used by the British was all Chinese export porcelain, which was scarce and hard to obtain. According to existing literature, the translator of the Dutch East India Company's trade records, T. Volker, believed that in 1639, the Dutch East India Company's order included a description of "two hundred teapots, with lids, handles, raised ribs, and referring to sample number four." It can be inferred from this record that the relevant sample was probably sent with the ship.[21] The early Chinese porcelain imported to Europe were often through private trade, among which the most common type was probably Yixing purple clay teapot. Jane Pettigrew, an export on British tea culture, wrote in her work that Yixing purple clay teapots started to appear on British tea tables in the 1660s. These teapots were not large in size and were made of vermilion or purple clay. There was also a type of glazed pottery, which was reddish brown or black brown in color and had a fascinating design.

It is said that the first Yixing purple clay teapot was made in about 1500, and was originally exclusively aimed at Chinese market. From the

[20] Same as footnote 5, pp. 53–54.

[21] [American] Shirley Maloney Mueller. Imagination and Diversity: The Teapot Trade in 17th Century China [J]. Translated by Wang Qian. Beauty Perpetuated Through Time, 2016(4): 59.

beginning of the seventeenth century, its reputation gradually surpassed the porcelain teapots from Jingdezhen. The tea-drinking culture began to form in Europe in the mid to late seventeenth century, bringing in Chinese tea sets. Among them the Yixing purple clay teapot was considered the most exquisite and imaginative, and gradually became the preferred choice for brewing tea since 1660s. In the seventeenth century, Dutch were the first to cultivate the European tea market and were also the first to introduce Chinese tea ware to Europe. According to the tastes, preferences, and habits of Europeans at the time, they redesigned the teapots and went to Yixing for custom-made pieces. The main types of clay materials include purplish-brown clay, reddish clay (also known as vermilion clay), and light yellow Benshan green clay (also known as Duan clay). After firing, the color variety is diverse, ranging from light yellow, purplish brown, red to black, and there are also some very rare ones that appear green, blue, or gray.

The first choice of Dutch merchant to crack open the European market was vermilion clay pots with stickers. Because the decorative technique of this pot is similar to a red ancient exquisite pottery that once prevailed in history, which was called Terra Sigillata. The history of Terra Sigillata can be traced back to the Gallic Roman period. From the first century BC to the second century AD, this pottery appeared in most European countries, along the Mediterranean coast, and even in India. Therefore, red-colored, ornamented pottery is often referred to as "Terra Sigillata." During the Renaissance, it revived in the market. For the Dutch, they also made necessary adjustments to the capacity size of teapots. As mentioned earlier, when tea was first introduced to Europe, it was rare and expensive. Therefore, only a small number of Chinese teapots appeared, all of which were common styles in Chinese market. At that time, even the upper class could only afford a small amount of tea each time. So the Dutch East India Company limited the capacity at around 250 ml when customizing, while the common capacity in China was 500 ml.[22]

For Europe, teapots were still a strange and exotic product. Due to a lack of understanding, they could not appreciate their shape, but focused on their surface decoration instead. Although these decorations were more complex and magnificent than that in China, the patterns were typical Chinese, often related to Buddhism and Taoism. So, it can be deduced

[22] [French] Patrice Valfrey. Yixing Teapots Exported to Europe [M]. Translated by Shi Yunqiao. Hangzhou: Xiling Seal Engravers Society Press, 2015: 24, 26.

that Europe was enthusiastic about the unknown world, and the exotic atmosphere in these mysterious images and characters perfectly met their curiosity.

According to the records of the Dutch and British East India Company, the trade of Yixing teapots dates back to 1679. In the archives of the Dutch East India Company at its former headquarters in Batavia, the first batch was seven boxes of red clay teapots were shipped from Zhangzhou, Fujian province. According to another record, there were 320 decorated ones arrived, and another 1635 teapots that arrived at the port of Amsterdam were also identified as likely purple clay. And the British archives record 82 clay teapots that arrived in 1699.[23] However, there is also evidence to prove that the purple clay teapot probably entered Europe as early as the 1660s. For example, on an advertisement by Delft pottery factory in 1678, it was claimed that the ceramic master Lambertus Cleffius created the process of imitating India porcelain in 1672, and stated that he had been making teapot in red and other colors that could rival Indian teapots. The Indian teapot mentioned here is the Yixing vermilion clay teapot by the Dutch East India Company. This advertisement indicates that Yixing purple clay teapots had already been in the Netherlands before 1672. And there were also other colors besides red clay.

From old books and magazines as well as the collections of European royal families, we can glimpse the design and production of the exported purple clay teapots at that time. Simonis Paulli, the physician of the King of Denmark, published a book in 1665 titled *Commentaruis de Abusu Tabaci [...] et Herba Thee Asiaticulum in Europa Novo*, which was one of the earliest books to include Yixing teapots. The book includes illustrations and descriptions of Yixing teapots. The pots in the illustration are similar to Chinese domestic style, which may indicate that the teapots specifically for export had not yet begun, or were scarce in quantity. Poly introduced in the book: "the tea utensils (i.e. Yixing purple clay teapot) from China were expensive as gold, and were wrapped in silk. Only the best friends would present them as gifts. It is widely recognized that their value compares to diamonds, gemstones, or the most luxurious necklace".[24] A French merchant Sylvestre Dufour published *De l' usage du Caphe, du The et du Chocolat* in 1671. The book was revised and reprinted in 1685, adding a large number of charts and illustrations. The title was also

[23] Same as footnote 20, p. 27.

[24] Same as footnote 20, p. 49.

adjusted to *Train e s nouveaux & curieux du coffee house, du The et du Chocolat*. The book made a great hit, not only reprinted multiple times within 15 years, but also introduced in the UK, the Netherlands, and Switzerland, influencing the whole Europe. There are two printmaking illustrations in the book depicting Chinese officials drinking tea: the first one is the cover, the other is in content. In the second one, a purple clay teapot is placed in front of a sitting Chinese official, drinking tea. And the text along with it provided introduction: "Chinese brew tea with red pottery teapots, with printed decorations on the body. They believe that tea brewed by this teapot tastes better than others. I'm not sure whether it's true, but based on the illustrations in the front page, you can see that these teapots are beautiful indeed."[25]

Another influential book is *Le bon usage du The, du Caffe et du Chocolat* by Nicolas de Blegny, which for the first time included illustrations of exported teapots. The book also includes the author's introduction and comment on teapot: "In the East Indies and Europe, there are teapots specially designed for tea... see the teapot in my illustration... is a typical style, and their material can be silver, tin pewter or Chinese porcelain." In another page explains the usage: "the second teapot in the illustration is a Chinese one with simple carved decorations. The third, fourth, and fifth ones are made of the same type of clay, but with different styles. The alcohol temperature furnaces under these teapots are made of gilded copper, brass or purple copper, without gilding and with copper green on top. These teapots are not only decoration but also used for brewing, for that I don't have anything better to put onto cabinets and fireplace racks. And when teapots are put on table, they're more convenient for brewing and drinking."[26]

What's more interesting is that the largest teapot in this illustration looks no different from Yixing purple clay teapot, but it's actually a silver or tin teapot made by European craftsmen imitating Yixing. The other four are purple clay teapots decorated with typical molding or decal, rarely seen in Chinese domestic market, but rather an exporting style. Three of them are also equipped with metal chains in areas prone to collision and the lid, preventing damages caused by falling. The figure of the Yixing teapot appeared in the still life paintings created by Dutch painter Pieter

[25] Same as footnote 20, p. 50.
[26] Same as footnote 20, p. 50.

Gerritsz van Roestraten (1627–1698) living in England in the second half of the seventeenth century, a metal chain also appeared (Fig. 3.5).

In the seventeenth century, export teapots with medal chains were quite common in England. This can add to the value to the already precious porcelain, protect the porcelain, and better conform to the habits and aesthetic tastes of Europeans. But from another perspective, we can see it as a process of "de-contextualization and re-contextualization" of tea coming to Britain. In this way British infuse their own culture into Chinese tea sets and localize them.

Apart from purple clay teapot, another type appeared on English tea tables was blue-and-white porcelain. On the gift list of Devonshire Schedule there are two teapots given to the Earl of Devonshire, dating back to 1690. One of them is a small silver-plated teapot with a lychee-shaped design, described as "a small yellow teapot with a green handle,

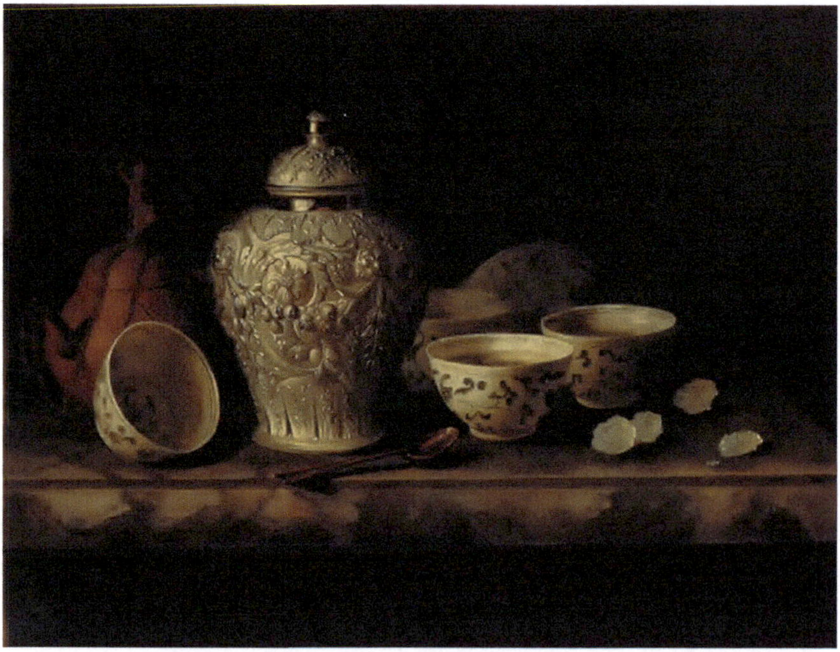

Fig. 3.5 Yixing purple clay teapot appears in the still painting by Dutch painter Pieter Gerritsz van Roestraten in the second half of the seventeenth century

base and spout adorned with a metal chain, novel and unique." The other is larger, with a metal handle, "a square large teapot with a square cover, adorned with metal chains on the neck, handle, and spout."[27] These two teapots are vastly different in size, shape, and decoration, but both are adorned with metal chains.

In existing literature, we can also see some "special" teapots whose functions have been "altered" in different contexts. For example, Chinese export wine pots may also be used as teapots, while Dutch may brew tea with local kettles or other containers.[28] A vase from Chongzhen period of the Ming Dynasty, was sawn off in the upper half, opened a hole on one side, added a lid, a spout and a handle (all made of medal and wood), and became a teapot.[29] There is also a special teapot: large in size and in the shape of melon, double flow. This may be a new type designed by Chinese craftsmen for export. This port has a partition in the middle, probably be used to brew different types of tea.

American scholar Shirley Maloney believes that the teapots in seventeenth-century England were: "big and small, square and round, decorated various elements from traditional Chinese patterns. The details are even more diverse, such as star shaped base, a positioning buckle lid, a convex edge of the pot body, etc. All require rich imagination and creativity. To a large extent, Chinese produced teapots pursue diversity and variability; none of them are identical replicas. They are typical Chinese style in their impression and characteristics, lacking Western style elements."[30]

Chinese teapots have flooded into Europe since 1680s. British also began to try making their own teapots, but they didn't get the hang of it in the beginning. They started in 1670, and the first teapot was silver, molded after the coffee pot used in the coffee houses in London (Fig. 3.6). The inscription on the body recorded its origin: "it was presented to the British East India Company by George Berkeley, the owner of Berkeley Castle, in 1670."[31] The tall cylinder makes this pot look like a coffee pot. This may indicate that during that period, the shape and structure of English teapots hadn't been fixed yet. In the early days, silversmiths made teapots by continuously hammering silver ingots, making them thinner,

[27] Same as footnote 19, p. 67.
[28] Same as footnote 19, p. 59.
[29] Same as footnote 16, p. 202.
[30] Same as footnote 19, p. 69.
[31] Same as footnote 6, p. 93.

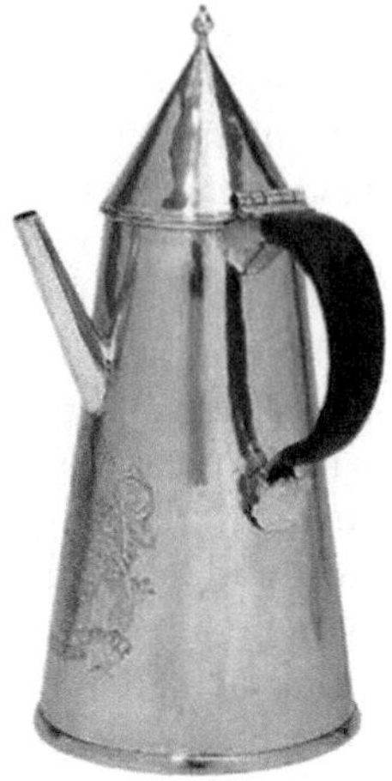

Fig. 3.6 Silver teapot made in 1670. (Its shape is similar to coffee pot, with inscriptions on its body. Currently housed in the Victoria & Albert Museum)

until it becomes thin as the thickness of teapots. Then they cut it into pieces, form the body of teapot, and polish it. The legs, handle, and spout need to be made separately, and then welded onto the body. The gift given by the Archbishop of Berkeley to the British East India Company was also produced in this period, reflecting the manufacturing techniques of British silverware at that time. Another early silver teapot in the shape of melon was made in 1685, and is currently housed in the Victoria & Albert Museum. It appears to be imitating Yixing purple clay teapot. This shape of teapot became popular in the early eighteenth century and has since become the mainstream of British teapots. This may indicate that the shape of British teapot gradually established by this time.

From a Teacup Without a Handle to a Teacup with a Handle

Ancient Chinese drank tea with bowls instead of cups. Before the Tang Dynasty, there was no clear distinction between tea and food utensils. In the Tang Dynasty, tea vessels were separated from wine and food vessels, becoming an independent system.[32] On tea parties at that time, all participants took turns to share a bowl of tea, and craftsmen have created

[32] Peng Zhaorong. Anthropology of Food and Drink [M]. Beijing: Peking University Press, 2013: 46.

different sizes of tea bowls according to their way of drinking and different occasions, such as party and drinking alone. Obviously, a handle couldn't fit in such a tea party.

During the Tang and Song Dynasties, boiling tea (Jian Cha, a special way of making tea, by putting ground tea into water the middle of boiling) and tea competitions (Dou Cha, competing the quality of tea by the color of tea soup and the appearance of bubbles) were very popular. On such events, there were no teapot, but only tea bowls. In the Song Dynasty, the openings of tea bowls were usually wider to better demonstrate the skills of participants. Tea bowls were called "Zhan," and saucers were created to prevent burns. According to Li Kuang's Ziqi Ji, during the reign of Emperor Baoying of the Tang Dynasty, the daughter of Cui Ning, the governor of Chengdu Prefecture, was fond of tea. She noticed that the tea cup was hot when poured into the hot water, so she melted wax and made a wax ring the size of the bottom of the cup, then took a small saucer under the wax ring, and tea cup on top of the wax ring: problem solved. After that, she had a painter make similar lacquerworks, and named it "Tuo."[33]

As an important part of Chinese culture, tea sets naturally embodies Chinese element as well. Each vessel has its own specific purpose and position, constraining each other without interference, but no repetition in function: reflecting the cultural connotation of "rhythm." From this perspective, handles will be redundant if there is already a tea saucer. During the Ming and Qing Dynasties, people drank tea with covered bowls with saucers: the lid represents the Heaven, the saucer the earth, and the bowl the human. This reflects the philosophical idea of "harmony among heaven, earth and human." This already has nothing to do with handles.

Besides, tea played a vital role in various ceremonies since ancient times. People have been treating guests with tea since the Tang and Song Dynasties; even ordinary people would use tea to greet each other or ask for a favor. In big events such as weddings, it is also common for the young couple to serve tea to the old. No matter to the elderly or to family or friends, the giver needs to show respect with both hands, and the recipient need to receive with both hands as well. Handle would be obstacles in such occasions.

[33] Liu Zhaorui. The Art of Drinking Tea in Ancient China [M]. Xi'an: Shaanxi People's Publishing House, 2002: 41.

Therefore, you can't see handles on Chinese tea bowls and cups. However, handles appear in almost all visual materials about British afternoon tea. So, when and why did British add handles?

The two tea cups on the tea table in the secret room of Ham Villa, the most historic tea space in the UK, may prove that there were no handles when tea was first brought to the UK. William Hogarth's painting "The Wollaston Family" completed in 1730 depicts the nighttime entertainment of aristocrats. There are several women sitting around tea tables, sipping tea without handles (Fig. 3.7). From this we can see the posture and demeanor of people holding cups: they wrap their fingers around the edge of the cup, gripping the bottom tightly, or placing their thumb at the bottom of the cup and their middle finger at the upper edge. In the 1768 painting "Paul Revere" by John Singleton Copley, a painter who

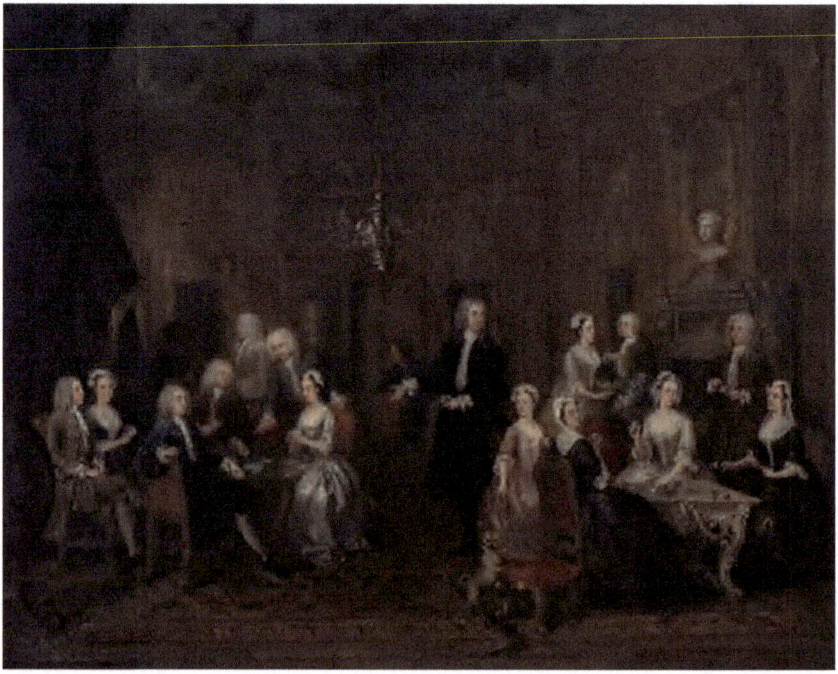

Fig. 3.7 William Hogarth's painting *The Wollaston Family* completed in 1730 depicts the nighttime entertainment of aristocrats. (There are several women sitting around tea tables, sipping tea without handles)

immigrated to London, the woman holds a tea saucer with single hand, and a cup filled with tea on the saucer. She holds the lower edge of the saucer with her thumb and middle finger, with her index finger resting on the upper edge and little finger slightly risen. Regardless of postures, the key is agility and elegance. For women, drinking tea is a chance to show their elegance as well as their porcelain. Later Wedgwood took advantage of this and launched the Black Rock tea set. The black teapot contrasts sharply with fair arms, highlighting the skin color and the beauty of women. There is currently no definite evidence to prove when handles were added; probably the mid to late eighteenth century, when local porcelain manufacturers got hold of the key techniques. However, among currently available materials, cups with handles first appeared in 1750.

Traditional British drinking utensils all come with handles. For example, Posset Cup that is used for hot drinks have one handle on each side, preventing burns. When handles on Posset Cups are "planted" onto Chinese tea cups, British tea culture expert Jane Pettigrew praised on her book *Tea Design*: "How thoughtful this design is!"[34]

In the UK, a teacup without a handle is called a "teacup like a saucer," while a teacup with a handle is called a "saucer like a teacup." Although Chinese had created saucers, they still put handles onto cups. Obviously, their understanding of the function of saucer is largely different from British. How did British use saucers when tea was first introduced there? Although Swedish writer Per Kalnr mentioned in his *Account of His visit to England* that British women drank hot tea directly from a teapot rather than pouring into saucers to cool it before drinking. In fact, they do drink with saucers probably because they're not accustomed to drinks that are too hot. The book *Tea Design* also holds a similar view, and it mentions the emergence of a saucer specifically designed for tea from the late eighteenth to early nineteenth century. This point is supported by a poster in 1772. It is titled *Lady Nightcap at Breakfast*, depicting a woman wearing a nightcap drinking tea from a tea saucer (Fig. 3.8). The traditional British drinking posture is to hold the tea cup and saucer together to the mouth, elegantly and balanced; hold the saucer with left hand and the cup right hand, with the little finger risen.[35] As can be seen, grace is the key.

[34] Same as footnote 6, p. 82.

[35] Same as footnote 32, p. 97.

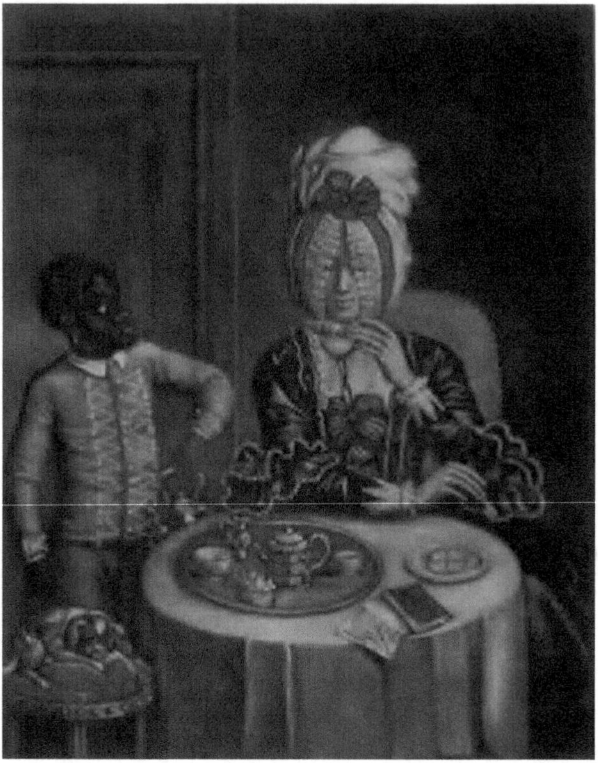

Fig. 3.8 A poster titled *Lady Nightcap at Breakfast*, depicting a woman wearing a nightcap drinking tea from a tea saucer

When British tea culture began to take shape, British would imitate China as much as possible, not only in drinking ways, but also in the usage of tea utensils and the arrangement of tea space. They were passionate about Chinese tea, as well as utensils and tea furniture. The inconvenience of transport and peoples' thirst for tea led to the extreme rarity of tea utensils, just like the extreme rarity of tea itself. As French philosopher Pierre Bourdieu expressed in his masterpiece *La Pistinction: Gritique sociale du juglement*, the cultural practice in daily consumption, from drinking, clothing, body to music, painting, and literature, all express the individual's position in society. For British aristocrats, elegant demeanor, behavior, and lifestyle are compelling evidence of their background, and mastering etiquette is self-explained. As a result, while tea symbolizes simplicity and integrity in China, it has transformed from meditative to expressive and from simple to luxurious when integrated into Britain, forming a brand-new cultural system. Drinking tea has become a medium for showcasing identity, showing off wealth, and self-promotion, facilitated and illustrated by utensils and manners of drinking. The difference in the drinkers' identity as well as way of drinking has created the unique British tea culture as well as tea set, with "nobility" as its back color.

CHAPTER 4

Moving Toward Mass Consumption

1 From Harbors to Coffee Houses

> Mrs. Jesse poured the tea. The oil lamp threw a warm light on the tea tray. The pot was china, covered with little roses... And there were sweet biscuits... Sophy Sheeky watched the yellow-amber liquid pouring from the spout, the steam and the aroma rising slowly. It was a wonder: that the leaves had been picked by yellow-skinned men and bronze-skinned men, packed in lead-lined chests and wooden chests, taken on board white-sailed ships, fought over by tempests and whirlpools, borne through the stars of the Southern Cross to be here at last, made in a china teapot from good clay, moulded by clever craftsmen in a city of porcelain, fired in a furnace at great heat....
>
> —A.S. Byatt, "Possession"[1]

The painter Samuel Scott (1702–1772), who was active in the second half of the eighteenth century, painted a work called *A Thames Wharf*, describing busy work scenes on the dock. Ships returning from long voyages crowded along the shore, with cargo piled up everywhere. Between the cylindrical and box filled with goods, there is a light-colored container tied with a rope, with a unique trademark of the East India Company and a number "316" on it. In the center of the painting, there is a

[1] [UK] Alan Macfarlane, et al. Green Gold: The Empire of Tea [M]. Hu Xilin, translator. Beijing: Social Sciences Academic Press, 2016: 87.

C. Zhang, *Beyond the Teacup: 18th Century Sino-British Tea Trade and Design Cultural Exchange*,
https://doi.org/10.1007/978-981-97-7691-7_4

foot-powered crane lifting a barrel into the warehouse. After arriving from the distant East, tea would enter the warehouse in London like this.

In the early days, people often transported tea with drums or jars, but later changed to boxes. These containers would be labeled with the name of the ship, and tea barrels or boxes would be numbered for the convenience of searching and statistics. Tea was stored in different locations according to its types, and classified according to quality before being sold. For example, OS represented odd smell, W represented woody, B represented burnt flavor, and SM represented smokiness. When sales began, these symbols would be written into the catalog for buyers to choose. Of course, tea would be reclassified and labeled after entering the retail market.

Since the 1680s, the British East India Company had formed a tradition of holding auctions in March and September each year. The auction adopted limited-time sales, lightening a candle when it officially started; the auction was over when it went out. The goods from the East were sold, including tea, ceramics, textiles, etc. The quotation was usually based on their cost, including freight, labor remuneration, insurance, import fees, etc.; the price pushed up during auction was the profit. And the bidding for tea was done by licensed tea brokers who represented their respective owners.

The collaboration between French illustrator Augustus Charles Pugin and British cartoonist Thomas Rowlandson in 1808 titled *Interior of Sale Room in East India House, During Sale* showcases the chaotic scene inside the auction venue: tea brokers flock to win their desired goods; the companies' representatives making gestures on the stage; the chairman leaned against a chair; the auctioneer stands on the stage; and a group of clerks downstairs concentrate on taking notes.

Tea entered the retail market through auctions. However, this was only true since the late seventeenth century. But in the middle seventeenth century, when tea trade hadn't been officially launched, tea was sold in retail in coffee houses. In fact, this was the place where Chinese tea, African coffee, and American chocolate gathered. For the tea trade at that time, the domestic market was particularly important. British traditionally drank beer, so they didn't have to learn; on the contrary, tea was a stranger to almost everyone, so it was a challenge faced by the British East India Company that how to make the public understand tea, fall in love with tea, and become accustomed to tea, so as to ensure continuous profit.

Some scholars believe that Britain ushered in a consumer revolution in the eighteenth century. With the continuous strengthening of the economic power and social status of the middle class, they hope to distance themselves from the lower class by imitating the lifestyle of the upper class, thus proving their identity. During this period, the luxury consumption group gradually shifted toward the affluent middle class. Historian Lorna Weatherill analyzed the consumption issues in Britain from a cultural and social perspective, examining over 2000 probate inventories. From these, she found a significant increase in consumption by the mid-eighteenth-century middle class, as their concern for social status led to the formation of new material culture and consumption behaviors. They began to try more commodity and services, using consumption as a means to showcase.[2]

According to her research, the earliest mention of tea drinking in the Halifax probate records dates back to the 1720s. The person who made the will was named George Mewson, a local lawyer. He had a tea table, a silver teapot worth £12 2 shillings, and a small amount of porcelain. In 1725, the wool merchant James Kitson of Halifax passed away, leaving an inheritance that included 67 "porcelain" items, a tea table tray, and a teapot. By the mid-eighteenth century, all surviving family ledgers recorded expenses for tea or coffee consumption, and teacups and other ceramic utensils appeared more frequently in wills. Weatherill concluded, after analyzing these probate inventories, that in the eighteenth century, especially in the mid-eighteenth century, tea had become extremely common among the middle class, and the quantity of ceramic tea ware also correspondingly increased. This reveals that drinking tea and coffee had become part of the daily routine of the middle class.[3] Faced with the growing market, it became a new challenge faced by tea merchants that how to cultivate consumption habits and how to make their brand known.

As Alan McFarlane observed, "Based on hundreds of years of retail experience and skills, people invented and improved a series of strategies, including advertising, storage, packaging and distribution. During this tea played many roles, one of which was a medium to establishing a new consumer society."[4] Indeed, in eighteenth-century Britain, modern

[2] Wu Guanzhong. The Origins of Modern Consumer Society - A Study on Consumption Issues in 17th and 18th Century Britain [D]. Nanjing: Nanjing University, 2014: 5.

[3] Lornia Weatherill. Consumer Behaviour and Material Culture in Britain, 1660–1760, Routledge, 1996: 37.

[4] Same as footnote 1, p. 21.

promotion methods including newspapers, ads, business cards, and storefront decoration came up, becoming a major force to stimulate consumption.

The earliest existing tea advertisement was published by Thomas Garway, the owner of Sultaness Head in London, in the *Mercurius Politicus* from September 23 to 30, 1658. It is believed that this was the first ever advertisement of product that appeared in newspapers in London.[5] The ad only included a few words, but it pointed out that this globally popular beverage was originated in China. In 1660, he designed another tea poster, which was also the earliest existing tea poster in Britain. In the seventeen century, British still used old woodcarving printing, so the composition, layout, and decoration of printed materials were often the same.[6] This poster is no exception, very similar to other posters at that time: it was composed of text and images, with text as the main focus and images only occupying a small corner, showing the growth of tea in its native place–China. The text was over 1300 words: the first paragraph explains that tea originated in China, while the rest introduces the growth, name, origin, efficacy, picking and drinking methods of tea, as well as the cultural character bestowed and its magical healthy effect.

Coffee, which was born in Ethiopia in the tenth century, also came to Britain in the seventeenth century. In the mid to late seventeenth century, coffee house was one of the most commonly invested commercial projects by merchants who traded with East. The first coffee house in London was founded by Greece Pasqua Rosee in 1652 and later called the "Cape of Turkey." By 1683, the total number of coffee houses in London exceeded 2000, including the Queen of Sudan Coffee house mentioned earlier.[7] Coffee houses from Turkey not only sold coffee, tea, and hot chocolate, but also provided tobacco and frozen fruit juice. According to the account books of the Queen of Sudan, the guests were mostly nobles and business elites, and police officers from the Royal Exchange, stockbrokers, lawyers, officials from the mayor's office, as well as merchants, investors, and shop owners nearby. In addition, there are also intellectuals such as writers, journalists, doctors, scientists, and politicians attracted by the power and

[5] Same as footnote 4, p. 122.

[6] Xiang Xiang. A Study of Modern Western Printing Media - From Gutenberg to the Enlightenment [M]. Shanghai: East China Normal University Press, 2001: 127.

[7] Stephen H. Twining. Twinings, Two Hundred and Fifty Years of Tea and Coffee, R. Twining & Co.LTD, 1956: 6.

wealth of the region. The huge profit in this industry attracted the government, and the parliament allowed the royal family to impose a consumption tax of 4p per gallon of coffee. It is interesting that the consumption tax on tea is 8 pence, twice that of coffee, which implies that tea was sold at higher price.

For regular customers, thirst and excitement alone were not enough to make them frequently visit the shop. No matter how refreshing the drinks were, what truly attracted them was information. For example, Thomas Gawai provided a large number of books, advertisements, and briefings in the coffee house, and there were always engaging discussions about news. Merchants were doing business, capital companies searching for investors, and speculators looking for opportunities. Everyone was analyzing information from overseas trading companies and events on financial, trade, or politics in Europe. Regular customers were usually men; although there were women as well, they were usually waitresses rather than consumers. Therefore, coffee houses were usually associated with male socialization. Here, tea was soaked in large wooden barrels and sold in large cups like beer, and was traded with tokens, printed with the name and address of coffee house. At that time, what really mattered was not tea drinking or tea utensils, but the commercial and financial information obtained during drinking.

2 "Fine Teas on Sale!"

With the further development of the trade in the British East India Company, products imported from the East gradually became indispensable among British nobility. Exotic daily necessities like tea, porcelain, furniture, and silk aroused the desires of new consumers. Since the late seventeenth century, markets were replaced by shops as the main scene of consumption. Shopping became a new leisure activity and lifestyle for the urban elite. People started to enjoy the pleasure of shopping, and fell into the trap of pursuing the beauty, delicacy or convenience, or products.

In the early eighteenth century, it was coffee houses, medical herb merchants, ceramic shops, silk merchants, and hat designers who sold tea. But when it came to the mid-eighteenth century, tea retailers preferred the title of "grocery and tea merchants." With the development of large-scale printing technology and the decrease in paper prices, shop owners started to boost sales through newspapers, flyers, trade cards, and notices.

Among them trade card was widely used. Apart from tea, retailers selling porcelain, cloth, wallpaper, clothing, and metal vessels all advertised by trade cards. They were usually etched and decorated with exquisite carved prints, describing the industries, trade names, addresses, business scope, and prices. Owners usually claim their prices as the lowest or most reasonable to impress customers. With both illustration and text, this form of advertising was more precise, direct, and wide compared with verbal communication. In tea sales, owners usually drew decorative patterns such as the origin of tea, trade situation, and sales methods onto the cards. This was also public education to some extent, allowing British to have a more comprehensive knowledge of tea and tea culture.

By studying these trade cards, we can also take a glimpse of the perception and consumption of tea at that time. In the 1740s, there was a shop named Parkinson from Twinings, its card stated that all the products it sold were "from Twinings." Several different sizes of fonts were in the Rococo styled frame, indicating the address and the source of its goods. The card design is consistent with the store's logo (Fig. 4.1). Another card from Raittes Tea Warehouse stated that the store sold a variety of high-quality tea, coffee, and chocolate, both wholesale and retail. This card was printed around 1757 and 1758. The store is located in St. Martin's Lane, Coventry Gardens, and its logo is a green tea can. This can appeared on the card as well (Fig. 4.2).

More cards incorporate Chinese elements to emphasize the imported nature of tea. In the 1840s, a tea merchant John Heigham Gresham made a card for his shop, with two tea jars on it, one labeled "High quality Xichun tea" and the other labeled "High quality Kungfu tea." There was a frame between two cans that resembled a tea can, with three Chinese characters inside. Two of them were holding umbrellas, while two of them holding some plant, symbolizing a bountiful harvest of tea. In the 1750s, the porcelain and glass shop Jane Toyloe & Son located on Pall Mall also had a card with Chinese characters. In the picture, two people were talking, one was a Chinese wearing pointed hat and loose-fitting clothes, and the other was a European businessman wearing a suit and holding a cane, symbolizing civilization. There was also a huge tea box filled with Chinese writing. Another example is the card of the tea merchant William Barber, displayed a patchwork scene in which a European woman holding a fan and a man wearing an official hat in Qing Dynasty, both were reclining, drinking tea, and chatting; on the other side there was a Chinese watering

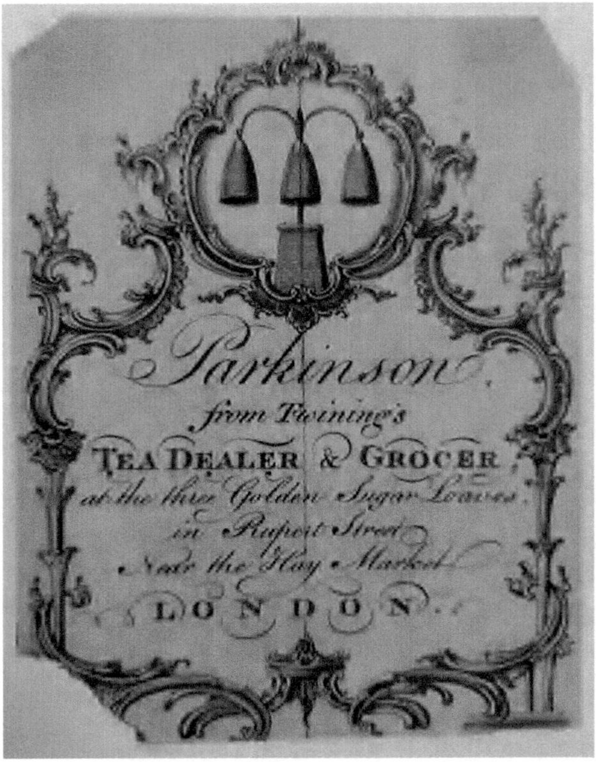

Fig. 4.1 In the early eighteenth century, there was a tea shop named "Parkinson from Twinings" with a business card that stated that all of its products were "from Twinings." (The card featured a Rococo-style border with several different sizes of English fonts, indicating the location and source of the tea shop's goods. The design of the card was generally consistent with the store's signboard)

a tea tree. The distant mountains in the picture are undulating, close to the landscape of tea-producing areas in southwestern China. The distant view on the left side was a Chinese pagoda standing in mountains. And in the center was a monument with the shop's name and address, and a locust. It is said that the image of locust has long been related to commercial activities in London; another interpretation is that locust is the logo of William Barber's store (Fig. 4.3).

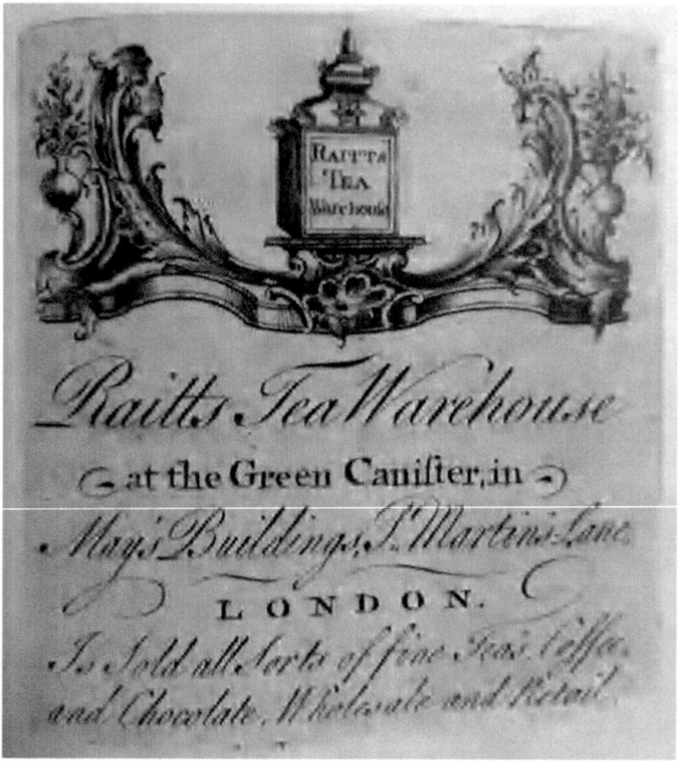

Fig. 4.2 Raittes Tea Warehouse stated that the store sold a variety of high-quality tea, coffee, and chocolate, both wholesale and retail. (This card was printed around 1757 and 1758. Its logo is a green tea can. This can appeared on the card as well)

Another tea merchant in Bristol, George Harris, connected Guangzhou and London on his card, both are important port cities in the Sino-British tea trade. Guangzhou was represented by ancient pagoda and a sampan, and London represented by the East India Company. The Pearl River and Thames River flew together on the picture, sparkling imagination of tea lovers about the cultural exchange between the two. In the middle is a Chinese imagined by Western, carrying a banner with words "Fine Teas" on it (Fig. 4.4).

As a form of advertising, commercial cards in tea shops became popular in the mid-eighteenth century, and their usage was further expanded. They were treated as trademarked letterhead, receipts, bills, and merchants

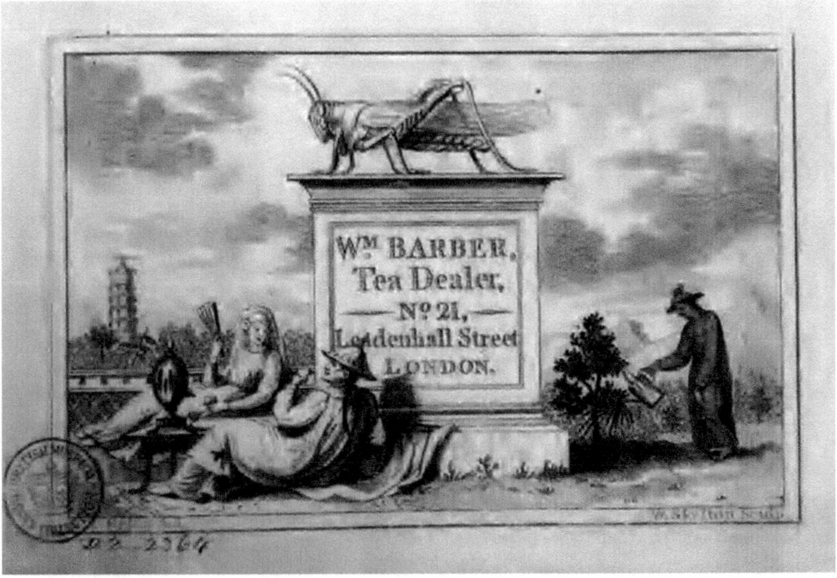

Fig. 4.3 The card of the tea merchant William Barber displayed a patchwork scene in which a European woman holding a fan and a man wearing an official hat in Qing Dynasty, both were reclining, drinking tea, and chatting; on the other side there was a Chinese watering a tea tree. (The distant mountains in the picture are undulating, close to the landscape of tea-producing areas in southwestern China. The distant view on the left side was a Chinese pagoda standing in mountains. And in the center was a monument with the shop's name and address, and a locust. It is said that the image of locust has long been related to commercial activities in London; another interpretation is that locust is the logo of William Barber's store)

intentionally print them on thin paper to pack tea. For example, Thomas Twinings began using decorative packaging paper with specific marking since the 1830s. The paper had a lion standing on its hind legs, and the words "Thomas and Daniel Twinings" in Roman font underneath it. And they simultaneously launched the same series of blank documents, flyers, etc. This allowed Twinings's brand name and the image of golden lion appear repeatedly and leave a deep impression on customers. These measures can be seen as pioneers in enterprise visual recognition (Fig. 4.5).

However, Twinings's innovation in building a new consumer experience goes far beyond this. In the eighteenth century, the thriving of shops expanded peoples' space and ways of consumption, interpreting a new

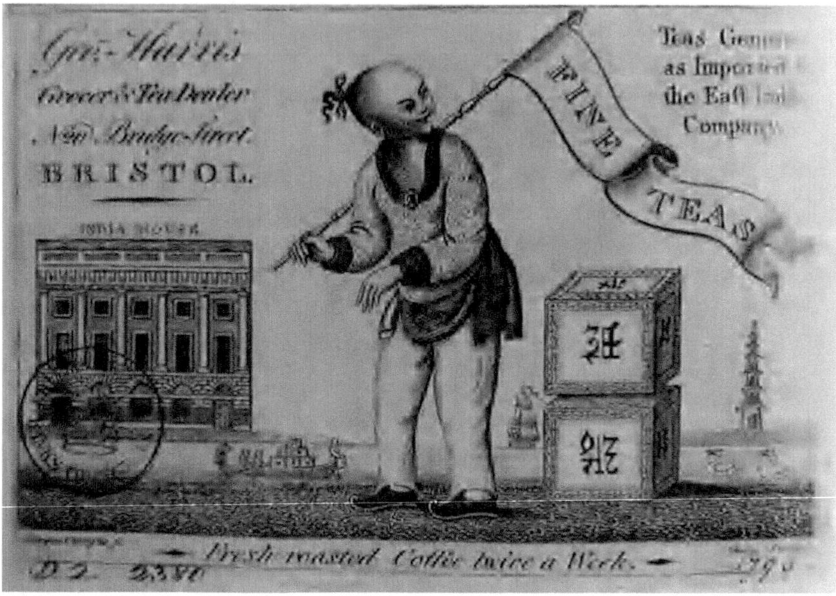

Fig. 4.4 George Harris from Bristol, connected Guangzhou and London on his card, both are important port cities in the Sino-British tea trade. (Guangzhou was represented by ancient pagoda and a sampan, and London represented by the East India Company. The Pearl River and Thames River flew together on the picture, sparkling imagination of tea lovers about the cultural exchange between the two. In the middle is a Chinese imagined by Western, carrying a banner with words "Fine Teas" on it)

atmosphere of prosperity and civilization, and becoming a new landscape in the city. To attract consumers, shop owners in the city have come up with unique sales strategies, forming a distinctive style of architectures for retail stores: the storefront signs, hanging signs, prominent display windows, and ads in front of the store became the most eye-catching features.[8] Some savvy shop owners would try their best to decorate a comfortable leisure space, encouraging consumers to stay long, experiencing new products.[9]

[8] Claire Walsh. Shop Design and the Display of Goods in Eighteenth-Century London. Journal of Design History. 1995(8): 157–176.

[9] Stobart Hann. Site of Consumption: the display of goods in provincial shops in eighteenth century England. in Cultural and Social History, 2005 (2): 181–186.

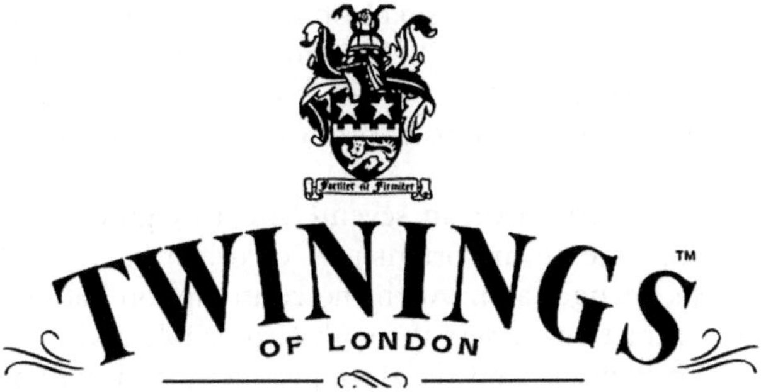

Fig. 4.5 The logo of Twinings

The best among them was Twinings. At that time, coffee houses were still exclusive to men. In 1706, Thomas Twinings invested in a coffee house named Tom's Coffee House, wholeselling tea and coffee to many coffee houses in London, and retailing loose tea as well. Ladies in upper class often ask their husbands or male servants into shops for tea, they themselves would wait outside in a carriage or sedan chair. Twinings saw the business in this, and bought the house next to the café in 1717, converting into a tea and coffee house for women. The innovation lies in providing women with a public space for communication, breaking the tradition of being exclusive to men.

At that time, both shops and residential buildings had door numbers; but if people wanted to search one of them, they needed a specific identifier or symbol. Thomas Twinings named its shop "Golden Lyon," after the king of beasts. This tea shop is still open on its original site—216th Strand Street. The storefront retains the design of the first generation of logo from over 300 years ago, with two officials in Chinese Qing Dynasty attaching to the elegant and noble Golden lion on both sides. This is the most historic brand logo still in use today.

On a certain day between 1715 and 1720, Mr. Warren of Bath purchased a set of ceramic tea plates, as recorded in Twinings's sales ledger. So, it can be seen that they sold not only tea but also tea sets. They also customize tea sets for genteel women. "Different types of tea have slightly different prices, ranging from 20 to 30 shillings per pound. The aristocratic ladies often go to Mr. Twinings' tea house in the Defro Courtyard together, just to experience the small Chinese porcelain cup and enjoy the refreshing, heavenly beverage..."[10] Twinings's teahouse liberated women. When men discussed matters in café, women could chat freely and exchange information in teahouses, promoting women's right in the public sphere.

From another perspective, in seventeenth to eighteenth centuries in Britain, shop became an important part of urban life, and the business model of shops changes along with the consumption habits of the elite. Shop owners attract customers through fashionable and elegant decoration, as well as exquisite and dazzling products, creating an image that satisfied their target buyers and letting them enjoy visiting in the store. The behavior of consumers entering the store is not only pure consumption, but also a way to showcase their identity. Meanwhile, the concept of "polite shopping" stood out in consumer culture. Consumer behavior became a way to emphasize peoples' taste and status, forming a part of the consumption venue. As an object of gaze through the display window, buyers were seen to be in a shop that suited their refined taste, which means that they had both aesthetics and consumptive power. The stores strived to create a "social space" for consumers that were elegant, comfortable, and filled with exquisite luxury goods. Just like Twinings's teahouses, noble women drink and chat here as a part of social activities.

In short, with the further development of retail industry, promotional methods such as storefront decoration, boutique display, and advertising emerged and became an important stimulation of consumption. Tea, an exotic beverage and beloved by the aristocrats, naturally became one of the hottest spots. As a medium, tea played a key role in establishing a new consumer society. To cater to the new market trend, tea merchants continuously purchased tea, providing a fundamental drive for the long-lasting prosperity of Sino-British tea trade. The conspicuous consumption of tea not only helped the elite to maintain their status and identity, but also differentiated them from other classes. Tea retailers played a crucial role in the development of new products, and their promotion and sales made tea a part of the quality life of Britain, further popularizing tea and enriching tea culture.

[10] [UK] Jane Pettigrew. The Design of Tea [M]. Translated by Liu Rong. Jinan: Shandong Art Press, 2013: 79.

3 Lifestyle Reshaped by Tea

As the supply continued to increase, the price gradually dropped. According to the appendix of the *Chronicles of Sino-British Relations*, which includes the selling price of tea per pound by the British East India Company in the first half of the eighteenth century, in 1705, the price of green tea per pound was 16 shillings and black tea 30 shillings. By 1748–1759, the average price dropped to 5 shillings 5 pence, and the drop in price accelerated the growth of sales in turn. The demand of tea encouraged the British East India Company to further expand tea trade, and the virtuous cycle between supply and consumption made tea affordable to more British people.

By the mid-eighteenth century, tea had become a common item on the bills of middle class and some working-class households, and it had even become a special "welfare" in some industries. For example, a traveler from Italy wrote in his travel record: "Even the most ordinary maid must drink tea twice a day to show her status, which they wrote into their contracts. The total cost of this special clause is equivalent to a maid's salary in Italy." There is a similar record in the salary ledger of Sochem Villa in Devonshire in the 1780s: "On February 19th, the 9-month salary for Jane Dowie is 15 pounds and 15 shillings. He was promised a pound of tea worth 16 shillings."[11]

The desire for tea in the UK bred smugglers. They came to exist not only due to the enormous commercial value, but also the heavy taxes that the government imposed on tea. Tea became a subject of taxation shortly after entering the UK. In a decree passed by the government in 1660, it was explicitly stipulated that a tax of 4 pence was levied for manufacturing and selling a gallon of coffee, and 8 pence for tea. This form of tax continued for the next 30 years, and the amount increased. In 1690, laws enacted during the reigns of William and Mary required an increase of 20% tariff in certain commodities, including tea. In the eighteenth century, tea remained one of the vital sources of taxation. According to Milburn's statistics in *The Business of the East*, the tax ratio of tea was between 70% and 200%, except for 36% from 1711 to 1712, 69% from 1745 to 1747, and 64% from 1768 to 1772.[12]

[11] Jane Pettigrew. A Social History of Tea [M]. National-Irust, 2001: 52.

[12] Liu Zhangcai. The 18th Century Sino-British Tea Trade and Its Impact on British Society [D]. Beijing: Capital Normal University, 2008: 108.

Due to the imbalance of supply and demand in the tea market, adulteration emerged besides smuggling. There were two ways of adulteration: coloring the tea leaves, and faking tea with other leaves or re-process the tea residue that had been brewed. "Green tea was easier to adulterate compared to black tea from Wuyi Mountain. As a result, European lost trust in green tea and favored black tea instead, which may explain why 80% of the world's tea consumption today is black tea."[13] The most obvious impact of tea adulteration was that black tea consumption surpassed green tea, becoming the most welcomed tea in the British market, laying the foundation of black tea culture. From another perspective, the smuggling and adulteration proved the huge demand. So, what exactly caused the frenzy of British for tea?

American sociologist Van Buren pointed out in his work *On the Leisure Class* that the wealthy leisure class influenced other class by showing off. The latter imitated the former to improve their social status; to be more specific, to imitate the consumption taste of upper class. With the abolition of sumptuary laws in early seventeenth century in Britain, social class became open and flowing, making it possible for people to blend into adjacent classes, and leading to the prevalence of "social imitation." Neil McKendrick, a scholar studying the history of consumption in Britain, believes that "social imitation" was an important factor of the birth of modern consumer society in eighteenth-century England. The luxurious consumption of elites drove all the levels of society, thus opening up a new era. "To emulate the upper class, middle class became more luxurious and frenzied; their behavior and ideas have driven other classes to compare and imitate. As a result, demand was inflated in an unprecedented way. Pushed by imitation and competition, both men and women were controlled by the desire of novel products. This caused the permeation of luxury goods as well as the vanity of possession into every corner of society, which used to be exclusive to the wealthy."[14]

Overall, after more than a century of dissemination and development, tea completed its transformation from an imported product to a localized beverage loved by all. In the early eighteenth century, before the reign of

[13] Beatric Hohenegger. The Story of Tea From the West to East. New York:ST. Martin's Press, 2006: 96.

[14] Neil McKendrick, John Brewer, J.H. Plumb. The Birth of a Consumer Society: The Commercialization of Eighteen-century England. Cambridge: Cambridge University Press, 2009: 10.

George I (1714–1727), tea was still a luxury drink; by the mid-eighteenth century, the consumption of tea had surpassed that of traditional British drinks such as beer and ale, and Scottish philosopher Sir Lord Kames found that even those who lived on welfare would drink tea twice a day. In 1751, Charles Deering described in his book the tea consumption in Nottinghamshire:

> It is not true that people here cannot afford tea, coffee and chocolate, especially tea. Tea has become so popular that not only gentlemen and wealthy businessmen who drink it, but also all sewing workers, women who starch clothes, and those who roll and stack fabrics. They would enjoy tea every morning... even ordinary laundry women believe that they cannot eat well in breakfast without tea and white bread with hot butter.[15]

By the end of the eighteenth century, the average annual consumption of tea in England exceeded one pound, reaching various levels including workers, farmers, and servants.

The popularity of tea fundamentally reshaped the diet of British, including dining times and methods, the use of tableware, and table manners. Besides tea drinking, the catering behavior evolved around tea also included breakfast. Before the seventeenth century, British people had no habit of sitting around and having breakfast together, just like they had never seen tea. The main meal was usually served in the afternoon or evening according to the profession and social status of the breadwinner. For example, farmers worked in the fields all morning, so they didn't eat until noon. William Harrison described this in his introduction to the life of English people in late sixteenth century. All people only ate in afternoon and evening except for the kids who couldn't stand the hunger from waking up to the afternoon.[16] In the mid-seventeenth century, some British people began to eat casually before their afternoon meal, but not considered a former meal. Samuel Pepys's diary records that he occasionally went for a morning draught on streets or bars. But this was neither a routine nor with his family.[17] It was in the mid-seventeenth century that aristocrats started the trend of breakfast. And by the first half of the eighteenth

[15] Same as footnote 8, p. 94.

[16] William Harrison. Description of Elizabethan England 1577, Whilefish:Kessinger Publishing, 2004: 140.

[17] "morning draught" was a term used in the seventeenth century that is not commonly employed today. It referred to the act of drinking alcohol early in the morning.

century, having breakfast with family became the norm of the day. In 1729, Scottish Mackintosh found a change in greetings: "in the past, when I went to my friends' house in the morning, they usually asked me if I had had breakfast bread; but now their questions changed to tea. Moreover, the big glasses of ale and toast bread, as well as a small amount of nice Scottish health wine disappeared, and replaced by teapot simmered on the stove, silver and ceramic utensils on the tea table, as well as jam and cream."[18]

In the mid-eighteenth century, tea began to prevail in breakfast in all families; the underprivileged would drink tea and eat bread, while some decent families even dressed up for breakfast. This gathering gradually evolved into a convention, fixed around 9 am, included tea, coffee, or hot chocolate, with newspapers, hot bread, butter, jam, and sometimes cream. Duncan Forbes commented on this, "The excessive consumption of tea has become so widespread that the working class, especially the poor, drink tea every morning and thus abandoned ale."[19] A Swedish described the scene of English breakfast tea: "My appetite was so good – I ate 3 hot buns and a pint of tea with cream at a heat… In the UK, it's almost ubiquitous that wealthy families have breakfast. They drink tea but not in the same way as in Sweden. We usually drink a lot of hot water on an empty stomach, but British take it in a more natural way: they eat one or several slices of oatmeal bread at the same time…Servants in London could also have breakfast like this."[20] In 1758, an article titled *The Good and Bad of Tea* described the popularity of tea in breakfast: "having tea in breakfast and tea brewing is already well-known and do not require any explanations; Some like to put both cream and sugar, some put either, and some put none…"[21]

In contrast, workers would buy breakfast tea on their way to work. There was an ad on a newspaper in London: "Ladies and gentlemen, please note that Spencer's earliest breakfast shop serves breakfast every day except Sunday, including high-quality tea, sugar, bread, and milk, at 4 pence per person…For the afternoon is 3 pence, with tea, sugar and milk.

[18] Ma Xiaoli. Research on British Tea Culture from a Multidimensional Perspective [M]. Hangzhou: Zhejiang University Press, 2010: 49.

[19] The comment of Dunkan Forbes, recorded in *Illustrations of Cheapness Tea*, p. 254.

[20] Same as footnote 20, p. 49.

[21] Same as footnote 20, p. 49.

The location is between the intersection of Denston and St. John's Street by the new river, opposite the Seydler Mineral Spring Sanatorium."[22]

Breakfast provided an opportunity for British families to communicate and get closer to each other. Members gather together to enjoy tea and snacks, which not only replenishes energy but also generates comfort and pleasure and brings them closer so as to create a good tradition of family. As a result, breakfast has become an important medium for decent families to maintain and showcase their dignities. However, due to the fact that most of the beverages and dishes in breakfast are imported like tea, some believe that it was the British East India Company that promoted breakfast for more benefit.[23] Indeed, there are a large amount of Chinese porcelain plates, pottery cups, and metal vessels on the breakfast table except for food and drinks. These imported necessities add grace and beauty to the table, and became the "standard" in peoples' minds.

As a result, tea shifted from a prop of wealth and power in the upper class to the foundation of the subsistence of working class. In 1797, British author Frederick Eder documented the tea-drinking activities of workers: "Anyone who accidentally walks into these farmhouses in Middlesex and Surrey during mealtime will find that the poor people not only drink tea in the morning and evening but also in dinner." For them, tea is a necessity, a beverage to swallow dry and hard food, and the only comfort in their bitter lives.

British anthropologist Alan McFarlane described the role of tea in the industrial revolution in his book *Green Gold: The Tea Empire in great length*. He believes that the tea break time of workers had a significant impact on modern British economy and society. "Tea breaks boosted peoples' endurance, gave workers hope and became the most valued social time of those who engaged in heavy and tedious work for a long period of time, in factories, small workshops, offices and mines."[24] More importantly, in addition to social functions, the hot tea changed British's habits of drinking alcohol or unboiled water, significantly improving their health. In addition, tea is also regarded to make people more restrained, kind, and gentle. The obsession of tea brought about unprecedented changed to the country.

[22] Same as footnote 20, p. 51.

[23] Smith D. Woodruff. Consumption and the Making of Respectability, 1600-1800. Routledge, 2002: 85.

[24] Same as footnote 8, p. 115.

In the mid-nineteenth century, historian John Davis wrote, “in terms of the revolutionary impact on nations’ habits, nothing can compare to tea in the UK in the past century.” Another point is from Sidney Mentz, a renowned anthropologist known for his research on material culture: “the first cup of sweetened hot tea by British workers is a landmark event, as it foreshadowed the transformation of the society, and a complete reshaping of the economic and social foundations.”[25]

Tea from China had been through strangeness and skepticism in the eighteenth century, had broken the upper echelons and embraced by middle and lower class, and eventually became the national beverage of Britain. Tea greatly changed the way people live and social. Especially for the impoverished, tea was off the altar and became a comfort, allowing them to take a break from their busy lives. As a result, tea, once an exotic beverage and a luxury item, was finally integrated into popular culture.

[25] Same as footnote 8, p. 123.

CHAPTER 5

Challenge and Integration: China's Response to Western Market

1 Changes in Trade Patterns: The Establishment of 13 Factories in Guangzhou and Tea Export

Tea is a traditional Chinese beverage. As mentioned in Chap. 1, the development of tea from medicine to commodities occurred during the Western Han Dynasty, and it was during this period (206 BC to 25AD) that tea began to be exported. At that time, China traded in countries in South China Sea, and tea was one of the most important commodities. China's tea export sales also dominated the world tea market for a long time, and it was initially transported from Guangzhou through waterways. In the late fifth century, Turkish began to barter tea from the Mongolian Border. In the Tang Dynasty, foreign trade prospered and was managed by the Market Shipping Bureau, and the government began to levy taxes on tea, resulting in a significant increase in tea trading volume. Later in the Northern Song Dynasty, Market Shipping Bureaus were established in Guangzhou, Mingzhou (now Ningbo), Hangzhou, and Quanzhou, and tea was the main commodity in these places. And in the Southern Song Dynasty, merchants from Arab, Italia, Japan, and India came, making Quanzhou an overseas transportation hub. As a result, tea from the nearby Fujian Province was sold in large quantities. The Yuan Dynasty remained the same. In the Ming Dynasty, Zhenghe's seven voyages to the West further promoted its sale. It can be said that tea has been involved in overseas

C. Zhang, *Beyond the Teacup: 18th Century Sino-British Tea Trade and Design Cultural Exchange*,
https://doi.org/10.1007/978-981-97-7691-7_5

trade since the beginning, and long been prominent as a symbol of China's traditional material and spiritual civilization.

As discussed in Chap. 1, Sino-British tea trade was closely related to the trade policies of the Qing Government. In 1685, the 24th year of the Kangxi reign, the government established four customs to collect tariffs, located in Guangzhou (Guangdong Province), Zhangzhou (Fujian Province), Ningbo (Zhejiang Province), and Yuntaishan (Jiangsu Province), respectively. In 1757, the 22nd year of the Qianlong reign, foreign trade was restricted and the Canton System established, the Thirteen Factories became the only window.

There is no consensus in the academic community on the official date for the establishment of the Thirteen Factories. But a relatively convincing statement comes from *Research on the Thirteen Factories* by Liang Jiabin, a foundational work of studying the Canton System. The author believes that the Thirteen Factories was established earlier than 1720. According to historical records, the official factory of the Thirteen Factories started in 1719, but the name "the Thirteen Factories" and the system had already existed before that. The author also holds that the development of the Thirteen Factories into a complete foreign trade system was closely related to the Canton System. Anyway, the Thirteen Factories contributed to the unprecedented prosperity of foreign trade in Guangzhou. British merchant William Hickey described the grandeur of the time in 1768:

> The hustle and bustle in the Pearl River is like the Thames under London Bridge; while the difference lies in the form of sailboats, and there are large sailboats in the Pearl River. In the eyes of foreigners, nothing is more spectacular than sailboats lining up for several miles.[1]

According to existing records, in the early Qing Dynasty, Southeast Asia was a traditional trade partner of Guangdong. Countries like Luzon (now Philippines), Vietnam, Siam (now Thailand), Singapore, Java (now Indonesia) all came to Guangzhou for trade. And major western trade partners were the UK and the US; other countries included Denmark, Portugal, Mexico, the Netherlands, Peru, Hamburg, Bremen, Austria, Italy, Chile, Prussia, France, etc.[2]

[1] Hu Qiaoli. Guangdong Local Chronicles and the Thirteen Factories – A Collection of Materials on the Thirteen Factories [M]. Guangzhou: Guangdong People's Publishing House, 2014: 222.

[2] Liang Jiabin. A Study on the Thirteen Factories in Guangdong [M]. Guangzhou: Guangdong People's Publishing House, 1999: 354.

Among them Britain boasted the most trading ships. Hosea Ballou Morse wrote the book *The Chronicles of the East India Company Trading to China* based on his own experience. He wrote in the preface that "What I mean by British trade is only the literal meaning of Britain. In fact, it's the trade between Guangzhou and London, and London maintains strict exclusive power over the East India Trade Union Company, commonly known as the (British) East India Company."[3] For example, during the reign of Emperor Qianlong (1757–1795), at the beginning of the Canton System, a total of 517 British merchant ships came to Guangzhou, accounting for 38% of all ships. This data indicates a huge trade volume between China and Britain. Despite various restrictions, trade in Guangzhou flourished unprecedentedly throughout the entire Thirteen Factories system, making it the country's foreign trade center. The UK ranked the top in trade volume with China. In 1764, the value of imported British goods reached 1.208 million taels of silver, taking up 63.3% of the total value of imports from Western countries; from 1795 to 1799, the average was 5.373 million, holding 91%; by 1830–1833, the average grew to 7.335 million, and the proportion fell to 80%: still a huge proportion.[4] After carefully studying *The Selected Statistical Materials of Modern Chinese Economic History*, Yan Zhongping concluded that Britain had already been prominent in Guangzhou's maritime trade with the West. Other European countries included Prussia, France, the Netherlands, and Denmark, but their total import volume to China was surprisingly less than half of that of Britain.[5] In Macartney's personal diary, he also wrote that the trade with France, the Netherlands, Denmark, the US, and Sweden had sharply declined and disappeared within a few years.[6] From this we can see that the establishment and blooming of the Thirteen Factories were the result of trade, and Britain was not only the main partner of the Thirteen Factories but also the major trade partner of China.

Specifically, for export tea, Fujian has been a major producing area since ancient times. Before Guangzhou became the only foreign trade window,

[3] [US] Ma Shi. The Chronology of the British East India Company's Trade with China [M]. Translated by Qu Zonghua, Edited by Lin Shuhui. Guangzhou: Sun Yat-sen University Press, 1991: 6–7.

[4] Xu Dezhi. A History of Guangdong's Foreign Economic Trade [M]. Guangzhou: Guangdong People's Publishing House, 1994: 97.

[5] Yan Zhongping. Selected Statistical Data on Modern Chinese Economic History [M]. Beijing: China Social Sciences Press, 2012: 1.

[6] [UK] George Macartney, John Barrow. Observations of the Macartney Embassy to China [M]. Translated by He Gaoji, He Yuning. Beijing: Commercial Press, 2013: 57.

cities like Xiamen and Quanzhou were all important ports, and tea has always been the main commodity for export. When the Qing government changed its foreign policies and demanded "all foreign ships must be docked in Guangzhou" and all the tea from Fujian, Jiangsu, Zhejiang, and Anhui provinces "must be shipped by sea and gathered in Guangzhou."[7] Foreign merchants who wanted to purchase things like tea and silk had to entrust the Thirteen Factories. They did not need to buy on their own, but be handled by the official factory. That is to say, all tea must be sold to the Thirteen Factories before being sold to overseas. Tea was the most important export commodity in the eighteenth century, and among the 13 merchants in the Thirteen Factories, 10 of them were from Fujian Province, including the most renowned Pan Zhen and Wu Bingjian.[8] This has naturally linked tea from Fujian to the tea export in Guangzhou.

British traded with the Thirteen Factories through contracts. Usually at the end of the previous year, after all the ships of the East India Company left, the Thirteen Factories would discuss the quantity, grade, price, and other aspects of tea with the East India Company's chief officer who stayed in Guangzhou, and sign relevant contracts. Hosea Ballou Morse recorded that Chinese merchants and chief officer had "good connection," supporting and facilitating each other.

To ensure tea trade, some merchants set up tea packaging factories in Guangzhou, where tea was packed before sold abroad. Taking Fujian tea as an example, after long-distance travel through mountains and rivers, it usually arrived in Guangzhou after mid-October. The wholesaler would carefully take out the dampened tea and dried them before selling to the merchants. Due to the requirements for packaging, variety, classification standards, and other aspects put forward by foreign merchants, tea would be processed for the second time in packaging factories. There workers needed to first package the tea in different grades: the most exquisite tea was packed in appropriately sized lead drums; high-quality tea in small boxes; and inferior tea in large boxes. These boxes were customized, made by carpenters in advance; and their edges were wrapped with lead by plumbers. After that, packaging workers would put the tea into them. Boxes with high-quality tea also required painters to paint patterns on the outside, and those without patterns needed paper labels, with the name of

[7] (Qing) Zhou Kai. Xiamen Chronicles [M]. China Taipei: Chengwen Publishing House, 1967: 116.

[8] Based on the statistics in Chap. 3 of the second part of "A Study on the Thirteen Factories in Guangdong".

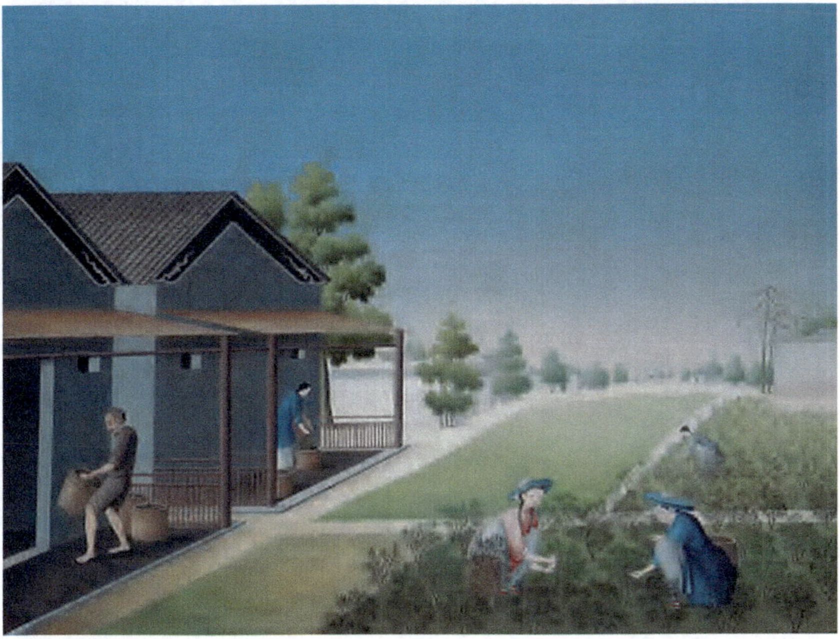

Fig. 5.1 Tea picking

the cargo ship printed in English, the type of tea, etc. Then they were wrapped and sewed with mats, and tied firmly with rattan. An additional label needed to be added outside for convenience. After all the packaging was completed, the boxes are ready to be loaded.[9]

The process of tea export is also depicted by Chinese artists specialized in export painting. This type of painting was particularly prevalent from the late eighteenth century to the early nineteenth century, both in business and in Western art market. These paintings were grouped in a dozen, depicting the various stages of tea production in Chinese painting style: hoeing, sowing, watering, tea picking, sorting, placing stacked tea into baskets or trays, spreading and drying leaves, frying, weaving tea containers, shipping in rivers, and repackaging and weighing them in warehouses in Guangzhou. Although these paintings (Figs. 5.1, 5.2, 5.3, 5.4, 5.5 and 5.6)

[9] Yao Xiangao. Historical Materials on Modern Chinese Foreign Trade (1840–1895) [M]. Beijing: Zhonghua Book Company, 1962: 264–265.

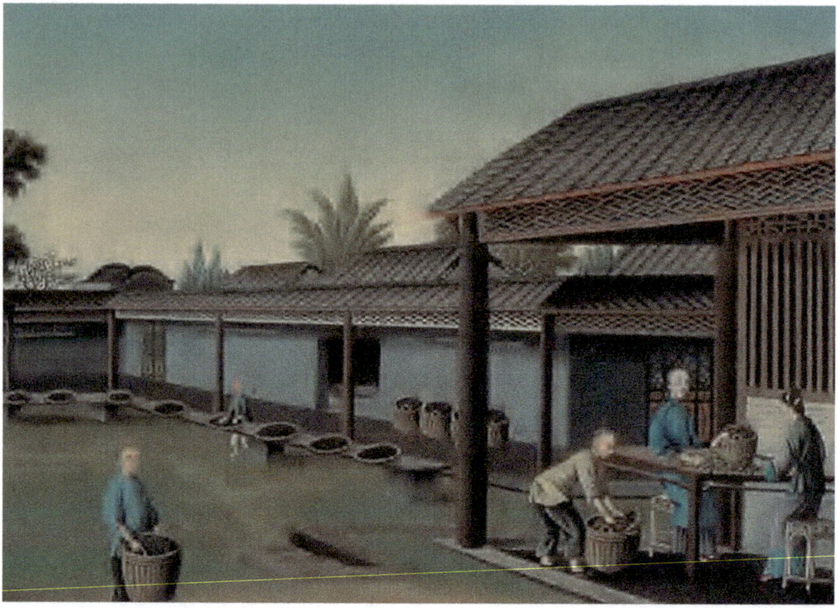

Fig. 5.2 Sorting

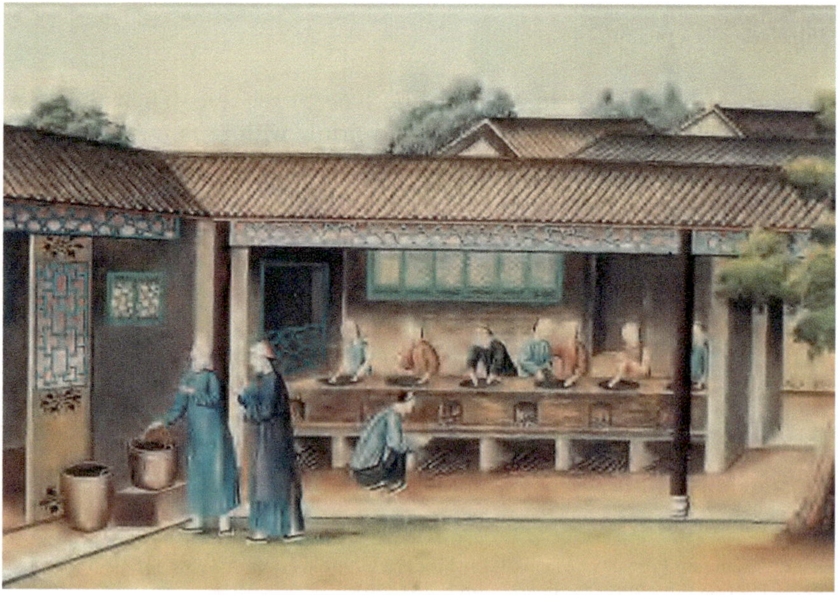

Fig. 5.3 Tea frying

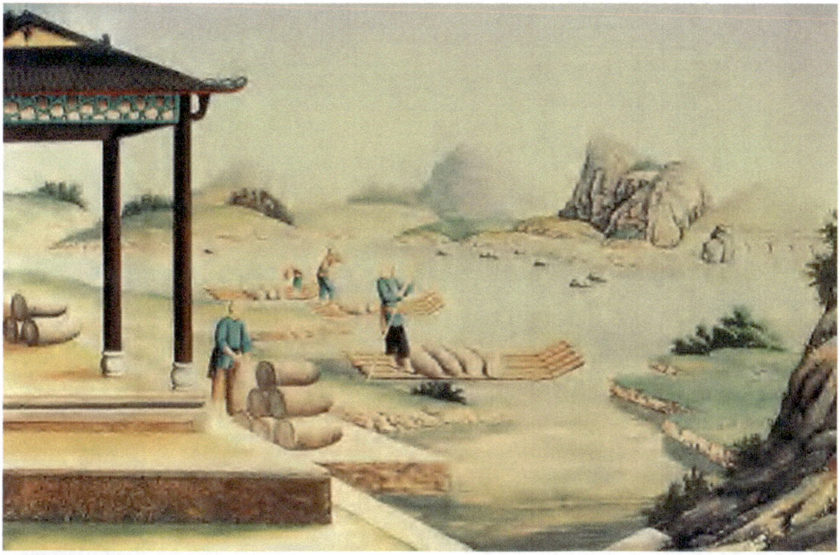

Fig. 5.4 Shipping by river

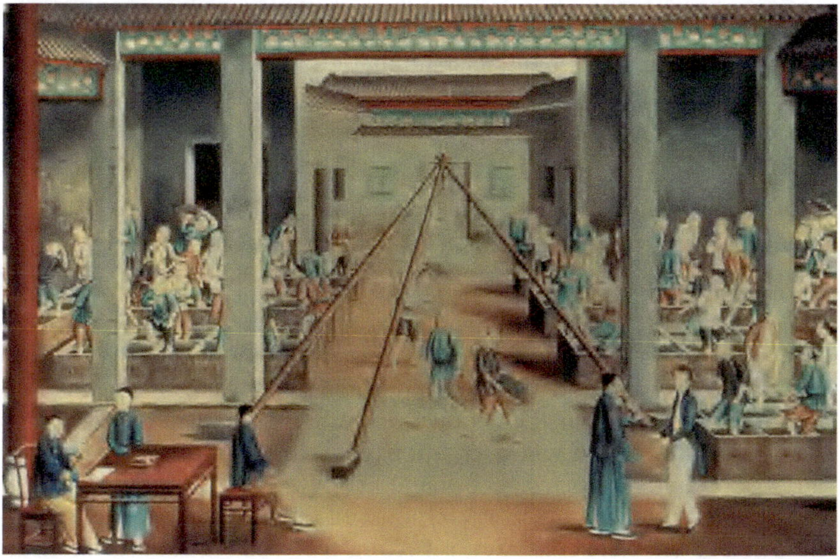

Fig. 5.5 Repackaging and weighing in warehouses in Guangzhou

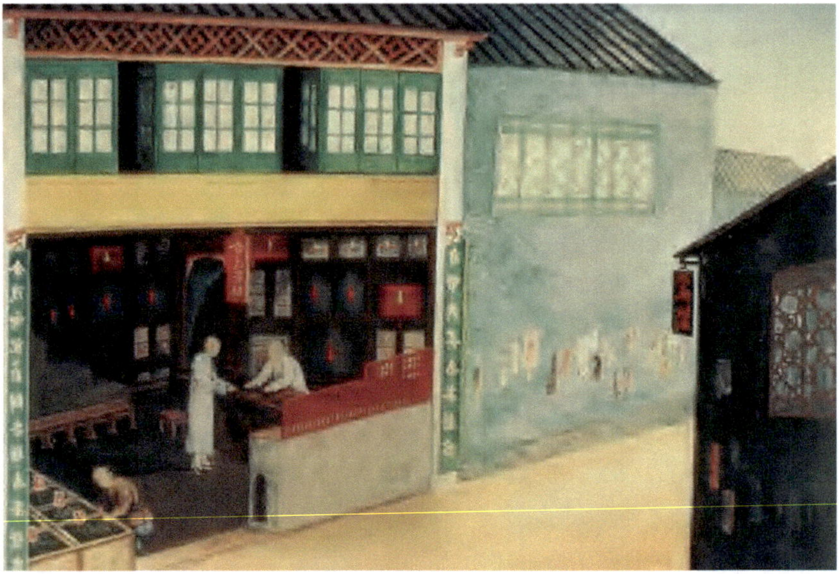

Fig. 5.6 Selling

depict the process in a concise way, they allowed Westerners to have a deeper and more concrete understanding of how tea was produced in the East, step by step. At that time, they were precious materials as public education about tea.

2 A Complete and Efficient Ceramic Production System in Jingdezhen

Among the bulk commodities from the Thirteen Factories, there were silk, porcelain, and various handicrafts except for tea. The handicrafts were mostly tea utensils and decoration in tea spaces required by the British. With the expansion of market demand, foreign merchants in Guangzhou have deeply involved in the production of these handicrafts, leading to changes in production and decoration. One of the most representative one was ceramics exported to Britain. The revolution in the production and decoration techniques was a response of Chinese ceramic industry to the demand of Western market, reflecting the exchange and collision in design between China and the UK.

The ceramic industry in Jingdezhen can be traced back to the Han Dynasty. Till the early Ming Dynasty, the porcelain production system was matured and renowned for its advanced craftsmanship and production scale. At that time, the central government established a factory in Jingdezhen to meet the needs of the imperial, as well as rewards and exchanges both domestically and externally. The founding of the Imperial Ware Factory has promoted the producing techniques, further refining the division of labor and coordination. In the Qing Dynasty, Cheng Tingji recorded in detail the division of labor in his book the *Fuliang County Annals*. There were a total of 23 works: "Big Bowl Works, Wine Bell Works, Plate Works, Writing Works, Color Works, Box Works, Mud and Water Works, Lacquer Works, Rope Works, Barrel Works, Dyeing Works, Eastern Dui Works, and Western Dui Works."[10] Such meticulous division formed an organization close to modern industry: the needs of excellence, efficiency, and maximizing benefits were inherent in the production mode.

This mode enabled Jingdezhen to cater to the demanding court, and prompted it to step forward to commodity production. With the production mode of official kilns radiating to civilian kilns, it improved the overall efficiency and level of techniques of Jingdezhen porcelain industry. The cost of a single piece was reduced, laying a solid foundation for commercialization. At that time, there were over 1000 kilns and 70,000 workers, making it the world's largest industrial production base.

In the mid to late Ming Dynasty, the corvee system was adjusted to "silver payment for labor," allowing Jingdezhen porcelain workers to break free from the restriction of government and be able to choose their own employers. This measure elevated the social status and enthusiasm of porcelain workers. Some of them turned to work in the folk kilns in Jingdezhen, which were the main body for export porcelain. These folk kilns could not be as comprehensive and complete as imperial kilns, nor could they reach the scale of the later. "Jingdezhen ceramics are made from the same source, and the 3 industries of the adobe workshop, the red shop, and the kiln workshop each carry out their own tasks and are divided into their own groups. The essence of their techniques was only passed down to their own group to maintain their business, with their spirits concentrate and hands coordinate with their mind...The professionalism of their duty is inherited from generation to generation, until they're known

[10] (Qing Dynasty) Zhu Yan. Translated and Annotated "Tao Shuo" [M]. Translated and annotated by Fu Zhenlun. Beijing: Light Industry Press, 1984: 138.

for their family names."[11] The above three industries can be further subdivided. The owner of folk kilns adopted a "specialization in each profession approach," with division of labor and coordination, each house focused on a specific production unit of the entire organization, which not only improved the technical level but also ensured efficiency. In addition, there are service industries around ceramic production, including raw material, saggar, packaging and handling, leftovers repairing, tools, ceramic service, sales, etc. These industries formed a complete industrial chain, from raw materials, fuel supply, casting, glazing, painting, and red shop[12] to firing, then sold and transported by shops and merchants. *The Records on Jingdezhen Ceramics* described this phenomenon: "Ceramics have kilns, kilns have workshops. The craftsmen have their creations, and each creation is associated with a household. Pottery is the resource on which every household relies."[13] Besides, to meet market demand, each step followed their respective standards, industries depended on each other: the refined division of labor was the pioneer of modern assembly line manufacturing.

In 1712, in a letter sent back to Europe, French missionary Pere Francois Xavier D'entreolles recorded the working of the painters in Jingdezhen: "the painting is divided among many painters in a workshop. One painter is only responsible for the first colored circle on the edge, another paint flowers, the third coloring; some specialize in painting mountains and rivers while others in painting birds and animals."[14] Similar records are also seen in Lan Pu's the Records on Jingdezhen Ceramics-Painting: "The creation of blue and white porcelain involves both round and carved vessels. Producing a single piece often requires the efforts of ten or even a hundred people. Those who draw only draw without dyeing, while those who dye only dye without drawing. This division of labor ensures that each person can focus on their specific task without being

[11] Fang Lili. Civil Kilns in Jingdezhen [M]. Beijing: People's Fine Arts Publishing House, 2002: 145.

[12] Jingdezhen is a specialized industry that produces and markets painted porcelain. Specifically, it is divided into four categories: freehand painted porcelain, traditional painted porcelain, artistic painted porcelain, and Huangjiazhou decorated porcelain.

[13] Fu Zhenlun. An Exhaustive Annotation of Jingdezhen Pottery Records [M]. Beijing: Beijing Booklist Information Publishing House, 1999: 34–36.

[14] [French] Dominique Hurdeman. Jesuit Letters from China: Correspondence on the Jesuit Mission in China (Volume 2) [M]. Translated by Zheng Dide, Zhu Jing, et al. Zhengzhou: Big Elephant Press, 2001: 98.

distracted by other aspects of the production. In the workshop, there are designated areas for drawing and dyeing, ensuring that each step is carried out with precision."[15] The pattern on a piece required several people to complete: those who painted objects only painted objects, those who paint landscapes only paint landscapes, drawers never painted and painters never drew. The division of labor was strict and well organized. This meticulous division was to facilitate workers in every process to work quickly and with high quality, so as to improve efficiency while ensuring techniques. This production mode was both effective and organic, guaranteed the quality of products. *The Annals of Jiangxi Province* records the composition of craftsmen at a large kiln in Jingdezhen during the Wanli period, Ming Dynasty. There were roughly 4 masters with 39 assistants, 16 porcelain craftsmen with 86 assistants, 4 painters with 19 assistants, 3 glazing craftsmen with 3 assistants, 5 craftsmen writing the year, 3 masters made saggar with 24 assistants, and a group of strong men making clay with 1 master. In the process, each link was further separated into independent steps. For example, in painting, each complex pattern was subdivided into multiple simple patterns. Beginners started from the simplest, and then learnt another one when they mastered. They learnt as they grew. This mode allowed even green hands to quickly participate in production, to work with experienced, skilled masters, providing a clear career path. However, seen from another perspective, this has turned craftsmen into replaceable screws on this production line. They did not need core skills; if one left, others could be substitutes, so as to prevent delay.

The craftsmen in the folk kilns were ordinary workers who lacked cultural awareness and aesthetics. Their painting skills were nothing but experiences to make a living, so they never sought innovation. Over a long time, the techniques inherited from masters to apprentices had formed a relatively stable program in terms of content, subject matter, form, color, and technology. They were only responsible for what they were similar to, followed the existing production mode, and produced according to orders. This reduced the technical demand, therefore ensuring the sufficiency of human resources: a low industry barrier made it easier for more labor to join.

With the expansion of porcelain industry, the prosperity of Jingdezhen was described as "craftsmen come from all directions, and artifacts go to all parts of the world." As Yin Hongxu recorded, "it is reported that there

[15] Same as footnote 12, p. 19.

are 18,000 workshops in Jingdezhen, with some big commercial factories occupying a large area and employing a huge number of workers. It can be said that there are over 1 million souls here, consuming 10,000 kg rice and 1000 pigs every day… In addition to the high cost of living, Jingdezhen is also a destination for many impoverished families who find it difficult to survive in the surrounding cities. Workers include children and physically weak people, as well as the blind and cripples. The disabled make a living by grinding materials."[16]

For thousands of years, the techniques in Jingdezhen had been taught strictly within fathers and sons, or masters and apprentices. This was the convention and the law. The skills were taught verbally, and the number of apprentices and time length were also strictly limited, varied according to the demand of different industries. For example, in "Red Shops," large stores could take around a dozen disciples while small stores at least 2 to 3 at a time. The apprenticeship period lasted at least three years, and only with the approval of their masters could they graduate. And they were not allowed to switch careers later on. This contributed to the stability of human resource, and secured the inheritance of skills. These family workshops were scattered in blocks in Jingdezhen, according to the demand and their types of work.

Spanish monk Juan Gonsales Merdoza recorded in *Historia del Gran Rei no de la China*: "Craftsmen and workmen of the same profession live on designated streets; different specialties are not allowed to live together. If you come to the streets and see, you will know the entire street is of the same profession."[17] These craftsmen lived as organized and worked as organized: year after year, their working hours were scheduled. According to the *Jingdezhen Ceramics Chronicle*, "from the spring equinox to the autumn equinox, they work every day from 6 a.m. to 5 p.m. The night work is limited to 10 p.m. And from the autumn equinox to the spring equinox, they work every day from 7 a.m. to 6 p.m. The night work is limited to 11 p.m. There is a noon break in summer and autumn, but only limited in painters and billet workers. But for the kiln workers, they have to burn the kilns day and night, they only take shifts but without Sundays."[18]

[16] [US] Moira Pen. The Great Divergence: Development of the Economies of Europe, China, and the Modern World [M]. Translated by Shi Jianyun. Nanjing: Jiangsu People's Publishing House, 2004: 77.

[17] [Spain] Mendosa. History of the Great Chinese Empire [M]. Translated by He Gaoji. Beijing: Zhonghua Book Company, 1998: 33.

[18] Same as footnote 11, p. 218.

"Every year, the work started from March 1st in the lunar calendar to December 13th. They worked throughout the year, and only took breaks on the Dragon Boat Festival in May, the Hungry Ghost Festival in July, the Mid-Autumn Festival in August, and the Labor Day in October. Workers must complete a fixed workload within a certain period of time, depending on the type of work. For instance, the workload of billet workers depended on the size of the vessel. For large ones they must complete 10 blank drawn parts every day; for small ones the number was 50; and for bowls and plates, the number was 100. This management was precise, promoted the timely completion of orders and facilitated scheduling."[19]

In short, regional specialized production, clear labor division, and complex information networks created a highly developed industrialized city in Jingdezhen. This enabled the entire industry to maintain its speed, efficiency, and exquisiteness, developing tremendous production capacity. This included manufacturing, labor division and specialization, commercialization, and adaptability to the global market. By the late Ming Dynasty, Jingdezhen civilian kiln porcelain had already spread "throughout the country and even to foreign lands, wherever ships and carriages reached, there were no exceptions to the Rao porcelain." It not only sold well within Chinese but was also extensively exported overseas. In the seventeenth and eighteenth centuries, the detailed division of labor constructed an organization that laid a solid foundation for meeting the overseas market needs for porcelain quantity, quality, and specialization.

3 The Shift of Production Sites of Chinese Export Tea Utensil Decoration

Liu Zifen, a writer in the Republic of China period, wrote in His *Bamboo Garden Pottery* that "in the middle of the Qing Dynasty, there were many foreign vessels, and the business was prosperous. Europeans valued Chinese porcelain, so our business men made white porcelain in Jingdezhen, transported them to Guangzhou, and hired painters to paint them in Western way; then they fired them on the south bank of the Pearl River, made them into colored porcelain, and sold to Westerners. Since they were painted in factories on the south bank of the Pearl River, they were given the names 'Henancai' (colored porcelain from the south bank

[19] Mou Xiaolin. The Impact of Overseas Demand on Ming and Qing Jingdezhen Porcelain [D]. China Academy of Art, 2014: 66.

of river) and 'Guangcai' (colored porcelain from Guangzhou). This type of porcelain originated in the reign of Emperor Qianlong, and reached its peak during the Jiaqing period. Recently, the Rar porcelain sold in Guangdong still includes those with additional colored decorations, which are slightly different from the traditional Rar kiln polychrome porcelain due to the use of Western color materials. These pieces are exquisitely painted with dazzling and vibrant colors, resembling the famille rose style of the Yongzheng and Qianlong periods."[20] Liu Zifen's summary essentially established the academic understanding of Canton enamel, indicating that Canton enamel was popular during the mid-Qing Dynasty for export to the West. The porcelain body originates from Jingdezhen, featuring luxurious styles, rich colors, and employing Western painting techniques, with patterns incorporating both Eastern and Western visual elements, and distinctive cultural characteristics of Guangdong.

So there are three key factors that contributed to the birth of Canton enamel: first, Guangzhou was the only gateway for foreign trade at that time, with a large market demand due to the concentration of foreign merchants and external orders; second, the meticulous division of labor in ceramic production made remote processing and decorations possible; third, the perfection of various systems and overall framework in the Thirteen Factories formed a clear design entity specifically targeting the Western market led by Britain, enabling the gathering of resources to meet challenges and produce exquisite craftsmanship that not only reflected Chinese characteristics but also met the demands of the Western market.

As mentioned earlier, the British used tea as a means of flaunting, and as a result, the customized armorial porcelain tea sets became popular. Before relocating the main decoration site to Guangzhou, the armorial porcelain was primarily made in Jingdezhen. Although the orders came with detailed instructions, Chinese craftsmen were not familiar with the patterns and did not understand English, so mistakes were inevitable, and some patterns may have experienced deliberate or unintentional alterations or reinterpretations. Additionally, a lack of understanding of the theme could result in the patterns on the outer borders greatly differing from the center, leading to inconsistent styles. More seriously, frequent pattern and spelling errors caused huge losses. To prevent this, some Cantonese merchants began setting up factories in Guangzhou to conduct

[20] Liu Zifen. Bamboo Grove Pottery Discourse [M]. Self-printed thread-bound edition, 1925: 46.

secondary processing and decoration on the white porcelain bodies from Jingdezhen.[21] This led to the birth of Canton enamel.

Zeng Yandong (1751–1830) once completed the book *Travel Record of the Southern Region* based on his travels in Guangdong. In his book, he recorded a visit to the Thirteen Factories in the forty-sixth year of the Qianlong Emperor's reign (1781) and being entertained by foreigners. This is the earliest Chinese record regarding Canton enamel to date.[22] During the meal, "the dishes were presented. The utensils were also made of Yuzhang kiln porcelain, but they were painted in gold and green, with colorful designs, different from practical items. Each could hold a liter, and when filled with chicken pieces, the head, claws, and wings were all complete, not chopped, using an iron fork as chopsticks."[23] Zeng Yandong identified the porcelain body at the banquet as "Yuzhang porcelain," the white porcelain from Jingdezhen, with patterns painted in "gold and green, with colorful designs," and "different from practical items." In other words, this style was not for daily use, but rather showcased a splendid and luxurious color palette that was completely different from the decorative style presented by Jingdezhen. Also, the context and user of these items were completely different.

4 The Production and Trading of Canton Enamel

In fact, Canton enamel was born out of market demand. Therefore, unlike other handicrafts, Canton enamel's decorative style is influenced by both consumers and producers. Throughout the process from production to sale, a dynamic network was formed among foreign merchants, porcelain traders, and workshops, constantly adjusting to market changes. Their interaction was the main driving force of Canton enamel. So, how did foreign merchants put forward their demands to Chinese and purchase? According to the rules in the Thirteen Factories, Westerners could not directly contact manufacturers, but through designated trading companies

[21] Jiang Ling. The Relationship between Decorative Processes and Place Transfer in the Decorative Process of Dingdezhen Pattern Porcelain in the Qing Dynasty [J]. China Ceramic, 2010(5): 78.

[22] Huang Shengzhi. Research on Export porcelain of Cantonese Painting [D]. Taipei: Taipei University of the Arts, 2012: 10.

[23] (Qing Dynasty) Zeng Yandong. Little Bean Pavilion [M]. Jinan: Qilu Book Society, 2004: 287. This book was completed in the 60th year of the Qianlong Emperor, which was in 1795, and only published in 1880 during the Reign of the Guangxu Emperor.

instead. How did these trading companies facilitate the cooperation between producers and buyers? Additionally, how did Guangcai workshops produce goods that met the demands of the Western market? These issues will be the focus of this section.

Every summer, merchant ships from countries including Britain and the Netherlands arrived in Guangzhou carried by the southwest monsoon and moored at Whampoa Port. Subsequently, the foreign merchants transferred to smaller Chinese pilot boats on the Pearl River and reached Guangzhou. After obtaining permission from the Canton Customs, they traded with the designated Chinese merchants appointed by the Qing government. Before the end of the northeast monsoon season, they had to complete all trade and pay customs duties to the Canton Customs before setting sail back. This means that all goods, including tea and tea sets, had to be delivered within the limited trading season, and there were also corresponding requirements for the types and qualities of the goods. After the direct trade between China and Britain and the Netherlands began, the porcelain trade, which was closely related to tea drinking, was conducted through direct purchase and special customization. Direct purchase was relatively simple; once the procurement personnel arrived in Guangzhou, they immediately sought porcelain that met the listed requirements, purchased enough, and then transported it to the ship for ballast, so that they could return on schedule after the tea arrived. However, special customization went through a gradual refinement process.

Dutch scholar Christiaan Jorg, who focuses on the Dutch East India Company and Chinese and Japanese export porcelain, believes that the initial orders from the Dutch East India Company to China were mostly in the form of written descriptions, which gradually evolved into design sketches with shapes and patterns, and even models. In 1734, the Dutch East India Company invited Dutch designer Cornelis Pronk (1691–1759) to design four Chinese-style figure patterns, which were originally designed for porcelain and later became one of the most representative Chinoiserie-style patterns. However, due to the complexity of these patterns and the high risk of production, production ceased in 1739. Another representative custom-designed porcelain artist was Dutch engraver J. P. Certon, who once traveled to Guangzhou to supervise the painting of porcelain to ensure quality.[24]

[24] Same as footnote 22, pp. 21–22.

The British East India Company was a major consumer of custom-made porcelain. According to records, "British colonizers estimated that in the early 18th century, they transported between 25 to 30 million pieces of porcelain to Europe, and after the 1730s, they would dominate the trade with China."[25] Moreover, in the eighteenth century, there may have been over 5000 sets of armorial porcelain specifically tailored for the British market. It is evident that the British had a preference for sets of customized porcelain, including tea and dinner sets. The custom-made porcelain was primarily tailored for officials stationed in London, India, and China by the company.[26] In other words, most of the custom-made porcelain was the result of private trade. Employees of the East India Company typically conducted private transactions with merchants in Guangzhou or purchased porcelain from shops, rather than having them listed in the company's inventory.[27]

The list and products of armorial porcelain customized by the British Charles Peers, now collected in the British Museum, serve as evidence that Guangzhou merchants produced customized porcelain for the British.[28] In addition, within Britain, the private custom porcelain business ordered ready-made porcelain styles from native ceramic stores through the British East India Company and ceramic merchants. Customers only needed to provide the relevant coats of arms and patterns they desired.[29] Most of these sets of customized porcelain were finished in Guangzhou with enamel painting.[30] However, the trade mode of the British East India Company later underwent changes. According to Hosea Ballou Morse in his *Chronicles of the East India Company's Trade with China*, by 1774, the British East India Company signed contracts with Guangzhou merchants, shifting the previous mode of spot cash transactions to a prepaid order system, so that the trading ships arriving the following year could obtain goods as scheduled. This indicates that the British East India Company

[25] Zhu Peichu. Ming-Qing Export Porcelain and the Exchange of World Cultures [M]. Beijing: Light Industry Press, 1984: 198.

[26] Lü Zhangshen. The Charm of Porcelain: Masterpieces of Porcelain from the British Museum and the Victoria and Albert Museum [M]. Beijing: Zhonghua Book Company, 2012: 17.

[27] Same as footnote 22, p. 22.

[28] John Goldsmith Phillips. China-Trade Porcelain. Harvard: Harvard University Press, 1956: 38–39.

[29] Same as footnote 22, pp. 34–35.

[30] Same as footnote 24, p. 22.

later also had custom-made orders. However, this prosperity only lasted until the end of the eighteenth century. In 1801, porcelain disappeared on the British East India Company's product list. This was because the European ceramic manufacturing industry in Britain had matured and was able to produce porcelain as good as China, and at a reasonable price.

By examining the British ceramic trade with China, we can infer that the primary objects of trade at the time were utilitarian items. In other words, these ceramics was for tea drinking and dining. The increasing presence of complete sets of tea and dining ware on the orders reflects the further popularization of tea drinking in Britain. It also suggests that the eating habits of the British were profoundly influenced by tea, leading to the adoption of porcelain. The development and popularization of tea culture spurred the growth of custom porcelain, resulting in the emergence of Canton enamel workshops that were relatively affordable, responsive, and accurate.

At the time, ceramic merchants had two different business models: one was to act as a buyer, accept orders, and find subcontracting factories; the other was factory direct, that is to set up their own factories.[31] After receiving an order, the porcelain factory would assign it to cooperative factories, including the Jingdezhen porcelain workshops responsible for making the unglazed tire and the Guangcai workshops responsible for enamel painting and decoration. Therefore, porcelain merchants often shuttled between Jingdezhen and Guangdong. The outsourcing, purchase, and customizing of porcelain merchants in Jingdezhen became a common theme in export paintings. For example, in 1966, the German Walter A. Staehelin published a set of 34 export paintings, each with a title and seal impression, describing in detail the process of porcelain production from mining the clay in Jingdezhen to selling it in Guangzhou, which matched the processes described in documents like ceramic books, local chronicles, etc. From this set of paintings, we can infer that the sale and production of export porcelain followed a sequence of "ordering" first and then "starting the enamel work." The 20th painting, titled "Ordering," depicted a sign on the wall of a porcelain shop reading, "A word now is final, prices differ at different times of the day." Only after did they start to enamel the designs according to the customization requirements, i.e., "starting the enamel work." The 30th painting was titled "Enamel,"

[31] Huang Qichen. Guangdong Merchants' Association [M]. Hefei: Huangshan Bookstore, 2007: 176.

referring to the processing of Guangcai. The final "Opening the Shop" depicted the scene of foreign merchants shopping for porcelain in a store.

In *Jingdezhen Porcelain Records*, Lan Pu pointed out the differences between export porcelain, Chinese official kiln porcelain, and domestic market porcelain in terms of porcelain body: "There are two types of foreign porcelain: smooth foreign porcelain and coarse foreign porcelain. The former is made from talcum, which requires more craftsmanship; while the latter is made from porcelain stones, with slightly less craftsmanship. ... Talcum as the body material, its only advantage is smoothness, but it does not enhance the glaze color like porcelain stone does, not so bright and easy on eyes. Therefore, official kilns seldom used talcum, while foreign porcelain used it partially; and it was mainly used for carving and inlaying small accessories. However, the painting on talcum porcelain is also not as good as that on ancient official kiln porcelain."[32] Talcum, also known as soapstone, is a type of high-grade Kaolin found near Jingdezhen. It contains a high percentage of aluminum and has a smooth texture, making it a raw material for producing coarse porcelain. Porcelain stone, on the other hand, has been crushed and washed, and can be used for making both coarse and fine porcelain.[33] The term "official kilns" refers to Jingdezhen official kilns or fine porcelain imitating official kiln products.

Where were these plain porcelain bodies painted after being transported to Guangzhou? Zhao Guoyuan's "Stories of Canton enamel" recorded the oral accounts of previous generations of craftsmen in Guangzhou: The initial production organization of Canton enamel was in the form of family workshops, concentrated in the West Gate of Guangzhou, such as Hualin Temple and Changshou Temple, north of the Thirteen Factories. For example, the old site of the Guangcai Guild "Lingsi Hall," established in 1778 (in the 43rd year of the Qianlong reign), was located in the Yugi San Lane next to Hualin Temple (which no longer exists). The external painting titled "Porcelain Production" held by the Victoria and Albert Museum confirms the time when Lingsi Hall appeared, which is consistent with the oral accounts of Canton enamel craftsmen. The West Gate area outside Guangzhou city gathered various handicraft productions and occasionally witnessed conflicts. Additionally, due to the need to fire and paint the glaze, fires would often occur in Canton enamel production.

[32] Same as footnote 30.

[33] Same as footnote 11, p. 265.

Therefore, later on, the Canton enamel workshop moved to the Henan Island across from the Thirteen Factories on the southern bank of the Pearl River. Henan Island became another advantageous location for Canton enamel workshops due to its convenient water transportation, with the channels and streams on the island forming tributaries of the Pearl River.[34] In 1777 (i.e., the 42nd year of the Qianlong period), Irishman William Hickey (1749–1830) was invited by the British East India Company to visit a Canton enamel workshop in Henan Island and completed his memoirs titled *Memoirs of William Hickey*. According to this memoir, there had been Guangcai workshops with over a hundred workers operating on Henan Island till 1777. He also recorded his observations: "We visited the entire processing of porcelain. We saw over a hundred people working on each unique piece, painting various patterns. Some parts were done by older people, while others were done by adolescents, and even children as young as six or seven participated."[35]

Another record of the production of Canton enamel comes from the diary of American merchant Samuel Shaw (1754–1830) in Guangzhou, describing the scene of custom-made armorial porcelain he saw in Guangzhou in 1784:

> There are many painters in Guangzhou, but someone told me that they do not have a talent for design. I would like to have the emblem of Cincinnati Association printed on the set of porcelain it ordered. My idea is that the porcelain should adopt the style of the goddess Minerva, from whom the organization received its emblem and made it public. I have two statues of the goddess and a beautiful portrait of a soldier, and I have provided the painter with a copy of the emblem that I own. This painter is well-known among the Guangzhou painters, but despite his ability to accurately replicate these patterns, he has been unable to integrate them well after multiple attempts.[36]

[34] Guangdong Folk Art Museum. Centennial Transformation - Guangcai from the Hong Kong and Macau since the 19th Century [M]. Guangzhou: Lingnan Fine Arts Press, 2008: 3.

[35] Guangzhou Cultural Bureau. The Maritime Silk Road - Guangzhou's Cultural Heritage [M]. Beijing: Beijing Cultural Relics Publishing House, 2008: 332.

[36] [US] Philip Chadwick Foster Smith. China's Empress of the Seas [M]. Translation by Guangzhou Daily International News Department Legal Office. Guangzhou: Guangzhou Publishing House, 2007: 187.

American Samuel Wells Williams (1812–1884) wrote in *The Chinese Commercial Guide*:

> White porcelain shipped to Canton is painted according to (Westerners') requirements. Workers outline the patterns with ink, then color them with watercolors mixed with strong glue; this porcelain are repeatedly placed in a kiln for about half an hour, taken out to cool, and then soaked in cold water. These kilns are made of bricks of different sizes according to the size of the porcelain.[37]

In 1793, John D. Barrow, who accompanied the British Macartney mission to China, provided a more detailed observation and description of the decorative process of Canton enamel:

> The ceramic factory shipped a large quantity of all-white porcelain to Guangdong, leaving buyers to paint them in the styles they preferred. These samples prove that they are not bad imitators. However, it was observed that their historical and natural objects were often depicted inaccurately. For example, flowers on one tree were on the stem of another tree, and leaves on a third tree. In the past, this may have been the case because the samples they used were flawed, or they were able to alter nature; but they realized that foreigners valued natural object paintings more and paid close attention to the subject matter. We found that they were meticulous imitators who not only painted the exact number of petals and stamens for a flower, but also the number of leaves and their thorns or spots on the stem. They even worked out how many scales a fish had and presented them in the painting, but they were unable to reproduce the lush colors of nature. I brought back several plant, bird, and insect prints that were praised for their authenticity and color similarity. However, they lacked proper shading and contrast. The European color prints exported to Guangdong were faithfully copied there.[38]

Like other crafts in ancient China, the artisans of Guangcai did not leave their names in history. However, based on the oral history of LingSi Hall, we can take a glimpse of the training of Guangcai craftsmen. Zhao

[37] S. Wells Williams. A Chinese Commercial Guide. 4th ed., Canton: The Office of the Chinese

Repository, 1856: 170.

[38] [UK] George Macartney, George Barrow. Macartney's Mission to China: Observations by Macartney and Barrow [M]. Translated by He Gaoji and He Yuning. Beijing: The Commercial Press, 2013: 313–314.

Guoyuan wrote in *Stories of Canton enamel* that becoming an apprentice in LingSi Hall provided the opportunity to become a Guangcai craftsman. Unlike the traditional pattern of inheriting from father to son, entering the hall required an introduction by a skilled craftsman and payment of an entrance fee. Only the one who paid the most could be admitted. In the case of inheriting the family business, a fee called "Father-to-Son Fee" had to be paid, with two taels of silver for the eldest son, five taels for the second son, and daughters could apply after marriage through their husbands.[39] Furthermore, craftsmen in the association had to pay a monthly membership fee called "registration fee" to LingSi Hall to take on orders. If they accepted orders without registration, they would be fined and possibly have their registration revoked, and would have to wait until the next month's registration. This system reached its peak during the Tongzhi and Guangxu reigns, with over a thousand people registered, indicating the flourishing of Guangcai export porcelain. This may also explain that a comprehensive organizational management system provided assurance for the large-scale export of Canton enamel in the eighteenth century.

5 The Fusion Between Chinese and Western Style in Canton Enamel Patterns

The birth and development of Canton enamel was closely related to the export market of Chinese porcelain, and it also served as a medium of the exchange of patterns between the East and the West. On the one hand, orders from the West introduced European visual culture to China, and the decorative style of Chinese porcelain constantly changed with the market demand. On the other hand, Europe did not simply purchase Chinese export porcelain; in fact, Western craftsmanship also influenced the Chinese porcelain industry through trade. At the beginning of the eighteenth century, European enamel painting led to the emergence of over glaze porcelain in China. This style more closely catered to European tastes, which laid the foundation of the further development of export porcelain. During the processing of customized porcelain, Guangcai craftsmen repeatedly operated and combined Western visual elements,

[39] Zhao Guoan. Study on Guaner Studio Guangdong Artworks [M]. Guangzhou: Lingnan Fine Arts Publishing House, 2008: 19.

integrating them with Chinese and Guangdong local patterns to gradually form a unique Chinese Guangcai craft and patterns. By analyzing several types of Guangcai works, this section will discuss how patterns and design from both China and the West, as well as various visual expressions, communicate and blend in Guangcai.

The Decorative Techniques and Patterns That Are Half Chinese and Half Western

The early Guangcai armorial porcelain with characters in decorated frames not only integrated Western techniques, but also frequently used Western elements in themes, especially some scene patterns. The design and patterns fully integrated Western painting composition and different life scenes between the West and the East. For example, a Guangcai armorial binaural bowl with characters in decorated frames, which is currently on display at the Guangzhou Museum, shows a Chinese official wearing official hats in Qing dynasty and two Chinese figures carrying heavy loads, but the background is a western building with perspective. The Chinese-style tree trunks and leaves are also accented with light and shadow; the rocks and distant mountains in the foreground use the Chinese painting technique of brushing strokes, while the sloping ground and ground behind are carefully depicted with short diagonal and vertical lines.[40]

Figure 5.7 is a pair of large bowls produced between 1750 and 1775, each of which depicts a scene of Chinese and Westerners drinking together. It can be seen that ceramic patterns had already demonstrated the cultural exchange between China and the West. On the bowl, the hat placed beside the characters indicates their identity—government officials. In addition to the blue-and-white porcelain wine cups in their hands and on the table, there are several dishes that they seem to be enjoying without any awkwardness. The servant was waiting on them with respect, whereas the Western dining table feels chaotic, with a large blue-and-white porcelain wine bowl in the center surrounded by people sitting around it, and others lying on the ground next to the table.[41]

[40] Same as footnote 22, p. 40.

[41] Yu Chunming. Chinese Calling Card: Exploring the Origins and Collection of Ming-Qing Export Porcelain [M]. Beijing: SDX Joint Publishing Company, 2011: 131.

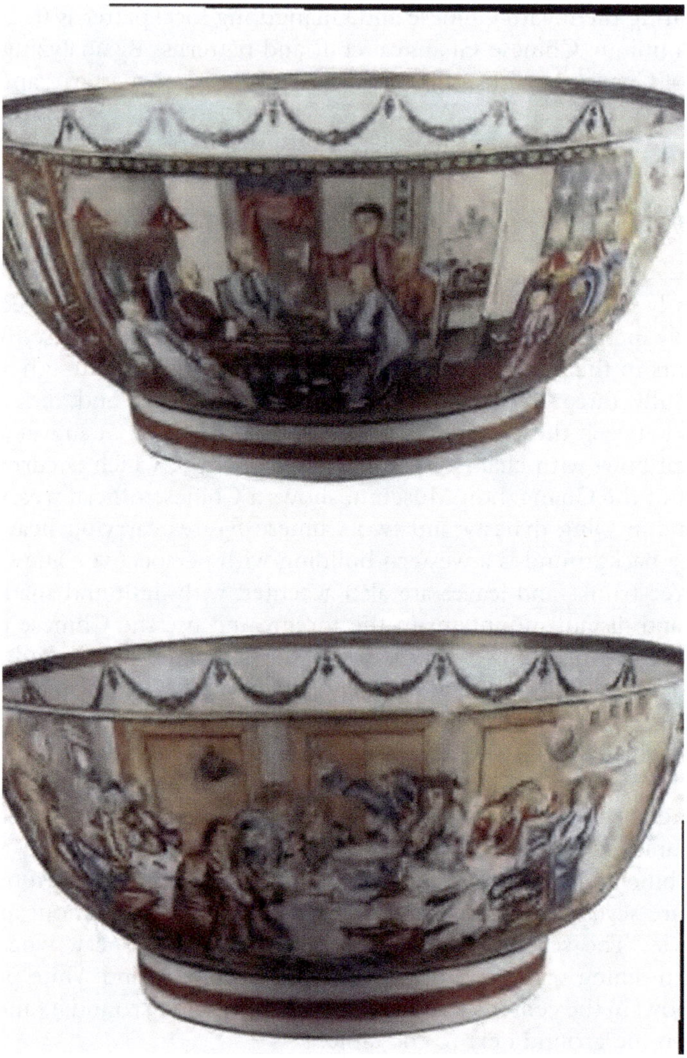

Fig. 5.7 Canton enamel big bowls made between 1750 and 1775

The Export Porcelain with Themes Related to Foreign Trade Was Popular for a Time

One category of Canton enamel featured decorations depicting foreign merchant ships, landscape of Guangzhou, and scenes of foreign trade. These patterns included foreign merchant ships, the Pearl River estuary, the Thirteen Factories trading center, and shops in Guangzhou. In his book *Yinliu Zhai Talking about Porcelain*, Xu Zhiheng mentioned, "Among the paintings of buildings and towers during the Jiajing and Daoguang reign, many were of West Lake, and some depicted the 10 Scenic Spots of Mount Lu. There were also paintings of Zhuhai, which were ordered by Cantonese people from the Jingdezhen kiln rather than the Guangzhou kiln. There were also similar paintings of the Eight Scenic Spots in the City of Sheep." (*Note: The City of Sheep is another name for Guangzhou.)[42] These ships, port landscapes, and trading scenes were rarely seen on Chinese paintings and domestic porcelain, but were commonly found on Guangcai for export, indicating that these were unique to Canton enamel. Most of these patterns originated from the designs brought by Western merchants for customization.

This type of ship-patterned porcelain for export to Europe was popular in the mid-eighteenth century, with the most typical example being a ship pattern dish in 1756, with the image of the Dutch East India Company's ship "Vrijburg" (see Fig. 5.8). The bottom of the dish depicts a merchant ship sailing on the sea, with a blue, white, and red flag on the mast, indicating its Dutch identity. The rim is decorated with scrolls and flowers painted in an imported red paint that is mixed with mastix oil and camphor oil, and in the center of the dish, there is an oval-shaped frame of scrolls and plants painted in blue. Inscribed in Dutch is "CHRIST: SCHOONEMAN OPPR STUERMAN OP: T: SCHIP VRYBURG: TFR: REEDE WANPHO IN CHINA INTIAAR. 1756." This means "Christian Schooneman, second mate of the Vrijburg, departed from Huangpu, China, in 1756."[43] This porcelain is now in the British Museum, and the details and painting techniques in the picture are commonly used in eighteenth-century Canton enamel.

[42] Xu Zhiheng. Yinliu Zhai Talking about Porcelain [M] // Collection of Chinese Ceramic Classics. Beijing: The Bookshop of China, 1991: 157.

[43] Lü Zhangshen, ed. The Charm of Porcelain: Fine Porcelain Collections of the British Museum and the Victoria and Albert Museum [M]. Beijing: Zhonghua Book Company, 2012, 89.

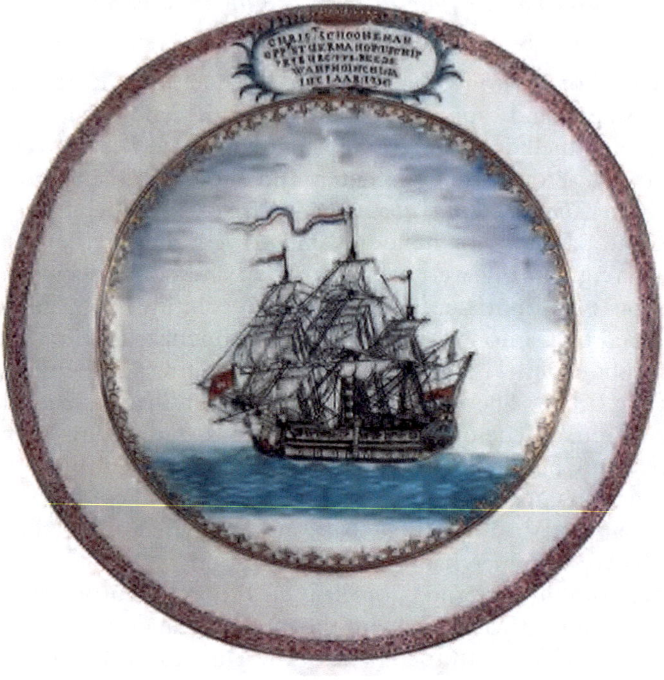

Fig. 5.8 The ship pattern dish of Vrijburg

Several museums in Europe have the same style of ship-patterned dish mentioned above, but the texts may vary due to customization, and the size and orientation of the ship also differ. Scholars speculate that these patterns may have been based on the same draft. In the diary of Edward Barlow, preserved in the National Maritime Museum in the UK, there is a sketch of a merchant ship sailing at sea, which closely resembles the one on the dish mentioned earlier (see Fig. 5.9). Barlow served in the Royal Navy and also worked for the East India Company. It is highly possible that the porcelain dish pattern came from Barlow's diary.[44]

Harbor landscape theme was popular in the mid-eighteenth century, but had already appeared in the early eighteenth century. An armorial piece from the family of Eldved Lancelot Lee, sold at Sotheby's Amsterdam

[44] Same as footnote 43.

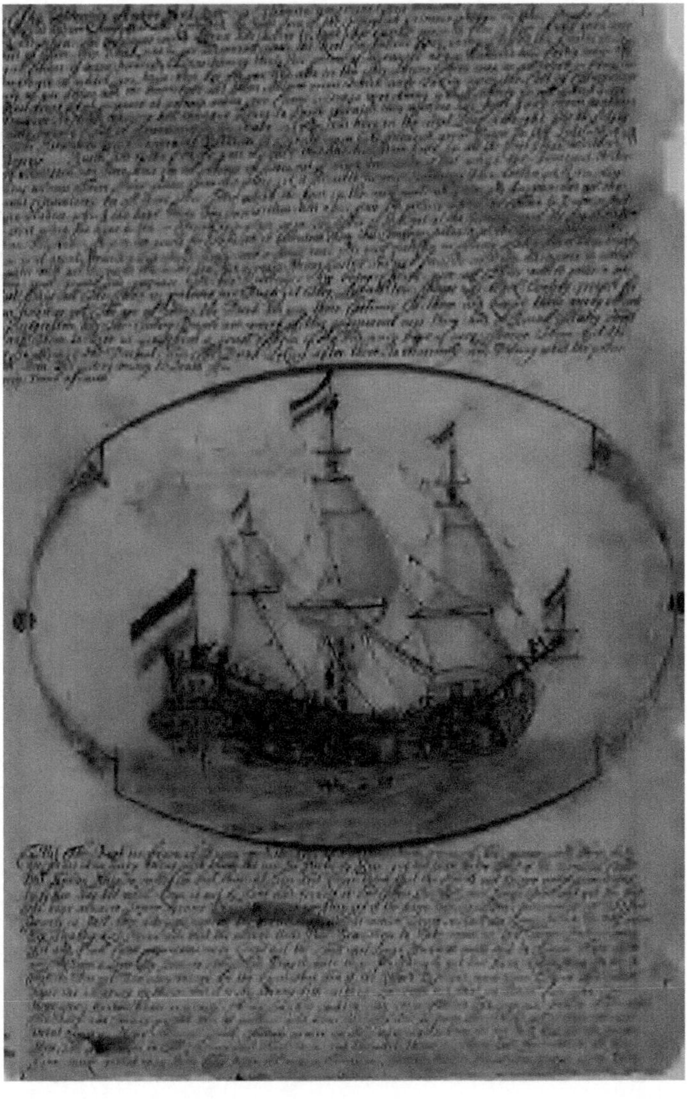

Fig. 5.9 The sketch of a merchant ship sailing at sea in the diary of Edward Barlow

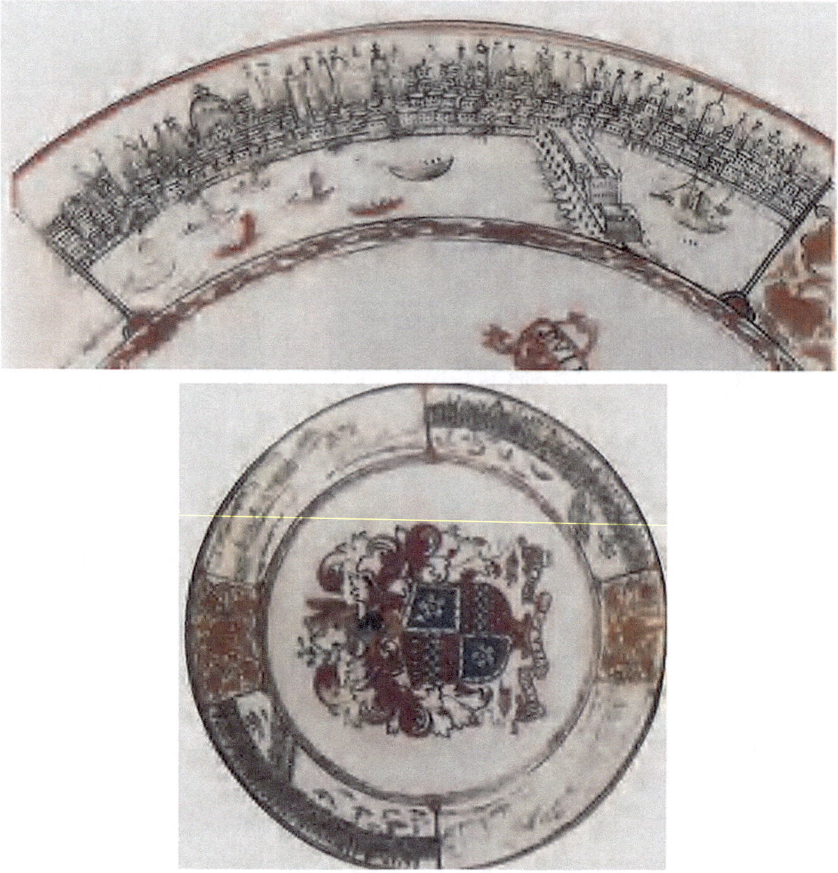

Fig. 5.10 An armorial piece from the family of Eldved Lancelot Lee features a pattern of harbor scenes

auction in May 2005, features a pattern of harbor scenes on the plate center (Fig. 5.10), with the patterns in the four frames on the rim representing the harbor landscapes of Guangzhou and London, symbolizing the trade connection between the two countries through porcelain.[45] Designers depicted the London Bridge, towers and church spires, as well as the Pearl River Garrison in the frames. British experts David Howard

[45] Same as footnote 41, p. 61.

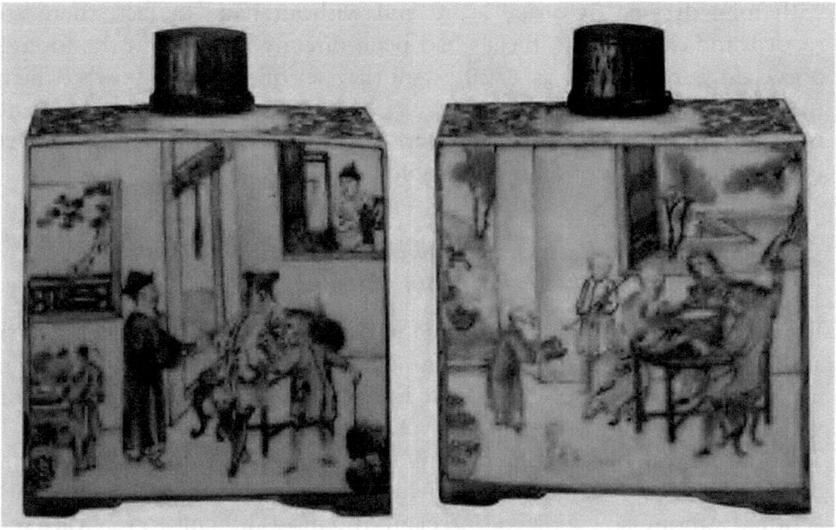

Fig. 5.11 A square tea caddy decorated with patterns on both sides illustrates European merchants engaging in tea trade with Chinese

and John Ayers believe that the River Thames in this plate were likely inspired by European copperplate engravings from the late seventeenth to early eighteenth centuries.[46]

The theme of the Thirteen Factories, along with the export trading scenarios, is a distinctive category of the Canton enamel, among which porcelain shops and tea houses are the most common. Figure 5.11 shows a square tea caddy decorated with figures produced in the 1740s. The patterns on both sides illustrate European merchants engaging in tea trade with Chinese. In the foreground of one side, a Chinese wearing an official's hat is conversing with a foreigner, and in the corner of the background, one can see the accountant inside the house eavesdropping on them, with two boxes of tea already packed at the bottom right corner. On the other side, the two main characters are sitting together drinking tea, seemingly celebrating the success of their collaboration. Compared to the previous image, the overall atmosphere of this picture is more relaxed,

[46]David Howard, John Ayers. Masterpieces of Chinese Export Porcelain form the Mottahedeh Collection in the Virginia Museum. New York: Sotheby Parke Bernet, 1981: 45.

with men dressed in casual attire and without hats. In fact, there are records indicating that officials had been directly involved in the foreign porcelain trade as early as 1720.[47] Another set of porcelain bowls depicts the entire process of tea, from picking, drying, processing, to packing and transportation. These porcelains were also exported to Europe and have become highly sought-after collectibles.

Exquisite Patterns with Skilled Imitations of Western Painting Patterns

John Barnard, an official accompanying George Macartney, the first British ambassador who visited China, commented on Canton enamel in his writings: "For any pattern exported from England, the craftsmen in Guangzhou will certainly copy it meticulously. The glaze they use is unimitable."[48] Therefore, it can be seen that the imitating ability of Canton enamel craftsmen had already been recognized by Westerners in the late eighteenth century. Among all exported porcelain, the most difficult to replicate was Western painting. After 1720, as Westerners' demands for customized porcelain increased, sketches and copperplate drawings provided more specific patterns for customization. In addition, at this time, oil painting techniques had been introduced to Guangzhou, allowing Canton enamel craftsmen to accurately imitate the drawings, with an exquisite quality that could be mistaken for works by Western native painters. These patterns can be divided into two types: imitating Western engraved copperplate paintings, which used lines to construct landscapes with single-color, partial color, and full-color expressions; and imitating Western oil paintings, which used block colors to express light and shadow and three-dimensional effects.

On a blue-and-white gilded dinner plate in the Victoria and Albert Museum, there is a scene of Jesus being baptized in the middle of the river (Fig. 5.12). In the distance, a dove is depicted as God's avatar descending from the sky. There are six Chinese-style landscapes around the plate's periphery, with fruit and flower patterns surrounding the edges and angels hidden among them. The central scene perfectly matches a copperplate

[47] Same as footnote 40, p. 154.

[48] [Britain] John Barrow. My View of the Qianlong Dynasty's Prosperity [M]. Translated by Li Guoqing, et al. Beijing: Beijing Library Press, 2007: 220–221.

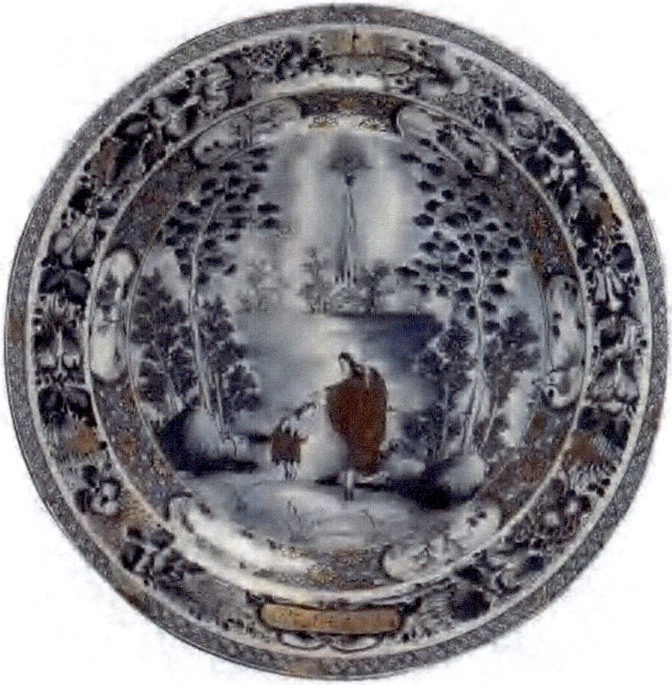

Fig. 5.12 A dinner plate with a scene of Jesus being baptized in the middle of the river

painting of "The Baptism of Jesus" in the British Museum (Fig. 5.13), indicating high level of matching.[49]

Another pattern that is completely faithful to the original copperplate painting appears on the dinner plate of Achilles (Fig. 5.14), which is currently housed in the British Museum. In the pattern, the newly-born future Greek hero Achilles is being immersed by his mother and maidservant into the River Lethe. On the left side of the picture, a goddess lying on her back on a toppled jar symbolizes the River Lethe. Behind him is the symbol of victory, the goddess Nike. On the right side of the picture is the Greek fire god and craftsman Hephaestus, who later forged armor for Achilles to participate in the Trojan War. This pattern imitates the design

[49] Same as footnote 42, p. 111.

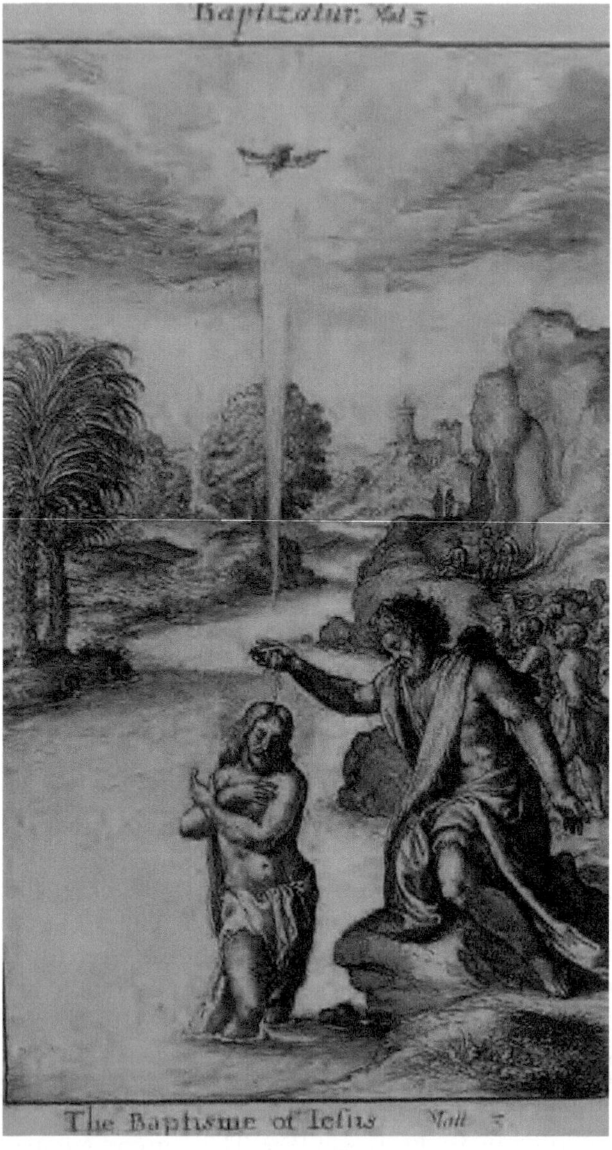

Fig. 5.13 The copperplate painting of "The Baptism of Jesus"

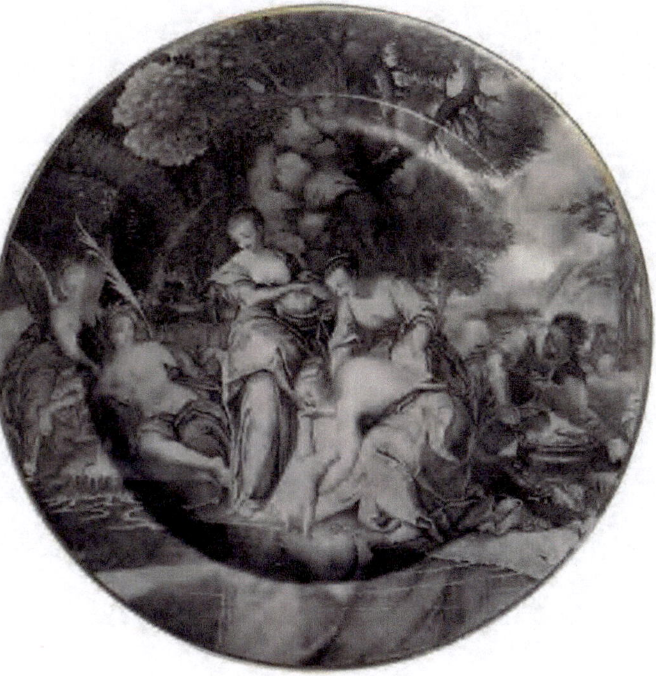

Fig. 5.14 The dinner plate of Achilles' being immersed

of Edme Jeaurat's engraving based on the original work of Nicolas Vieughels (Fig. 5.15). The ceramic pattern is almost completely identical to that of the print in color, composition, and other aspects.[50]

Characteristic Symbol Patterns Promote the Development of Ceramic Decorative Design

Among the numerous Chinese export porcelain collections in the Victoria and Albert Museum, a stamped pattern plate is unique. Unlike other plates with various landscape or figures, this plate only has a few patterns. The edge is composed of two bands, each band consisting of four patterns, and there are numbers 21, 22, 23, and 24 between the two bands (Fig. 5.16).

[50] Same as footnote 48, p. 113.

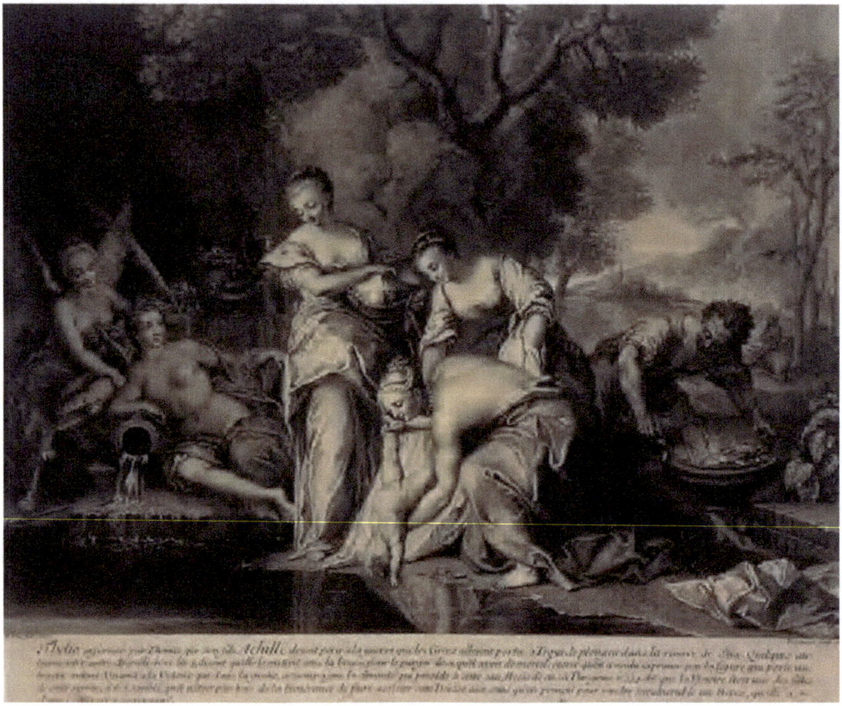

Fig. 5.15 The original copperplate painting appears on the dinner plate of Achilles

There are two groups of patterns in the center of the plate, both in oval shapes. One group consists of stylized English letter combinations such as "FE" and "IM," while the other group is "WF." The museum also has a similar plate (Fig. 5.17) with a variety of decorative patterns on the edges, which are numbered from 17 to 20.[51] The patterns on these plates can be considered as the ancestors of standardized edge decorations, allowing users to easily see the patterns appearing on the porcelain. These design patterns have promoted the modern decorative patterns being applied to ceramic decoration design, and are a direct manifestation of ceramic pattern design moving toward standardization.

[51] Same as footnote 48, p. 143.

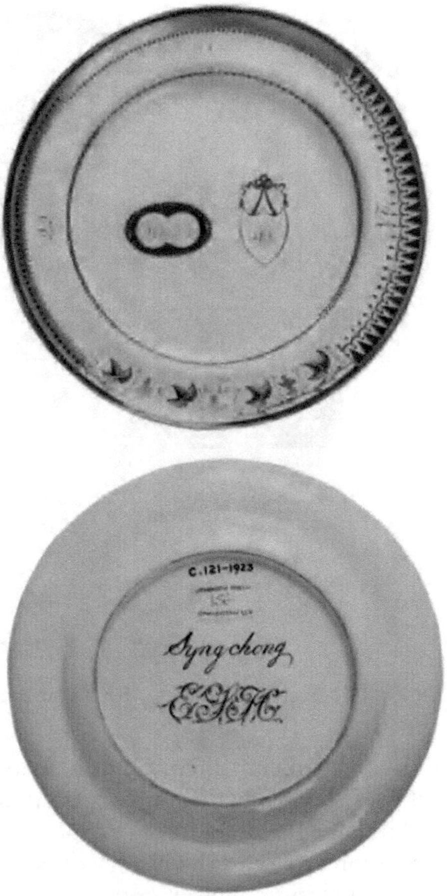

Fig. 5.16 Symbol plate with impressed seals

In summary, around the eighteenth century, the Chinese ceramic industry actively adapted to the market demand from the West by making adjustments in industrial layout and production methods. To reduce unnecessary losses, improve efficiency, and increase benefits, the design of decorative patterns for exported porcelain was transferred from Jingdezhen to Guangzhou. The establishment and perfection of the management system of the Thirteen Factories in Guangdong facilitated the development of Canton enamel. With the efforts of foreign merchants, local merchants,

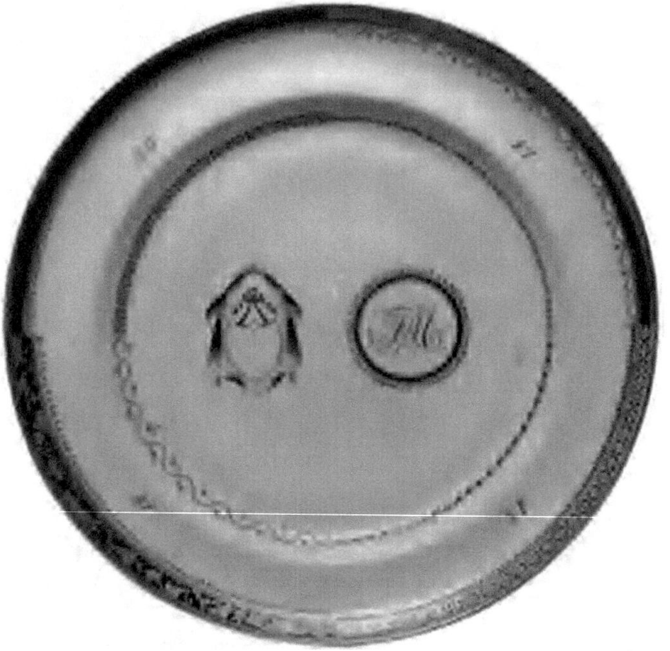

Fig. 5.17 A porcelain dish with a combination of various decorative patterns

and porcelain craftsmen, Canton enamel integrated Eastern and Western cultures, breaking through the traditional design of Chinese porcelain, and became the main force of exported porcelain in Qing Dynasty, leaving a profound mark in the history of porcelain between China and the West.

By analyzing typical examples of Canton enamel, we can see that Canton enamel has achieved innovation through the combination of Chinese and Western painting themes, techniques, decorative themes, and visual elements. The birth and development of Guangcai patterns are precisely the result of the Guangcai craftsmen's keen observation of the trends in the Western market. They actively explored the Western fashion trends and developed a fusion style and pattern design that met the needs of Western customers, which promoted the exchange of design between China and the West.

CHAPTER 6

Imitation and Innovation: The Rise of Tea-Related Industries in Britain

1 The Signification of Imitation

In 1756, as Hanway wrote in his book *A Journal of Eight Days' Journey to Which is Added an Essay on Tea* that, "The people are so poor that not a single family has all the necessary implements for tea drinking. They can only carry their own equipment for one to two miles before gathering together to make up for this magical pastime."[1] As tea drinking became increasingly popular, tea and tea sets gradually became essential items in the daily lives of the British. The vast quantities of tea sets imported by the British East India Company from China still couldn't satisfy everyone's needs. The working class couldn't afford the expensive imported tea sets, so they had to bring their limited tea utensils to a common location for tea parties.

Along with tea, other products from the East consumed during tea drinking transformed the consumer culture of the British elite and middle class, as well as the material lives of craftsmen and laborers. These imported goods, which flooded into Britain, posed a threat to the related British industries, compelling them to strive to regain the market and establish their own uniqueness. They were forced onto the path of innovation. In the developing eighteenth-century Britain, faced with the growing

[1] [British] Jane Pettigrew. Tea Design [M]. Translated by Shao Lirong. Jinan: Shandong Picture Publishing House, 2013: 196.

C. Zhang, *Beyond the Teacup: 18th Century Sino-British Tea Trade and Design Cultural Exchange*,
https://doi.org/10.1007/978-981-97-7691-7_6

domestic demand for international consumer goods, policymakers and planners had to prioritize the improvement of domestic industrial craftsmanship and find ways to develop the industry.

In the eighteenth century, the British longed for art pieces that were tastefully designed and had a sense of style. They hoped that British goods could beat imported luxury items from Asia and other parts of Europe, and open up foreign markets.[2] Consequently, the government and entrepreneurs began to imitate foreign manufacturing. Additionally, based on the recognized principles in the eighteenth century, they admired and embraced imitation and replication, considering it a key principle of beauty. For instance, Adam Smith discussed aesthetic principles of beauty and elegance in *The Theory of Moral Sentiments*, highlighting the importance of style, color, diversity, rarity, and the ability to imitate. William Hogarth believed imitation was inherent to human nature, while Alexander Gerard and Joshua Reynolds believed creativity was built upon replication. Denis Diderot held a similar viewpoint, considering invention to be a cumulative and collective endeavor based on imitation.

The British government began to explore various ways to promote national industry, including providing substantial scholarships and encouraging collaboration between national and private institutions through patent grants, with a particular focus on design education. Against this backdrop, a series of private institutions related to design were brought to the forefront, with the most representative being the Society for the Encouragement of Arts, Manufactures, and Commerce, established in 1753. Founded by William Shipley, this society aimed to promote excellence in craftsmanship, manufacturing, and commerce. The society hoped to integrate design, art, and mechanics with business skills, working together to improve styles and find new uses for raw materials produced in Britain or its colonies. They opposed promoting innovation through patent licensing, and instead proposed establishing awards. These awards covered a wide range of products, including weaving, embroidery, and white cotton printing, as well as cabinetry and coachwork, and extended to designs in porcelain, pottery, iron, and copperware.[3]

[2] [British] Maxine Berg. Luxury and Pleasure: Material World of Eighteenth-Century England [M]. Translated by Sun Chao. Beijing: China Workers' Press, 2019: 106.

[3] Same as footnote 2, p. 110.

With the development of printing, in the seventeenth and eighteenth centuries, a group of books discussing technological inventions and the aesthetic taste of citizens emerged in England. Encyclopedias and dictionaries included a large number of entries related to the progress of decorative techniques, and scholars conducted discussions on the connotations of the term "art." Among them, some scholars such as David Hume distinguished between "manual or industrial craftsmanship" and "free or artistic craftsmanship," believing that the former was practical and manual, while the latter was free art or refined art. Historians generally believed that in the late eighteenth century, refined arts and industrial arts separated into respective paths.

Through the relevant entries on "imitation" in these encyclopedias and dictionaries, we can see the contemporary views toward this concept. William Henry Hall wrote in *The New Royal Encyclopaedia*, "The essence of imitation is to obtain experience from others as much as possible, to increase the variety of our products or improve them, without causing any loss."[4] During that period, the authors of encyclopedias and dictionaries almost unanimously believed that invention and creation were based on the productive recombination of existing knowledge rather than individual talent. Adam Smith even referred to imitative activities as "the source of miracles," considering it to be one of the key factors of the birth of modern British consumer goods.

Against this backdrop, new British products emerged one after another through the imitation of imported goods, including tea furniture and tea sets. The process of product innovation in Britain involved imitation, replication, and innovative redesign, allowing the middle class and ordinary consumers to enjoy a refined material life to some extent, similar to the upper echelons of society. During this process, internationally renowned brands such as Wedgwood emerged. These brands not only combined practicality and innovation but also possessed aesthetic appeal. By the end of the eighteenth century, a French term "anglomanie" associated with these English luxuries became popular, pushing "British design" into the global market.

[4] William Henry Hall. The New Royal Encyclopaedia, 3 vols, London: C.Coohe, No.17, Pater-Noster Row, 1788: 710.

2 Imitation and Innovation of Ceramic Tea Utensils

Compared with other European countries, the porcelain industry in the UK started relatively late and relied entirely on ordinary people instead of royal family. In a time when ceramic manufacturing technology was limited, the British ceramic industry had to compete with the goods imported by the British East India Company by imitating Chinese porcelain to gain market share (Fig. 6.1). In 1724, Daniel Defoe wrote in *A Tour through the Whole Island of Great Britain*, "We passed through Mile End to a village called Bow, where there is a very large pottery factory that has already produced a large quantity of teacups, saucers, tea trays, tea plates, covered bowls, and other kinds of practical porcelain…."[5] From Defoe's travelogue, we can confirm that the Bow pottery factory was one of the earliest manufacturers of tea porcelain in Britain, and the budding of the British ceramic industry was closely related to tea drinking.

In the eighteenth century, factories producing soft-paste porcelain began to appear in locations such as London, Derby, and Liverpool.

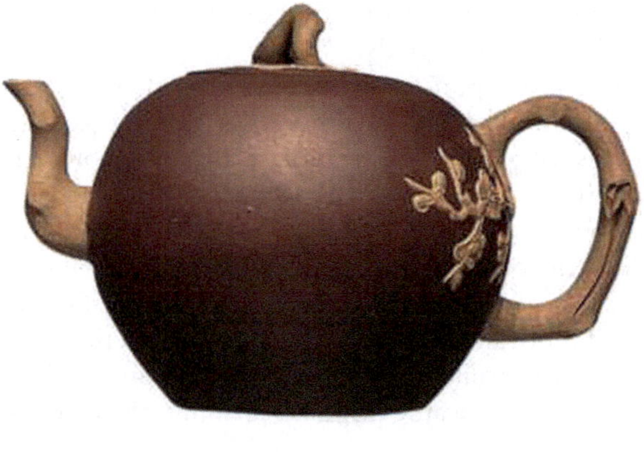

Fig. 6.1 This may be part of the first batch of teapots imported to Europe through the Dutch East India Company, produced between 1720 and 1760. (The twig-like decoration was very popular in China at that time and was one of the main objects imitated by Western ceramics. Photography: Li Leren)

[5] Ma Xiaoli. Research on British Tea from a Multidimensional Perspective [M]. Hangzhou: Zhejiang University Press, 2010: 43.

Among them were the Deby Ceramics Factory, the Worcester Ceramics Factory, and the Chelsea Ceramics Factory. "From almost the beginning of large-scale production of porcelain in the mid-18th century, English potters imitated the shapes and decorations of Chinese blue-and-white porcelain,"[6] which is evident from the production of "New Canton," a product initially produced by the Bow Ceramics Factory. Among the existing collections at the Victoria and Albert Museum, there are six ink-stone inscriptions commemorating the launch of "New Canton," with five dating from 1750 and one from 1751. In the eighteenth century, the main product of this factory was imitation of the white porcelain and glazed decoration of Dehua style in China (Fig. 6.2). The Chelsea factory also produced white porcelain in Dehua style at that time. This porcelain with its unique charm was known as Blanc De Chine, with pitchers, cups, and plates all being pure white with only raised floral patterns.

In 1763, an article published in the Oxford Magazine praised the porcelain produced by the Worcester Ceramics Factory, stating that they could now rival Chinese porcelain:

> The body of Worcester porcelain is even more refined and pure, to the point where it can almost rival the finest Chinese porcelain. And it is also harder

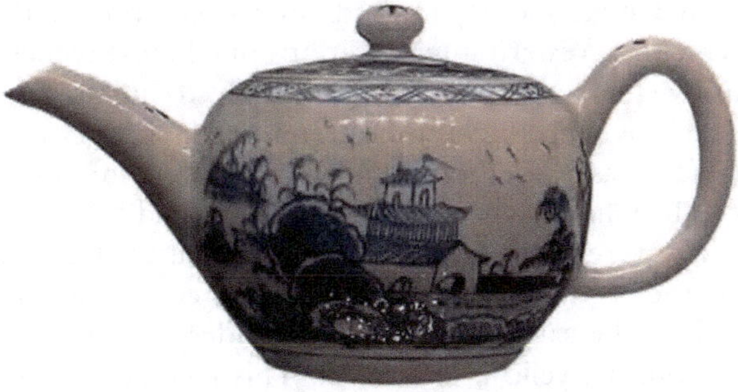

Fig. 6.2 This teapot was produced by the Bao Ceramic Factory between 1752 and 1755. (At that time, this cobalt blue-and-white ceramic decoration was popular in Europe. Photography: Li Leren)

[6] Rose Kerr, Nigel Wood. Ceramic Technology. Science and Civilization in China. Cambridge: Cambridge University Press, 2004: 749.

and more durable. Its glaze does not crack or peel unless subjected to strong external force. Additionally, it does not turn yellow, a flaw commonly found in ordinary Chinese porcelain and other types of porcelain after use. It is clean and transparent to perfection, which distinguishes it from other European wares. The more delicate varieties adorned with enamel colors resemble Oriental porcelain (be it Chinese or Japanese) so closely that they are often used as alternatives to replace damaged pieces in sets. The differences between Worcester and original ones are so subtle that even connoisseurs cannot tell, and Worcester is occasionally mistaken for foreign products.[7]

Between 1749 and 1751, Benjamin Lund, a ceramic manufacturer in Bristol, invented a new formula using block soapstone instead of feldspar to produce hard-paste porcelain. In 1751, the factory was taken over by the Worcester Ceramics Factory, located on the banks of the River Severn. After the takeover, the factory continued to use this block soapstone formula. This ensured the stability of firing, and the porcelain body was able to withstand higher temperatures compared to other soft-paste porcelain, avoiding deformation in the kiln and resulting in a stronger and more durable porcelain. This allowed Worcester factory to gain a significant market share in the eighteenth century.

The Worcester factory began producing Oriental-style ceramics from its inception, with some products closely imitating the vibrant enamel decorations of China and Japan, and others featuring underglaze blue paintings depicting Western interpretations of Chinese scenes. Both types received positive market response. Interestingly, to imitate Chinese porcelain or give their own products an Eastern flair, the factory used fabricated Chinese characters as decoration, some of which were intentionally altered. For example, the Chinese character "明" (Ming) and "玉" (jade) from the Ming Dynasty were both subject to bizarre alterations before being imprinted on the products.[8] The factory pioneered the technique of transfer printing from the early days, including underglaze blue and overglaze prints in red, purple, yellow, and black. This technique was later widely

[7] Hou Tiejun. The Others' Things and Self's Things: Porcelain Study in 18th Century British Literature [D]. Wuhan: Wuhan University, 2015: 69.

[8] [British] Hugh Hunter. Chinese Style: Discovering the Lost Elements of China in the West for 800 Years [M]. Translated by Liu Aiying, et al. Beijing: Peking University Press, 2017: 139.

adopted by the British ceramic industry, including the Spode factory in Staffordshire and the Wedgwood factory.

The early tea ware designs of Worcester were influenced by Chinese five-color porcelain and famille rose porcelain. However, not all cups were finished during manufacturing. The most expensive tea wares were often decorated by external artisans, with James Giles being a notable figure. He established his own decorating company in London and collaborated with factories such as Bow and Worcester. He would receive white porcelain or unglazed ceramics with only a blue background from these factories to decorate, greatly enhancing the quality and aesthetic appeal of the pieces. Other independent decorating artisans included Robert Chamberlain and his son Humphrey, whose workshop was also located in Worcester. They often obtained "in white" ceramics from the Caughley factory in Shropshire for decoration. Additionally, Thomas Bax's workshop in London would complete the decorative work for some plain-bodied ceramics from other factories, including those from Jingdezhen. Some ceramic factories even left richly Eastern-styled patterns or motifs on their cups to give customers the impression that their tea wares were on par with those imported from China.

The willow pattern is perhaps the most popular in eighteenth-century Britain. To be precise, it is the most widely applied pattern by ceramic factories, large and small, across Britain. It is the result of imitation, deconstruction, combination, and re-creation based on the landscape patterns found on Chinese export blue-and-white porcelain. It can be said that it originated from the Western imitation of Chinese porcelain, representing a derivation of Chinese porcelain in Europe and the result of cultural exchange as well. From the late eighteenth century to the nineteenth century, this pattern became popular in various products of major ceramic factories in Britain, and later even found its way back to China, exerting a reverse influence on Chinese export porcelain. The willow patterns have played an indispensable role in shaping Europeans' impression on China.

As for this study, the reason why these patterns are important is that, on the one hand, they are significant in cultural exchanges, and on the other hand, their origin is closely related to tea drinking. The first British porcelain factory to use the blue ink technique to mimic this pattern was the Coghill Pottery in Shropshire. This pattern was named "Nanjing," later was used to refer to the blue-and-white porcelain in Qing Dynasty. Coghill Pottery stipulated that this pattern could only be used on tea sets. In the 1790s, the similar decorative patterns were adopted by Josiah Spode of

Staffordshire, with the main content being a small Chinese bridge, with pedestrians on it, willows beside the bridge, a wattle fence, a solitary tower in the sky, and birds flying around. This pattern quickly gained market favor, and its success was closely related to Coghill Pottery. Thomas Lucas, a pottery painter who worked at Coghill in 1783, later switched to Spode Pottery, where he assisted in making Spode a renowned creator of this classic pattern. Although some people believe that the willow pattern was invented by Thomas Minton, there is no controversy regarding Spode Pottery's production as the most famous one.

According to Spode's explanation, there were two factors that prompted him to imitate and repeatedly use such patterns. First, customer demand. His clients would often suggest him to produce ceramics that could match their Chinese porcelain, so that if any of them was damaged, they wouldn't have to go through the hassle of purchasing replacements from Guangzhou. Another reason was that the new pottery painter he hired had some knowledge on imitating Chinese designs. In short, the booming of the British pottery industry was fueled by tea drinking. As there was a need to produce ceramics that could complement Chinese tea sets and replace broken pieces, British craftsmen became familiar with and gradually able to imitate the original works from China.

Thomas Turner, a potter, was the first to seize this market opportunity. According to his book *Rag Book*, he had copied six or seven popular Chinese patterns. Josiah Spode quickly followed in his footsteps: he faithfully copied 22, making him the one who copied the most Chinese patterns. Additionally, he also adapted many patterns based on his understanding of Chinese style. His earliest copies included "Ox," "Two People," "Rocks," and "Mandarin," and among the earliest released patterns were "Pearl River Cottage," "Hydrangea," and "Temple Scenery." The "Willow" pattern was introduced around 1795, while the others were after the nineteenth century. As it is difficult to determine the exact time for patterns being introduced from the late eighteenth to the early nineteenth century, it cannot be concluded that "hand-painted patterns on creamware must have been earlier than printed ones"; however, as a decoration method for blue-and-white porcelain, hand painting was very common in the early eighteenth century.

Overall, tin-glazed pottery produced in port cities such as London, Bristol, and Liverpool primarily featured blue and white, while North Staffordshire first used cobalt blue on salt-glazed earthenware. Salt glazing was likely inspired by German stoneware and later introduced to Britain. The technique of German stoneware involves cutting or scratching the clay and then filling the resulting gaps with powdered compounds such as cobalt blue glaze.

During the firing, cobalt blue glaze produces a charming decorative effect. This type of porcelain was mostly produced between 1850 and 1875. Creamware requires two firings, making it particularly suitable for hand painting. Prior to the nineteenth century, it is likely that hand-painted blue-and-white creamware had already been mass-produced. Most of this type in existence has a shell-edge shape, with undulations on the edges and deep scratch marks on the outer wall that gradually converge from the edges to the center, resembling a scallop shell. Most of these pieces do not have signatures. Ceramic fragments excavated at the site of Spode's factory exhibit a characteristic shell-edge shape with blue patterns, which have been fired again to harden but not glazed. This may indicate that the potters were painting directly onto the pottery. The British Museum and the Victoria and Albert Museum once jointly conducted an exhibition called "The Symphony of Porcelain" that sent pieces from their collections to the National Museum of China, where some of the exhibits belonged to this category of imitative blue-and-white porcelain.

In addition to blue-and-white porcelain, the British also had a major subject to imitate: purple sandware. Hilary Young, a British ceramic expert, believes that the popularity of tea and the demand for red earthenware teapots led the Dutch Delft factories to start producing red earthenware before 1678, which influenced the ceramic production in Britain. The earliest imitation of Yixing purple sandware in Britain was by the Elers brothers, John and David Elers, who were also pioneers in the British ceramic industry. In 1693, they established their own ceramic workshop in Fulham, west of London. In 1695, they made a few red earthenware teapots imitating Yixing purple sandware, which are still cherished in the Victoria and Albert Museum (Fig. 6.3). This teapot has the common plum blossom decorations found on Yixing purple sandware, with a long foot, a round handle, and a spout adorned with metal decorations. The father of British ceramics, Josiah Wedgwood, once mentioned the brothers' teapot-making technique in a letter: "Mr. Elers has innovated the craft of teapots by sifting and refining the common red clay into a slurry, and then injecting

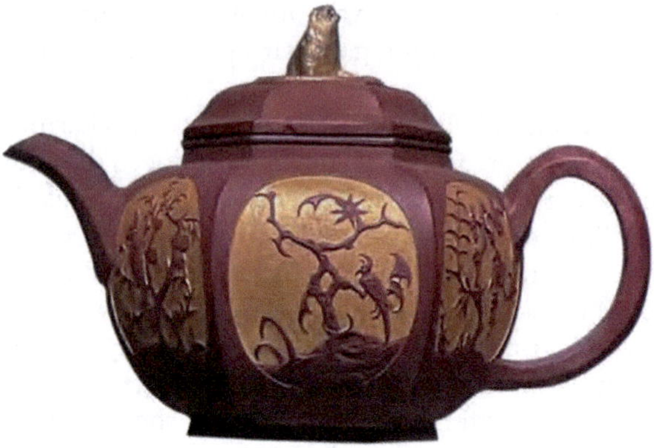

Fig. 6.3 This teapot was produced approximately between 1690 and 1698 and belongs to the earliest batch of teapots made by the British themselves. (Its creators are the brothers David and John Philip Elers. This teapot imitates the Chinese Yixing purple sand teapots imported to Europe in the seventeenth century through the Dutch East India Company. Photography: Li Leren)

it into a gypsum mold."[9] And the ceramic teapots of Wedgwood were also influenced by Yixing teapots; his designed black basalt and red clay teapots resembled those from Yixing.

In general, during the early stages of its development, the British ceramic industry closely followed behind China. British ceramic researcher Joseph J. Portanova proposed this point in his work, stating, "From the mid-18th century when British porcelain production began on a large scale, British potters had been imitating the shapes and decoration of Chinese blue and white porcelain."[10] These patterns imitating Chinese export ware have been widely applied in the production of tea ware in Britain. On the other hand, these decorative patterns that emerged from tea drinking had further permeated into the everyday lives of the British.

[9] [French] Patrice Van Vliet. Yixing teapots sold in Europe [M]. Translated by Shi Yunkui. Hangzhou: Siming Press House Publishers, 2015: 59.

[10] Joseph J.Portanova, Porcelain, the Willow Pattern, and Chinoiserie, http//nyu.edu/projects/mediamosaic/madeinchina/pdf/Portanova.pdf

3 Locked Tea Leaf Boxes

Similar to ceramic tea sets, wooden furniture such as caddies and tea tables have also been modified to adapt to the new cultural context after the introduction of Chinese tea sets in the UK.

How did the British store the tea purchased from the market? When tea first arrived in the UK, it was so precious that only the host of a family could brew, and purchasing could only be done by members of the household who were of higher status or trusted by the host, and was recorded on a special account. Tea was usually stored in red pottery vessels or porcelain from China that were kept in cupboards. Early on, they used teapots and ceramic covered jars that were popular in China at the time. The first tea jar to appear in Europe was from the red clay of Yixing, China, with a base that was rectangular or hexagonal and came with a small cylindrical lid that could be used to measure tea. There were no locked caddies back then, so the rich would hide their tea in cupboards (Fig. 6.4).

As tea drinking prevailed, people demanded more delicate tea sets. To prevent stealing, Chinese caddies were locked after coming to the UK. In 1695, a tea jar made by J&D Dales in Staffordshire, UK, was equipped with a lockable lid.[11] As summarized by Jane Pettigrew in her book *Tea Design*, in the early eighteenth century in England, "a complete set of tea utensils for brewing and serving tea would include a small round or pear-shaped teapot, a covered milk jug, a sugar bowl with a lid, a pair of scissor-shaped sugar tongs, a scoop for debris, a saucer, a teacup, a caddy with lock and key, and an iron fire pan for heating."[12] Dean Swift, in his book *Directions to Servants* published in 1729, wrote: "Small boxes and cabinets with locks and keys are used to store tea and sugar."[13]

Since the late seventeenth century, the British began to imitate Chinese tea jars and boxes. They not only attempted to develop their own versions of purple clay and porcelain but also created silver and wooden caddies. The Victoria and Albert Museum in the UK houses a caddy painted by British artist Marmaduke Cradock. This caddy was roughly made between 1685 and 1717 and has deviated from the typical Chinese tea jar design: it depicts birds and estate scenery with a distinctly British style.[14] Additionally, the museum also holds a silver-plated tea jar made in 1706,

[11] Jane Pettigrew. A Social History of Tea, National Trust. 2001: 32.

[12] Same as footnote 8, p. 194.

[13] Same as footnote 8, pp. 126–127.

[14] https://collections.vam.ac.uk/item/O79065/tea-canister-cradock-marmaduke/

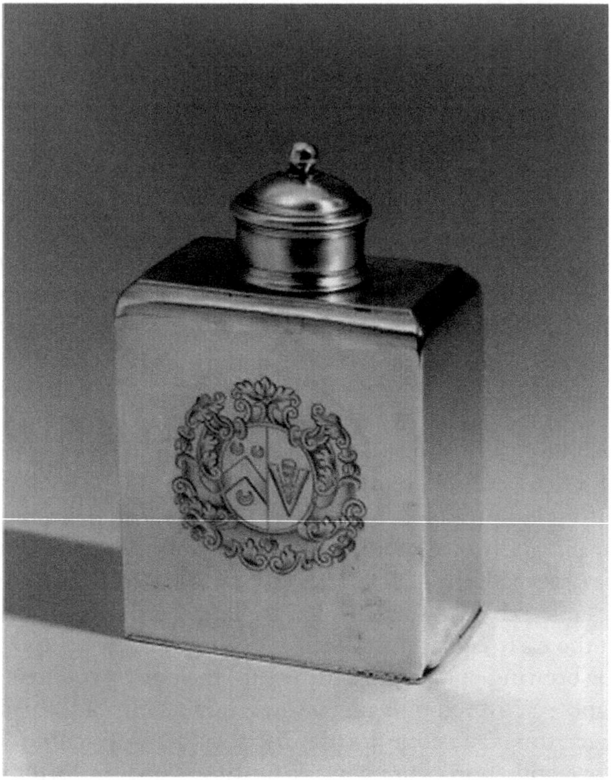

Fig. 6.4 This is a typical large silver tea caddy produced in the eighteenth century, with a coat of arms decoration on the surface. (The British believe that the early design of the tea caddy might have been inspired by the women's makeup boxes. Photography: Li Leren)

which appears similar to tea jars depicted in a still-life oil painting by Dutch artist Pieter Gerritsz van Roestraeten around 1695. However, its decorative patterns are completely different from those of tea jars from China (Fig. 6.5).[15] From this, we can observe the process of localization in the form and decorative patterns of caddies and tea jars.

[15] Li Zhuyu. A Brief Discussion on European Tea Caddies from the 18th to 19th Century [J]. Agricultural Archaeology, 2018 (2): 254.

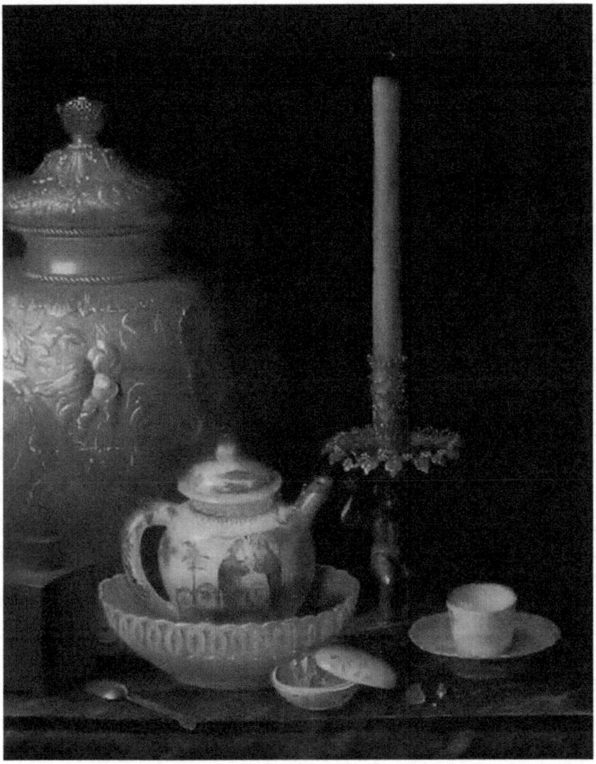

Fig. 6.5 A still-life oil painting created by the Dutch painter Peter van Rostrate around 1695, which features a tea caddy

The Saint Louis Art Museum in the United States holds a silver tea jar made in Europe. It is 12.1 centimeters tall and 11.4 centimeters long, with a long, oval shape. Its shape is quite similar to the bamboo tea crates used by the East India Company for shipping. As previously introduced, the crates typically have polished bamboo strips that are encased with lead and copper strips. This replica tea jar has designed the copper strips around the tea crate as intertwined tea leaves and bamboo forming a wreath. The circumference of the jar is covered with vertical lines resembling the bamboo strips of the crate. The lid of the jar has a tea branch and leaves design with flowers and buds attached. In the center of the jar, there is a coat of arms, with surrounding tea leaves and buds. There are also two Chinese characters "Te" and "Feng" engraved on both sides of the tea jar. Additionally, there are four Chinese characters "Heng," "Yin," "Lai," and "Tai" engraved on the side of coat of arms. Some scholars speculate that "Heng" may refer to Holmes, who may have been a merchant who frequently traveled between Guangzhou and England.[16]

In addition, tea jars specifically made for Westerners often had tea names written in Latin letters on the surface. Seeing from a different perspective, this provides us with evidence to understand the preferences of the British at the time and the state of Sino-British tea trade. Starting from the seventeenth century, the main tea varieties imported from China to the West included Bohea, Hyson, Singlo, Souchong, and others. The initials of these names would often appear on tea jars. In the late seventeenth century, a tea jar made of opaque white glass with the word "Bohea" on its body appeared in Bristol, England. This jar was one of a pair, and the other one could have been used to store another kind of tea.[17] Since then, European silversmiths began to replicate tea jars imported from China. They would also engrave the initials of these tea varieties' names on the bodies of the tea jars, such as "B" for Bohea tea and "G" for green tea (Figs. 6.6, 6.7 and 6.8). These tea jars were tall and thin in shape with flat sides. Some were similar to traditional Chinese jars, with a small lid on top. Others were adjusted, with sliding panels on the bottom or the top for accessing the tea.[18] The interior of the tea jars was usually made of lead, which helped to prolong the preservation time.

With locked caddies, hosts no longer had to worry about their tea being stolen by servants. It is recorded that after the advent of locked caddies, hosts often carried the keys to their caddies with them. For example, Jane Pettigrew mentioned this in her book *A Social History of Tea*: The famous poet William Cowper visited Miss Hesketh's house, but unfortunately, she was not home. Cowper complained that she had taken the key to the caddy with her, resulting in him not being able to have tea all day. A similar situation occurred at Mr. Bankes' Kingston Hall in Devonshire. Thus, it was not uncommon for people at the time to carry keys to their caddies with them when they went out.

[16] Reka Fisher. English Tea Caddy, Bulletin. St. Louis Art Museum, Vol.15, No.2, 1979: 174–175.

[17] Recent Accessions, The Metropolitan Museum of Art Bulletin, Vol.11, No.9, 1953: 260–264.

[18] Jane Pettigrew, A Social History of Tea, National Trust, 2001: 37.

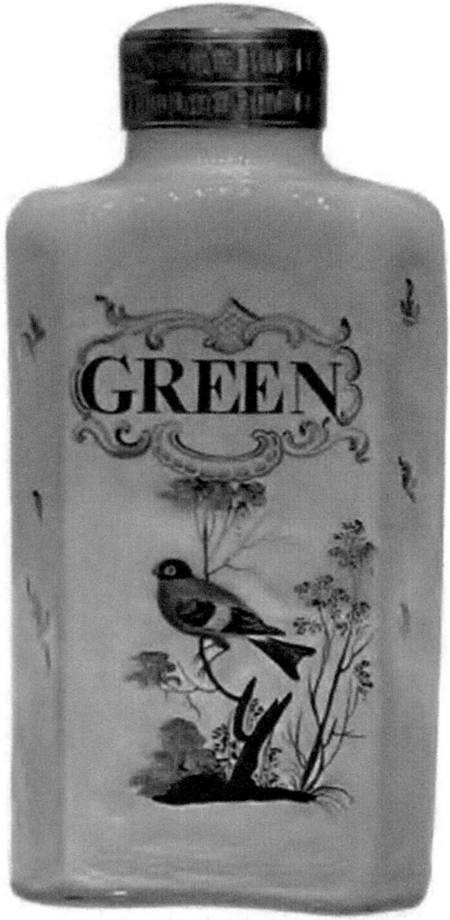

Fig. 6.6 This tea caddy was probably made between 1755 and 1760 and was designed to hold green tea. (It appears to be white porcelain, but it is actually made of white translucent glass. Photography: Li Leren)

From the book *Direction to Servants* by Daniel Defoe, we can further understand the way in which tea caddies were used at that time: "Servants gradually develop disgusting habits... With the invention of locked small boxes or drawers for tea caddies, the servants will be at a loss." In Duncan Campbell's *A Poem upon Tea* (1735), another scene is described: "My

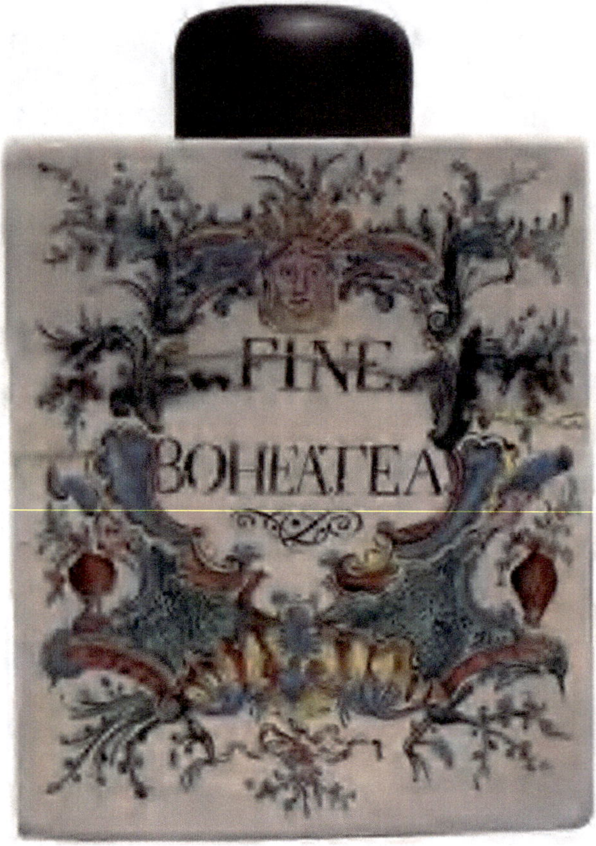

Fig. 6.7 This tea caddy was probably made between 1760 and 1770 and is relatively large in size, designed to hold Wuyi tea. (Photography: Li Leren)

Sukey Dean, Bess Trest, and my cook, they sit in the corner of the fireplace, I often find them drinking up the tea I have left…."[19]

In English, the box for storing tea is referred to as "caddy," which is derived from the Malaysian language "kati," means "one and two thirds pounds of tea." This word was only introduced into English in 1775. In 1788, George Hepplewhite, in his *Cabinet Maker and Upholsterer's Guide*,

[19] Same as footnote 8, pp. 126–127.

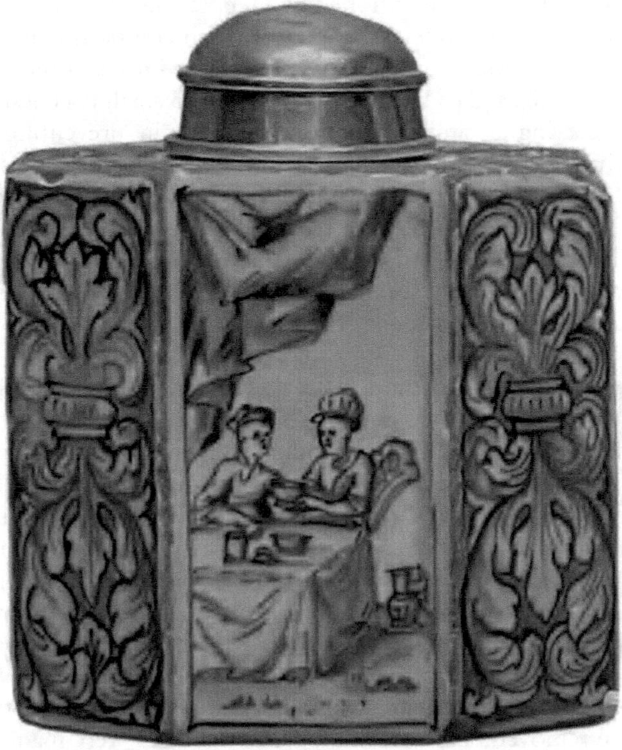

Fig. 6.8 This tea caddy was probably made between 1750 and 1760, possibly originating from Bristol. (The decoration on the surface was likely to be inspired by Chinese export porcelain. Photography: Li Leren)

wrote that "tea boxes are large boxes containing two or three movable small boxes, while tea caddies refer to one or two fixed, interconnected small boxes within the internal space."[20] Thomas Sheraton, on the other hand, believed that tea caddies could refer to various types of boxes, whether square, round, or octagonal. Although originally used to specifically refer to a type of tea container, by the early nineteenth century, it had become an umbrella term for tea containers.

[20] A. Hepplewhite and Co., Cabinet-Makers, The Cabinet-Maker and Upholsterer's Guide, Published By I. and J. Taylor, London: The Architecture Library, p. iv.

The type of tea boxes mentioned by Hepplewhite can be traced back to the period of Queen Anne (1702–1714), with compartments divided by two to three lead lines. Some tea boxes contained tea canisters or jars with markings, as well as glass bottles, silver cans, and small tea chests, with the markings serving a similar function to locks in preventing theft. As Hepplewhite mentioned, tea canisters were typically made as a set of three to be placed in the tea box, allowing people to store two different types of tea and sugar.[21] The materials for tea caddies were diverse, including porcelain, silver, tin, wood, and even glass and crystal. Among the surviving tea canisters, the majority are made of wood, many of which were used to store smaller canisters made of silver or other materials, and some can be locked.

The appearance of tea caddies on the business cards of cabinetmakers and furniture dealers in the eighteenth century indicated that the market was gradually accepting the tea caddies and canisters made by furniture makers. The simpler styles were rectangular boxes with small feet and thick brass rings as handles, while more elaborate designs were bomb-shaped with intricate Rococo-style carvings. Thomas Chippendale, in his 1762 publication *Gentleman and Cabinet Maker's Director*, drew eight design sketches for Rococo-style tea caddies. Most of these boxes were made of mahogany, occasionally walnut. The top handles and fittings were usually made of brass or silver. In the 1770s, with the emergence of Neoclassical style, wooden caddies began to adopt a more restrained aesthetic. The bases were removed, and some had pedestals. They were made of various fruit woods such as tulipwood, stained maple, and burr walnut, with a light-colored surface and inlaid with Neoclassical-style decorations.

Similar to blue-and-white porcelain imported from China, tea caddies, besides storing tea, were also displayed in tea spaces to flaunt wealth and taste. Therefore, the appearance needed to be impressive and exquisite. According to existing literature, we can also learn that in the late eighteenth century, people could add decorative details to tea caddies according to their preferences. *The London Cabinet-Maker's and Upholsterer's Guide of 1793* recorded the production and decoration details of an oval tea caddy:

> Approximately eight and a half inches long, five and a half inches wide, and five and a half inches high, with a rope running diagonally along its long

[21] Same as footnote 8, p. 132.

side, the lower part filled with cloth, and the top and edges of the inside made of wooden boards as before. A pillar approximately one and a half inches stands from the bottom to support it, with three grooves inside and two tea canisters embedded, each with a flat top, hinge, wooden board, and tin foil inside. (1 pound 4 shillings).

Additional decorations:

- -Lengthened or shortened by one inch: 10 pences
- -Double-sided wooden board: 8 pences
- -Lidded hole for adding sugar: 6 pences
- -Round cloth-wrapped handle: 5 pences
- -Small box for sugar, circular inside, square outside, with sloping top panel: 1 shilling 6 pence
- -Semicircular lid on a tea canister: 9 pence
- -Ribbon—see table above
- -Additional charge of 2 shillings 22 for adding film to tea canisters.

To enhance the beauty of the tea caddies, carpenters and goldsmiths would also use rare materials for embellishment and decoration. Silver and crystal were commonly used for inlay work, while carving, painting, lacquering, and gold and silver filigree techniques were employed to add luster and color (see Fig. 6.9). For example, Sir Richard Hoare of Stourhead in England once spent 7 pounds 17 shillings on a delicate tulipwood tea caddy. This caddy had rosewood edges, a lining of blue velvet, and a silver lock clasp. And Lady Francis Anne owned an eighteenth-century wooden tea caddy decorated with Chinese-style ivory motifs inside.

The British designed some tea tables that had both the functions of tea caddies and tables, which were also known as "Teapoy." Teapoy is considered to originate from the Persian or Indian word "three." In the eighteenth century, the British often served tea to guests in their living rooms, and various tea tables were used to place tea sets and snacks. During the mid-to-late eighteenth century, tea caddies were often placed on these three-legged tables.

Later on, the tea caddy was combined with the teapoys by the carpenters, giving birth to a kind of small teapoy with storage function. This type of tea table typically has only one pillar, with three legs at the bottom to ensure stability. At that time, this type was usually custom made, whose early styles resembled Queen Anne, with simple lines and forms. Around

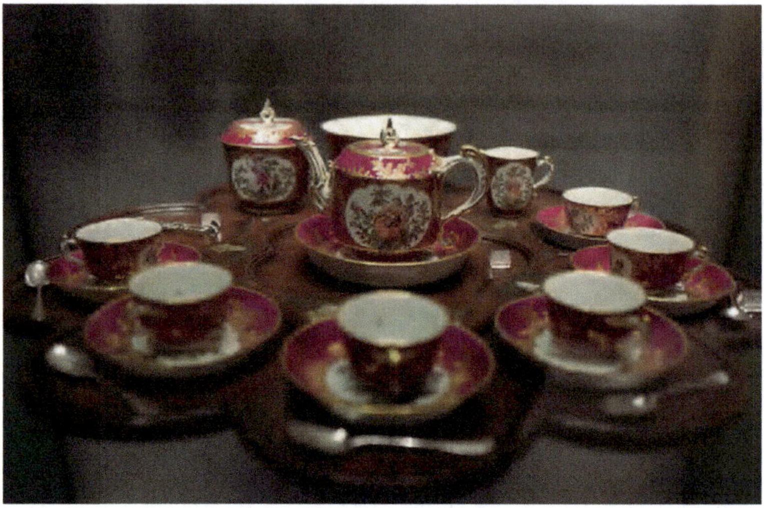

Fig. 6.9 This is a set of typical tea utensils used by wealthy families in the eighteenth century, including teapots, trays, teacups, tea saucers, milk pots, and sugar pots, produced by Chelsea Pottery between 1759 and 1769. (Photography: Li Leren)

1730, there appeared tables with carved borders and folding tables, where half of the table can be folded up. These teapoys were very common in the latter half of the eighteenth century, mostly made of mahogany, with patterns in Rococo or Neoclassical style (see Fig. 6.10).

Similar to the teapoy, there is another type of tea table that is also foldable and has storage functionality—the Pembroke tea table. Named after the Earl of Pembroke, this tea table is popular for its flexible dimensions and the dual function of tea caddy and tea table. Unlike the teapoy, the Pembroke tea table typically has a drawer under the table, which usually holds a custom-made tea caddy. Hepplewhite, in his book *The Cabinet-Maker and Upholsterer's Guide*, repeatedly praises the Pembroke tea table: "It is the most useful of this kind; its shape is various, with the most fashionable being rectangular, square, and oval. This kind of table is quite refined in workmanship and ornamentation."[22] And Sheraton, in *The Cabinet-Maker and Upholsterer's Drawing Book*, also mentioned this table,

[22] Same as footnote 20.

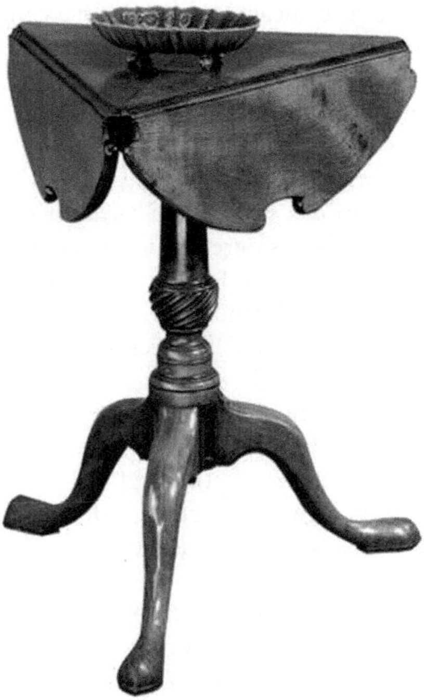

Fig. 6.10 Teapoy in Chippendale style from the reign of George III

considering it: "suitable for gentlemen and ladies to take breakfast. Its design is neat and elegant; often made of poplar, with the edges of the table painted and the drawers adorned with decorations."[23]

Wooden tea caddies and tea tables are both classified as tea furniture in Britain. Similar to ceramic tea ware, the tea furniture in Britain was all imported from China during the seventeenth century. The British furniture manufacturing industry sensed the pressure and, in 1698, the Joiners' Company petitioned the Parliament for government intervention on the import of furniture from the Far East, protecting the domestic industry. They wrote in their petition: "In these four years, 6582 tea tables have been imported into Britain."[24] Nevertheless, British furniture designers

[23] T. Sheraton. The Cabinet-Maker and Upholsterer's Drawing Book. London: T, Bensley, 1802: 412–414.

[24] Tea & Taste: The Visual Language of Tea. Tania M. Buckrell Pos. Beijing: Peking University Press. Translated by Zhang Chi et al.

were also aware of the business opportunities, and they began to draw inspiration from the imported Chinese furniture, incorporating the design vocabulary of Chinese furniture into their own designs, with this particularly evident in the design of tea furniture.

In the eighteenth century, the most heavyweight in the British furniture industry was Thomas Chippendale. In 1754, Chippendale published his seminal work, *The Gentleman and Cabinet-Maker's Director*. This book is considered a forerunner of the British furniture industry and includes several designs for tea furniture, among them there were a large number of Chinese-style designs, as well as Rococo and Gothic styles. Having observed the trends of the time, Chippendale writes in the opening pages of the book: "Elegant and useful household furniture, in the Gothic, Chinese, and modern styles, including: various breakfast tables, Chinese dining tables, tea caddies, trays....“[25] The book also describes the porcelain table—cornered with wooden or brass reticulated decorations, with hollowed-out edges; additionally, it is attached with seven plates with reticulated designs, and each table holds a set, which may be used as a tea table (Fig. 6.11).

Two other designers who have published books on Chinese-style furniture, as mentioned earlier, are George Hepplewhite and Thomas Sheraton. Hepplewhite's book *The Cabinet-Maker and Upholsterer's Guide* has influenced the entire British furniture industry. After his death, his widow Alice Hepplewhite continued to publish and republish the book under the name A. Hepplewhite & Co. in 1788, 1789, and 1794, respectively. The book contains over 300 elegant illustrations of furniture design and was often used by furniture craftsmen as a trade catalog. His book also includes a variety of furniture designs that were popular in Britain during the last ten years of his life. He endeavored through his writing to make these designs accessible to the average English carpenter, with a large selection of tea furniture, including tea caddies, tea jars, tea trays, single-legged tea tables, and folding tea tables, as well as advice on the types of wood and finishes to use (Fig. 6.12). In comparison, Sheraton's *The Cabinet-Maker and Upholsterer's Drawing Book* is more feminine, just fitting the expectations of the time for tea-related home designs. Another book is Sheraton's *Cabinet Dictionary*, published in 1803, with designs that catered to the styles of the Regency period, incorporating classical elements such as lion's paws, lion's single feet, and lion's heads.

[25] Thomas Chippendale. The Gentleman and Cabinet-Maker's Director. London: T. Osborne, 1754, title page.

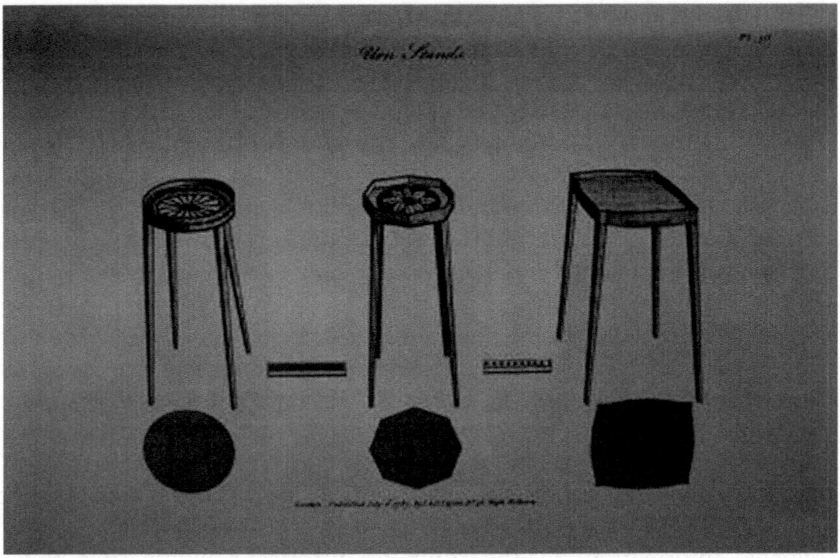

Fig. 6.11 Tea tray design featured in Thomas Chippendale's "The Gentleman and Cabinet-Maker's Director," around 1754

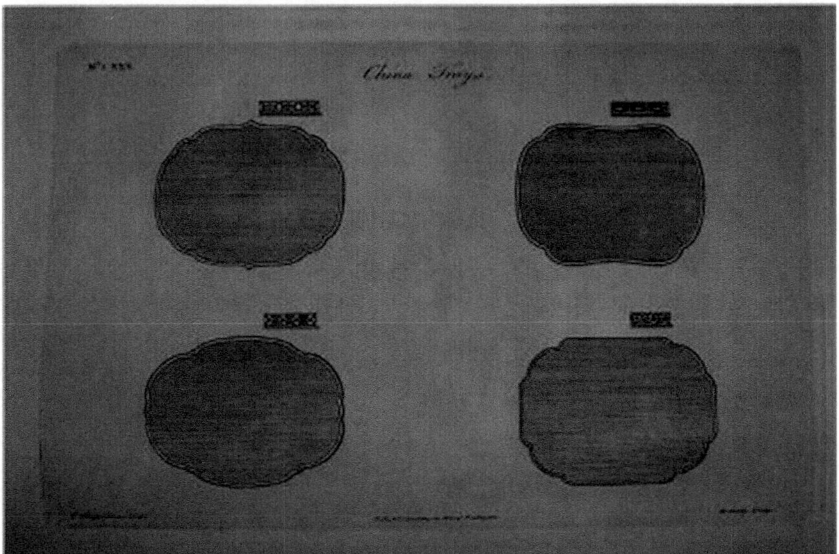

Fig. 6.12 Tea table designed by George Hepplewhite, used for storing tea urns, featured in a book titled "The Cabinet-Maker and Upholsterer's Guide," circa 1788

British cabinetmakers used hardwoods such as mahogany to craft delicate furniture that suited the tea-drinking culture, and these designs were well received on the European continent, leading to imitation by continental counterparts. As one commentator noted in an European magazine, "English furniture is generally sturdy and practical, while French furniture is more ornate and gaudy... there is no doubt that English furniture will continue to set trends for a considerable period of time."[26] It can be said that the British furniture design of the eighteenth century, which grew out of the tea-drinking culture, had fully developed its own unique style with international influence.

Around the same period, several other designers published books on Chinese-style designs. For example, *New Book of Chinese Designs Calculated to Improve the Present Taste* by Edwards and Darly, and *Designs of Chinese Buildings, Furniture, Dresses, etc.* by William Chambers. Chambers was one of the first Western designers in Europe to introduce the traditional Eastern material of bamboo into Western design. These books played a positive role in the dissemination of Chinese style in Europe and provided valuable information for the study of historical Chinese style today. However, it must be said that in today's perspective, many of the "Chinese styles" depicted in these books were largely based on the hearsay among designers, mixed with images from early Western travelers' travelogues or export porcelain, their own imagination, and created based on Western aesthetics. These creations were very far from the true Chinese designs of the time and were filled with stereotypes of Oriental culture.

4 The Rise of Wedgewood

The Birth of Wedgewood

Until now, the Wedgwood Ceramic Factory, founded in 1759, is still considered a national treasure. The founder, Josiah Wedgwood, is even praised as the "Father of English Ceramics." As a leading brand, the development of Wedgwood largely reflects the process of the British ceramics industry learning and borrowing from their Chinese peers, and integrating the

[26] P. Thornton, Authentic Decor. The Domestic Interior 1620–1920, Weidenfeld & Nicolson, 2000, p. 140.

technological advances of the Industrial Revolution to become a global leader. From its inception to maturity, we can see the innovation and accomplishment of the British ceramics industry in the Industrial Revolution.

Most of the ceramic businesses in the UK are concentrated in Staffordshire in the northwest, which is also jokingly referred to as the "Jingdezhen of Britain."

The history of ceramic production in Staffordshire can be traced back to the Saxon era, and some believe it began during the Roman rule. Initially, there were only a few scattered villages, with pottery workers of low levels of education and the lifestyle of gypsies, resulting in low-quality pottery. Fortunately, although there was no advantage in human resource, there were enough advantage in the geographical location. Staffordshire produces a unique type of coal with abundant reserves. The local geology is rich in limestone gravel, forming a valuable type of silica stone, which is the main material for ceramics. Besides, the water here is unique compared to other places, making clay easier to shape. Additionally, the tilted foundation and continuous mountain ranges in the area have weathered over time, resulting in rich clay deposits. All these natural conditions have become necessities for producing ceramics in Staffordshire.

Starting from the seventeenth century, Staffordshire gradually gained reputation in ceramic production, but it remained a handicraft industry until the late seventeenth century. Almost all processes of pottery making, such as selecting clay, forming vessels, firing kilns, and painting, were completed by a potter alone, and the process of making was exactly the process of shaping. Even at the beginning of the eighteenth century, there were not many workshops, usually only a few hired workers, and products were only sold locally. With the prevalence of tea, ceramic tea sets were in unprecedented demand and the industry here began to flourish.

Hillary Young, a British ceramic expert, wrote in her article *Europe's Response to Chinese Porcelain: Craft, Design, and Trade* that "The fine porcelain production in the UK is concentrated in the north of Staffordshire, an area that rapidly industrialized in the first 50 years of the 18th century and became one of the world's ceramic centers in the 19th century—a feat only matched by Jingdezhen. The initial momentum of industrialization in this place was more or less related to China: firstly, a fine white porcelain from the early 18th century to the 1780s was clearly influenced by imported Chinese porcelain. Secondly, with the growing fashion of drinking Chinese tea, Staffordshire began its prosperity driven by the demand for high-quality and affordable porcelain tea sets (larger and more complex tablewares were later)."[27] British scholar Adrian Forty also discusses this point in his book: "In the 18th century, The steady growth in demand for pottery was not solely due to population growth. The popularity of tea led to a growing need for ceramic cups (as pewter cups were not comfortable for drinking hot beverages), while colonial expansion opened up overseas markets. The entire industry benefited from this, with most manufacturers seeing an increase in their trade volume. Wedgwood, in particular, took the lead."[28] The introduction of the Wedgwood Museum, located on the site of the Wedgwood factory, also highlights the significance of tea in the Wedgwood Pottery Factory, as well as the entire British ceramic industry.

In 1795, Georgia Wedgwood, who was born in a local pottery family, founded the Wedgwood Pottery Factory. From the early stages of brand establishment, Wedgwood's invention of creamware gained some market influence due to its attractive appearance and competitive price. However, it was the Queen Charlotte's order in 1765 that truly made his name. This set was later marketed under the name "Queen's Ware" and developed into a series. There were several different styles of teapots in the early works of Wedgwood, which clearly reflects the influence of Chinese teapots and Chinese-style patterns (Fig. 6.13). It is said that Fig. 6.14 is the "first" teapot produced by Wedgwood, circa 1745, made from the red clay from the northern part of Staffordshire. The mouth and handle are shaped like wild apple branch, and the metal cap at the end of the mouth can be replaced. And the body and lid are decorated with peach blossom patterns. This teapot is now on display at the Wedgwood Museum in Staffordshire. Figure 6.15 is an early creamware, made between 1762 and 1765. The pattern on the lid is molded, with floral decoration. Figure 6.16 is a queen pottery teapot made in 1775, painted with colored Chinese figures. Figure 6.17 is a Wedgwood jasper Breakfast Tea set with light blue and white patterns circa 1785. The patterns on the teapot are derived from

[27] Lü Zhangshen. Elegance of Porcelain: Fine Porcelain Treasures from the Collections of the British Museum and the Victoria and Albert Museum [M]. Beijing: Zhonghua Book Company, 2012: 27.

[28] [British] Fowler. Coveted Things: Design and Society since 1750 [M]. Translated by Gou Xianxu. Nanjing: Yilin Press, 2014: 14.

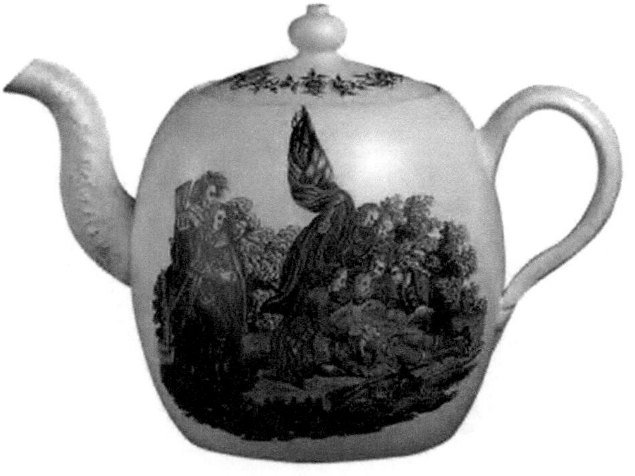

Fig. 6.13 A teapot from the "Queen's Ware" series, featuring a design depicting the "Death of General Wolfe" on its surface, produced in the late eighteenth century. (The spout is adorned with a cabbage pattern, and the top of the lid features a spherical decoration. The surface is printed with a black pattern. The transfer printing was processed by Sadler & Green company, and the craftsman William Woollett carved the design. The original painting was painted by Benjamin West)

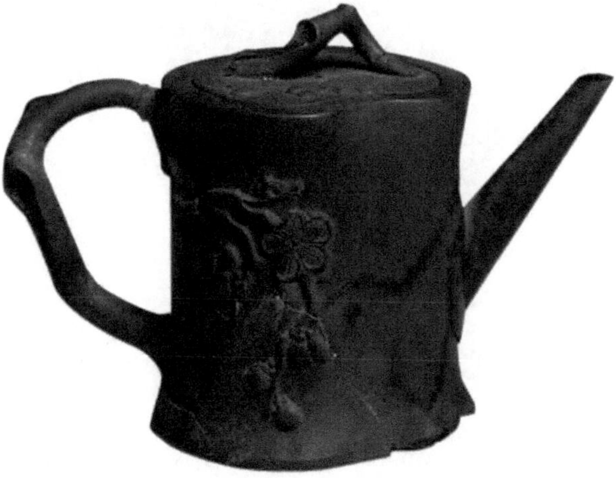

Fig. 6.14 It is said to be the "first" teapot produced by Wedgwood, circa 1745, made from red clay from the northern Staffordshire region. (The spout and handle are shaped like wild apple branch patterns, and the metal cap at the end of the spout can be replaced. There are also decorations of a cherry tree pattern on the body and lid of the teapot. This teapot is currently on display at the Wedgwood Museum in Staffordshire)

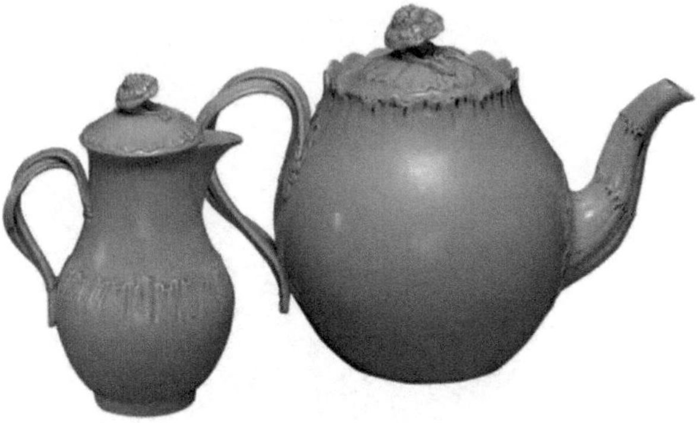

Fig. 6.15 This teapot belongs to the early creamware works and was made between 1762 and 1765. (The pattern on the teapot lid is molded, while the decoration on top is in the shape of flowers)

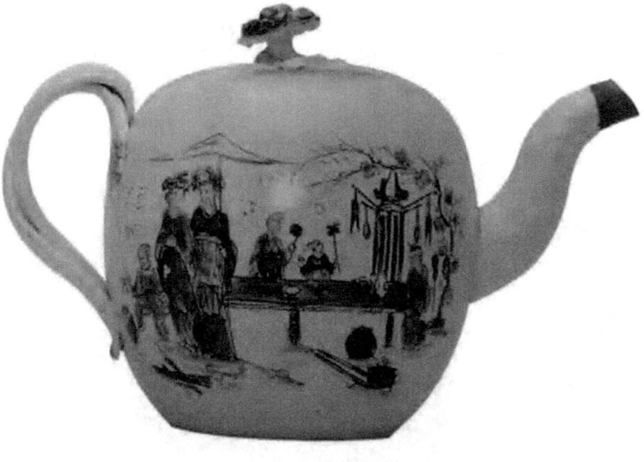

Fig. 6.16 A queen pottery teapot made in 1775, painted with colored Chinese figures

Christian "Poor Maria," on the sugar bowl is mother and child doing laundry, while the patterns on the cream container and teacup are of a playing Cupid. This tea set was designed by Lady Elizabeth Templetown for Wedgwood, with William Hackwood manufacturing the molds. Figure 6.18 is a molded sugarcane-colored pottery set designed to replicate bamboo, circa 1780.

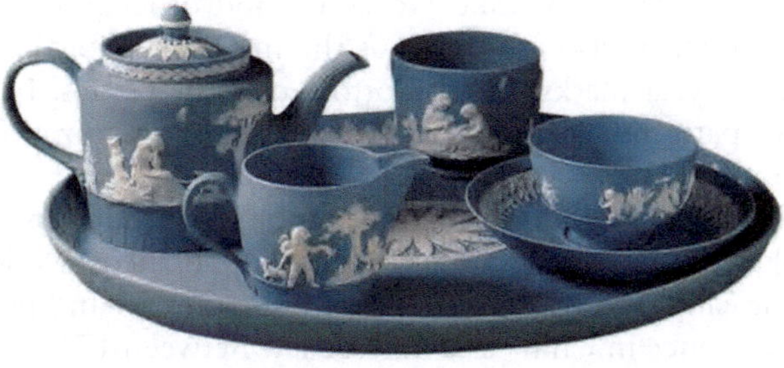

Fig. 6.17 Wedgwood jasper Breakfast Tea set with light blue and white patterns circa 1785. (The patterns on the teapot are derived from Christian "Poor Maria," on the sugar bowl is mother and child doing laundry, while the patterns on the cream container and teacup are of a playing Cupid. This tea set was designed by Lady Elizabeth Templetown for Wedgwood, with William Hackwood manufacturing the molds)

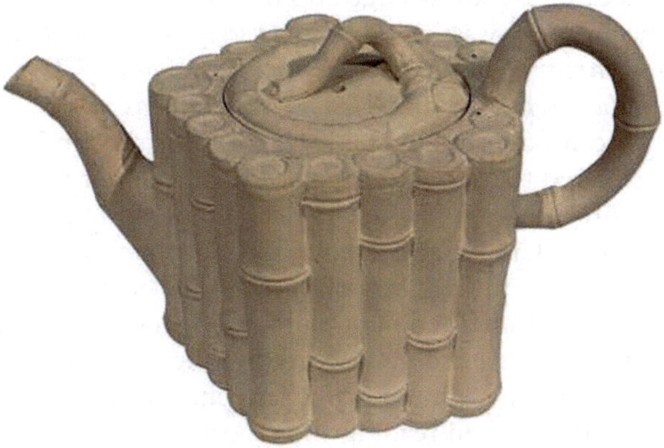

Fig. 6.18 A molded sugarcane-colored pottery set designed to replicate bamboo, circa 1780

Imitation and Innovation in Production Organization

Although Wedgwood claimed to reject the trend of Chinese after its brand had developed, it actually followed the same path as other British brands since their early stages, using Chinese ceramics as a standard. According to existing historical materials, Wedgwood once requested the Guangzhou agent of the British East India Company to send Jingdezhen clay to

Staffordshire for research. Like Worcester and other porcelain factories mentioned earlier, it also used blue as the main color for decoration and added Chinese year marks on the bottom of some vessels. In addition to shapes and patterns, Wedgwood's production organization was also learned from China.

Most of Wedgwood's information about the production of Chinese ceramics likely originated from the French Pere Francois Xavier D' entrecolles. In the early eighteenth century, he built a church in Jingdezhen and began his residence in China as a missionary. Between 1712 and 1722, he sent numerous letters to the French Indochina Missionary Department, reporting on various details related to the production of porcelain in Jingdezhen, including materials, techniques, production organization, and other aspects.

These letters were quickly compiled into a book, titled *Letters and Notes on the Chinese Marvels and Wisdom by the Jesuits*. The book consists of 34 volumes and is hailed as the first comprehensive masterpiece in Europe that provides extensive knowledge about China.

Later, this material was included in *Description of the Empire of China and Chinese-tartary, Together with the Kingdoms of Korea and Tibet Containing the Geography and History (natural as well as civil) of Those Countries* by Jean Baptiste Du Halde. It was published in France in 1735, commonly referred to as *The Complete Geography of the Chinese Empire*.

In the eighteenth century, the book became an important source of knowledge about China, and many European philosophers, including Voltaire, held China in high regard largely due to the influence of this book. The French Enlightenment thinker Diderot directly quoted Pere Francois Xavier D' entrecolles's words in the section on porcelain of Encyclopedia.[29] Sir Joseph Banks, President of the Royal Society of London at the time, when reading the report on porcelain production in the book, he asked Wedgwood to send staff to Jingdezhen to investigate into ceramic production. The German sinologist Rehdiger also mentioned in his book *All Things - Modular and Scaled Production in Chinese Art* that the innovation of Wedgwood's organization was inspired by the

[29] Robert Finlay. The Story of Blue and White Porcelain [M]. Translated by Zheng Mingxian. Haikou: Hainan Press, 2015: 22.

missionary 's letters. In fact, his description of the process in Jingdezhen, where a piece of porcelain was completed by over 70 artisans, did come true in Wedgwood. Inspired by this "revolutionary concept," Wedgwood "established the first porcelain production line in Europe that implemented a factory system and comprehensive labor division."[30]

In England, the dominant production organization during the original industrialization period was household workshop, which involved collaborative labor among the whole family, with each member specializing in a different task. This labor organization was prevalent in rural areas and industries including textiles and weaving. The rise of the household workshop system led to the thriving of rural industry in the sixteenth to eighteenth centuries, creating the necessary conditions for the industrial revolution, including the primitive capital accumulation, the first generation of entrepreneurs (capitalists) and skilled labor force (employees), shaping the employment in the industrial revolution, nurturing the market, while boosting the commercial agriculture. Based on the original industrialization, the real industrial revolution started in the second half of the eighteenth century. The first manifestation was the improvement of production tools, namely, steam engine. However, in addition to mechanization, industrial revolution also meant changes in organization: the factory system. "Technical changes in the eighteenth century is usually associated with the factory system,"[31] "which also plays a role in improving productivity and facilitating social change."[32] Without any doubt, the porcelain industry became a pioneer in adopting the factory system.

In 1769, Wedgwood established a new factory in Etruria. The choice of name was thoughtful, symbolizing the source of European culture. Wedgwood hoped to draw inspiration from ancient Greek and Roman cultures to reconstruct British aesthetic tastes. Therefore, the products

[30] [German] Rehde, Marlene. "Modularization and Scale Production in Chinese Art" [M]. Translated by Zhang Zong. Beijing: Life·Reading·New Knowledge Sanlian Bookstore, 2012: 143.

[31] [British] M.M. Postan. "The Cambridge Economic History of Europe (Volume 6)" [M]. Translated by Wang Chunfa, et al. Beijing: Economic Science Press, 2002: 260.

[32] Qian Chengdan. "A General History of Britain (Volume Four) - Transition Period: Britain in the 18th Century" [M]. Nanjing: Jiangsu People's Publishing House, 2015: 149–151.

from this new factory were mostly characterized by simple and cheerful shapes, simple styles of neoclassicism, including Etruscan painting, black basalt, and jasperware. These British-style ceramics appear to have broken away from the decorative style of Chinese ceramics. However, the division of labor in this factory still inherited that in Jingdezhen. Wedgwood reorganized the production process, implementing a more rational and refined division of labor, and applying steam engines to increase labor productivity. When Erasmus Darwin, a relative of Wedgwood and the grandfather of Charles Darwin, praised Wedgwood's new factory, Wedgwood attributed these innovations to the distant Jingdezhen: "The Chinese, with their artistry, have created brilliant works, such as construction, decoration, and tile laying, handling the entire pagoda and other various magnificent buildings."[33] He even suggested to Erasmus that he read the missionary's letters included in *Description of the Empire of China and Chinese-tartary, Together with the Kingdoms of Korea and Tibet Containing the Geography and History (natural as well as civil) of Those Countries.*

Specifically, in this factory, the ceramic production was separated into steps, such as mixing the clay, forming the pot, glazing, firing, and painting. Each worker was only responsible for one step—the ceramic artisans of the past no longer existed, only the workers responsible for digging and transporting the mud, mixing the clay, forming the potters' wheel, glazing, loading the kiln, firing, and painting. This is similar to the division of labor in Jingdezhen. Based on this, Wedgwood innovated the organization form by estimating the average workload required for each step, demanding a workload to each worker, and assigning different jobs based on their ages and genders.

In 1790, Wedgwood's factory employed a total of 278 workers, with all workers except for 5 general laborers being allocated to different workshops based on their respective roles.[34] To instill punctuality among the workers, Wedgwood pioneered a timing system in the ceramic factory, using bells to call workers to their tasks. He set specific times for various activities such as waking up at 5:45 am, having breakfast at 8:30 am,

[33] Same as footnote 30, p. 94.

[34] Neil McKendrick, Josiah Wedgwood and Factory Discipline, The Historical Journal, Vol.4, No.1 (1961): 33.

starting work at 9:00 am, and so on, with the bell ringing until it was too dark to see to call it a day. Wedgwood also hired a supervisor. The supervisor had to be the first person at the factory, "allocate tasks to the workers as they arrived, encourage those who arrived on time, and warn those who were late. If someone was repeatedly late for certain times, their pay would be docked."[35] Through modern factory operations and strict labor discipline, Wedgwood not only accelerated production but also improved quality. By "factory-ization," Wedgwood transformed and elevated the British pottery industry into the most organized pottery industry in Europe, significantly enhancing efficiency.

In addition to efficiency, clear division of labor further ensured quality. In this approach close to modern production lines, the making of a piece of pottery required the collaboration of multiple craftsmen, and no single individual could have a fundamental impact on the final result. However, each step could potentially resulted in deviations in the finished product, especially glazing, which could cause significant differences between products. Wedgwood once complained about this issue in a letter to his partner Thomas Bentley:

> ...and mixtures and color, no matter how much careful we are, too many unforeseeable risks and accidents can affect them, such as the clumsiness or lack of ideas of the workers. For example, when making a primitive and gorgeous pebble-pattern pottery with mixed clay, when putting the clay into the model, if the worker rotated the edge of the mold and did not keep the base plate stable, the vessel would show signs of fiber marks and lose the delicacy and color of pebble pattern.[36]

By training the workers, further refining the production process, and introducing a regulatory system, Wedgwood increased the reliability of the craft to a new level. Although this system was not welcomed by the workers, the higher professionalism led to better production. For instance, when making blue-and-white porcelain, glazing includes both glazing and decoration; but when making beige ceramics, glazing and decoration were

[35] Same as footnote 35, p. 41.

[36] [British] Fothergill, James. "Desirable Things: Design and Society Since 1750" [M]. Nanjing: Yilin Press, 2014: 14.

separated into glazing and enameling. There were clear instructions on how to complete their tasks, and a foreman regulatory system was introduced to ensure that instructions were carried out correctly.

The Innovation in Marketing

In fact, the impetus of the innovation in organization was market demands. At that time, ceramic craftsmen typically sent batches of products directly to the market or to wholesalers. While Wedgwood continued to use this access, he also worked out another channel: advance ordering. In 1759, he opened a product showroom called Wedgwood News on the bustling Greek Street in central London to showcase samples. In addition to displaying goods, this provided a social venue for old and potential clients, pioneering the European brand sample showroom concept (Fig. 6.19).[37] These samples were for display only, with no inventory inside the showroom; customers could only place orders after viewing the products. Subsequently, the orders were sent to the factory, and production began upon receipt of the order, with the finished products sent directly to customers. This method prevented funds from being tied up in inventory and avoided losses from producing unwelcomed products.

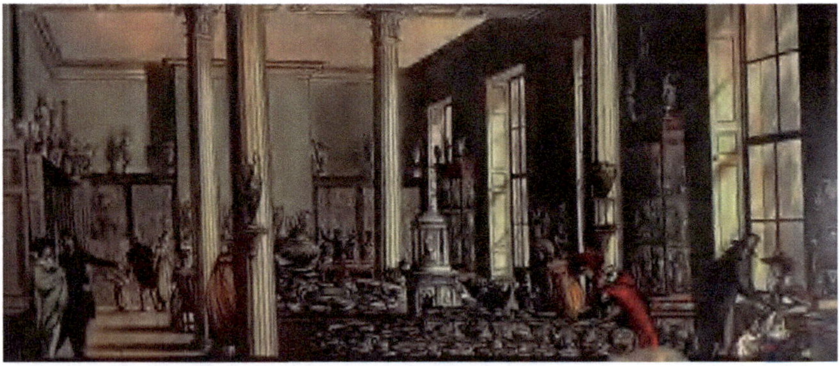

Fig. 6.19 In 1759, Wedgwood opened a product showroom on the bustling Greek Street in the center of London to display samples, pioneering the first European brand sample showroom

[37] Liu Lixian, et al. "Wedgwood's Design Management Thought and Business Practice" [J]. Decorative Art, 2020 (1): 78.

Later, Wedgwood further improved the advance ordering. In addition to sending salesmen carrying samples to other regions of the UK and overseas, he also published product catalogs for customers. However, this imposed higher demands on production. Customers would expect the items to be exactly the same as the samples they had seen. Maintaining absolute consistency is not a problem in the era of machine production on factory assembly lines, but it was still challenging in the predominantly handmade ceramic industry of the eighteenth century. Through arduous trials and continuous innovation, Wedgwood solved this problem, laying the core foundation of Wedgwood's production methods.

In the early 1760s, Wedgwood's main product was blue porcelain. Its decoration was achieved through the glaze on molded ornaments, with the final effect being determined by the skill of the glazing worker and the condition of the kiln. However, it was obvious that both factors were difficult to control, resulting in products of varying quality. In order to make the products suitable for advance ordering, Wedgwood conducted new experiments, leading to the creation and promotion of beige ceramics. Ceramic workshops in Staffordshire had been making a type of beige-glazed pottery since the 1740s. Under certain firing temperatures, this white earthenware could achieve more stable results, meeting Wedgwood's expectations.

In 1765, Wedgwood researched and developed a beige ceramic glaze that was as stable as white earthenware and could achieve uniform results. Another downside of blue porcelain was that the glaze used for decoration on the surface was easily affected by firing conditions. To address this issue, Wedgwood replaced colored glazes with plain glaze in beige ceramics, which were then decorated with hand-painted enamel after firing, and refiring at a lower temperature after painting. The process of hand-painted enamel had been used in porcelain and salt-glazed stoneware, but it was time-consuming and labor-intensive, not suitable for inexpensive ceramic products. The enamel decorations produced by Wedgwood in the early stages were typically intricate hand-painted designs, complex in design, difficult to replicate, and did not meet the requirements for Wedgwood's mass production. To utilize this technique in pottery while controlling the cost and outcomes, Wedgwood introduced transfer printing technology, where the enamel was transferred onto fired ceramic bodies. The illustrations on beige ceramics were mostly transferred, with hand-painting artisans only responsible for intricate borders and decorations that were not easily replicated accurately. As a result, the only instability remained was the skill of the hand-painting artisan.[38]

The Advent of New Professions

When an industry introduces finer division of labor and the entire production process needs cooperating, a new step would appear. In the ceramic industry, this refers to mold making, which can also be regarded as design, becoming independent from other steps. By the 1750s, this practice was relatively common and mold maker or designer came up as a real profession. Their job was to create prototypes. For example, William Greatbatch, who provided many prototypes for Wedgwood's celadon products, not only collaborated with Wedgwood but also held the position of mold maker at Whieldon.

The responsibility of a mold maker is to accurately convey instructions to workers through images, preventing them from random practices during production. This limited the variation created by craftsmen, making the role of the mold maker even more important. For those beige ceramics that pursue consistency, the greater the sales volume, the more the design is replicated, the more significant the value of the mold maker (designer). Because their work actually consolidates parts that each craftsman would be involved in during the handcrafting stage. Therefore, the value of a mold maker's work is equivalent to the sum of certain parts of all craftsmen's work. As a result, mold makers become the highest paid job in the industry. According to data published by Arthur Young in 1769, the annual income of a mold maker was 100 pounds, roughly two to three times that of a craftsman.[39] Additionally, business owners typically paid the mold maker a lump sum. Therefore, for business owners, the more molds produced, the greater the value created by the mold maker.

However, mold makers did not solve all problems, especially when it comes to changing design styles. For example, when Wedgwood wanted to introduce a new neoclassical style, ordinary mold makers, limited by traditional concepts in pottery shaping, were unable to meet their expectations. As a result, a new challenge emerged: finding suitable mold makers. Because Neoclassicism originated from fashion centers outside of Britain,

[38] Same as footnote 37, pp. 29–31.
[39] Same as footnote 37, p. 40.

mold makers living in Staffordshire did not have much access to this style. Wedgwood's eventual solution was to hire and consult with artists and designers from outside the pottery industry who understood neoclassicism to serve as ceramic designers.

Of course, this solution didn't run smoothly from the beginning. Artists liked to take their own courses and unwilling to comply with the factory's regulations, challenging Wedgwood's implementation of work rules and standards. To resolve this contradiction, Wedgwood's collaboration with these artists shifted to commissioning or purchasing designs. One example is his collaboration with John Flaxman. Flaxman lived and completed his designs in London, and sent the work to Etruria when finished. In this process, design was separated and was not bound by location.

Hiring artists for design also had another major commercial advantage. In the eighteenth century, Britain was at a crucial stage of the formation of the middle class, with an increasing number of individuals occupying the intermediate position between the upper and lower classes. To showcase their status, this new class was eager to emulate the lifestyle of the upper class, while also hoping to demonstrate their uniqueness through distinctive fashion tastes. However, the ceramic craftsmen living in Staffordshire all came from the working class and naturally lacked an understanding of these market trends. On the contrary, those artists typically belonged to this social stratum, and their aesthetic sensibilities were able to create products that were at the cutting edge of trends and catered to or even led the market.

In short, with the factory-based production organization that emerged with the Industrial Revolution, clear and detailed division of labor gave rise to design as a specialized activity in manufacturing. Design made it possible to create new products without increasing costs and ensured consistency in craftsmanship. Some design scholars believe that design is about creating products that perfectly balance between the requirements of production and consumption. For example, Jeffrey Meikle, in his book *Twentieth Century Limited*, stated, "The saturated market forces manufacturers to innovate; the new machine provides designers with easily applicable decorative patterns, and this fortunate combination, seen as 'modern' by the discerning public, has spurred design."[40] In this sense, the pattern makers at Wedgwood were fundamentally no different from professional

[40] Jeffrey Meikle. Twentieth Century Limited, Philadelphia, 1979: 39.

industrial designers that emerged in the 1920s in the United States. Their role was to create styles that met market demand by balancing market needs and manufacturing within the existing production conditions.

5 Macartney's Gift

By adopting the precise division of labor system from Jingdezhen, introducing machinery, and combining it with new marketing strategies, the British ceramic industry, led by Wedgwood, defeated the Jingdezhen porcelain industry, which represented the pinnacle of pre-industrial handicrafts. The poem *The Potter*, written around 1740, describes the Duchess Elizabeth Montfort holding a tea set from Staffordshire and praising: "On England, now three-fold delight, Thy clay shall work, and shine with gold, And honor to the Potter's Art."[41] The porcelain represented by Wedgwood, as a symbol of British technological and industrial advancement, was included in the gifts for the Macartney embassy's visit to China. The glory of the porcelain finally blossomed during the British Macartney mission's journey to China at the end of the eighteenth century.

In the late 1770s, due to rampant tea smuggling, the British government introduced the *Commutation Act*, which significantly lowered the selling price of tea in the British market, leading to a popularization of tea in Britain in real sense. Tea was placed in an unprecedentedly important position in the British East India Company's trade with China, and the trade volume of tea between the British East India Company and China saw a significant increase. Maintaining stable trade relations with China and expanding export while retaining or increasing import became a major concern for the British government. In this context, the British government dispatched the Macartney Embassy to China on the occasion of the 83rd birthday of the Qianlong Emperor, under the guise of offering birthday felicitations, in the hope of establishing diplomatic relations with China and expanding trade privileges. At the core of this mission was tea, as evidenced by Sir George Leonard Staunton in his *An Authentic Account of An Embassy from The King of Great Britain to The Emperor of China*.

The impact of ceasing foreign trade is not only a matter of the East India Company's inability to profit from it, nor is it simply a matter of British goods no longer being able to be marketed. While we may lose on

[41] Roger Lonsdale, ed. The New Oxford Book of Eighteenth-Century Verse, Oxford: Oxford University Press, 2009: 329.

one front, we can gain on another—with the diligence and bravery of British people, and under the prudent governance of the government, we can overcome these difficulties. The real problem is that, aside from profit considerations, there are Chinese products that are increasingly becoming essential for people at all levels of British society, which cannot be obtained elsewhere. Tea has already become a necessity in the lives of the British people, and until we can find an alternative source where we can purchase at the same amount and quality, with the same price, we must maintain our connections with China.[42]

One can conclude from this text that this visit was extraordinarily significant for Britain. So, the government was extremely serious in choosing not only the personnel, but also the gifts. These people and items symbolized the image and strength of the country, as Macartney said, all of which were related to "the glory of our nation."[43] They carefully selected 590 gifts in 19 categories, "exhibiting the pinnacle of artistic and civilized achievements of the British people to the Chinese."[44]

However, these exquisite gifts did not impress Emperor Qianlong—"every item listed within [the gift list] is unnecessarily exaggerated... just to boast the exquisite craftsmanship," what's worse, he even commanded the officials responsible for receiving the envoys to deflate their arrogance, ensuring that the British "would not dare to boast of their own marvels."[45] Under such circumstances, it is natural that the Chinese would appear indifferent to the British gifts. The Dutch envoys, who arrived a year later than the British delegation, witnessed the fate of these gifts: "They saw some of the gifts that Lord Macartney brought the previous year. They were carelessly dumped among a heap of other things and it is very likely that they had never been cared about."[46]

Of course, the fate of these gifts cannot be attributed solely to the Emperor. After visiting Qianlong's Summer Palace in Rehe, Macartney

[42] [British] George Leonard Staunton. "An Embassy to the Court of the Emperor Qianlong" [M]. Translated by Ye Yi. Beijing: Qunyan Press, 2014: 9–10.

[43] George Macartney. "An Account of the Embassy to China in the Year 1793" [M]. Translated by Liu Bannong. Tianjin: Tianjin People's Publishing House, 2006: 15.

[44] George Macartney, John Barrow. "Observations Made During the Embassy to China" [M]. Translated by He Gaoji, He Yuning. Beijing: Commercial Press, 2013: 10.

[45] Zhu Yong. "The Unopened Gates of China: Sino-British Relations during the Qianlong Period" [M]. Nanchang: Jiangxi People's Publishing House, 1989: 216–217.

[46] [British] John Barrow. "China under the Qianlong Emperor" [M]. Translated by Li Guoqing, et al. Beijing: Beijing Book Press, 2007: 157.

realized: "Here there are astronomical instruments, solar system models, clocks, and automatic musical instruments, all of them are exquisite in details and abundant in variety, there is nothing we can compare!"[47]

When Macartney took Wedgwood's porcelain to China, Wedgwood wrote to Bentley, "It is great pleasure to know that you are going to savor the joy of conquering Beijing."[48] And his pleasure was not overshadowed by the indifference of the Qing court. According to Macartney's records: "The officials in Beijing showed little interest in this... it could be said that the gentlemen who came to see the spherical instruments, solar instruments, barometers, and the chandeliers installed in the Yuanmingyuan all looked on them indifferently, as if these were not remarkable at all, and they already knew how to use them. However, when they saw the decorative vases on the Vulliamy's, they couldn't help but appreciate the elegance of our Derby porcelain."[49] The vice-envoy of mission, Staunton, also had similar records: "All their eyes were fixed on the vases, which were the most exquisite works of the late Mr. Wedgwood. When it comes to porcelain, every Chinese can be a judge. These beautiful European items received widespread recognition."[50]

According to John Barrow's account, officials at the time posed a question about the comparison between British and Chinese ceramics: "Between Chinese and British ceramics, which do we prefer?" This question actually reflected a comparison of the comprehensive strength of the two countries in terms of technology, art, and industry. Macartney's response was: "Our ceramics are truly precious, otherwise they would not be used as gifts for the Emperor, whereas the value of their ceramics can be reflected by the large quantity purchased every year by our merchants in Guangzhou."[51] This statement praised British ceramics, while his evaluation of Chinese porcelain was somewhat ambiguous, as he seemed to imply that China was nothing more than a "ceramic supplier" for Britain.

[47] Same as footnote 45, p. 187.

[48] Same as footnote 30, p. 335.

[49] Same as footnote 45, p. 63.

[50] Mr. Wedgewood passed away in 1795, when Staunton hadn't finished this book yet. George Leonard Staunton, An Authentic Account of an Embassy from the King of Great Britain to the Emperor of China, vol.2, London, Printed by W. Bulmer and Co., 1797, p. 163.

[51] John Barrow, Some Account of the Public Life and a Selection from the Unpublished Writings of the Earls of MaCartney, vol. 2, London, Printed for T. Cadell and W. Paries in the Strand, 1807, p. 223.

Macartney's mission did not achieve the desired results, as the Qing government did not agree to establish trade relations with Britain. However, Chinese porcelain didn't manage to prevent itself from declining in Europe, witnessing British porcelain sprouting in the international market.

The fate of Chinese tea is similar to that of porcelain. During Macartney's visit to China, his mission was requested by the British East India Company to visit the tea-producing regions of China and learn about planting and production. At that time, Macartney foresaw very far: "if cultivated properly, with local officials' promotion, Indian tea will surely prevail within a few decades."[52] In the second half of the nineteenth century, tea stolen from China was successfully planted in India, which had a huge impact on the export of Chinese tea, "changing the center of the world tea industry, impacting the established pattern of Asian tea production... sparking a technological revolution and making India the global center of tea technology."[53]

Simultaneously, the international status of China and the UK has completely switched. The UK completed its Empire on which the sun never sets in the nineteenth century. For the commercial interest, the UK launched the Opium War in 1840 and beat China. As a result, the latter fell into the abyss of semi-colonialism and semi-feudalism, and its influence plummeted. Although the UK no longer imported tea from China in large quantities, tea had already become an indispensable part of British culture. As tea evolved from a complete stranger to a national drink, Chinese culture has seeped into various aspects of British culture through the medium of tea.

[52] Same as footnote 44, p. 203.

[53] Tao Dechen. "The Rise of the Indian Tea Industry and Its Impact on the Chinese Tea Industry - From the Late Nineteenth Century to the First Half of the Twentieth Century" [J]. Chinese Agricultural History, 2007 (1): 70.

CHAPTER 7

Hybridization and Blending: Transition from Scene Construction to Spatial Aesthetics

1 Fantasies in the Tea Cup

> Sir Macartney said, for the thoughtful tea drinker, we know that the teacup contains not only memories of the outstanding compatriots of Mount Wuyi, but also memories of the entire Chinese nation and all its history. No, in this respect, there are also Ariosto and his beautiful stories about Angelica and Medoro, because Angelica is Chinese; followed by Chaucer's 'brave Kanbeskan' story about the Chinese neighbors and their conquerors; 'The Travels of Marco Polo' and others; Jesuits, Japanese, and our friend Groning; Ryukyuans, Confucius; we also have Chinese stories, Goldsmith's 'Citizen of the World', which brings you back to Johnson, and the old days of tea drinking; then there's 'The Rape of the Lock', with Belinda having breakfast; Lady Mary Wortley Montagu's pastoral at the tea table; family scenes in 'The Tatler' and 'The Spectator' magazines, recreating the contemporary fervor for porcelain. And Horace Walpole, who in this respect was like an old woman. All in all, there are a thousand other memories, both solemn and humorous, poetic and prosaic, all waiting for those who choose to read.
>
> —Leigh Hunt
>
> *The Subject of Breakfast Continued-Tea Drinking*

Researchers believe that material culture, in addition to its practical and aesthetic functions, is also a cultural symbol with important representation function. As objects created in a specific historical period and cultural context, they must also carry the history, culture, ideology, science and

C. Zhang, *Beyond the Teacup: 18th Century Sino-British Tea Trade and Design Cultural Exchange*,
https://doi.org/10.1007/978-981-97-7691-7_7

technology, and aesthetics of that era, as well as various demands, desires, or aspirations projected by the creators themselves, and its touch, sense, and appearance make it possible to imagine and perceive the customs and local conditions of its origin.[1] Since the middle and late seventeenth century, driven by huge interest, the Dutch East India Company and the British East India Company transported large quantities of tea, porcelain, silk, lacquerware, and other goods back to Europe. In addition to meeting the practical, aesthetic, and symbolic needs of people, these objects are also important media for Europeans to understand China. A scholar specialized in English perception of Asia, named Ulrike Hillemann, has pointed out in her book that early modern England obtained information about China mainly through two channels: "One is through missionaries in Beijing…The other is through goods, such as silk, porcelain, and tea."[2]

In the seventh and eighteenth centuries in Europe, the Enlightenment challenged the ideology of Christian theology, and people began to explore the mystery of nature. The light of reason was ignited, and scientific achievements influenced every aspect of society. People redefined values, pursuing equality, liberty, and democracy, and explored the meaning of life and new social order. Against this backdrop, Europe was thirsty for novel and exotic things.

As Said explicitly states in *Orientalism*: "The Orient is not only adjacent to Europe; it is also Europe's most powerful, wealthiest, and oldest colony, the source of European civilization and language, a competitor of European culture, and one of the most profound and frequently encountered images of 'the Other'…The Orient also helps Europe (or the West) to define itself against the Orient, regarding to images, concepts, humanity, and experiences."[3] Europeans sought external exploration in an attempt to pursue their own identity through the interactions with the outside world. From this perspective, for the British, their eagerness to understand and enjoy tea was driven by their desire for a broader world, their longing for distant civilizations, and their determination to develop themselves with global resources.

[1] Hou Tiejun. The Others' Things and Self's Things: Porcelain Study in 18th Century British Literature [D]. Wuhan: Wuhan University, 2015: 79.

[2] Ulrike Hillemann, Asian Empire and British Knowledge, China and the Networks of British Imperial

Expansion. New York: Palgrave Macmillan, 2009, p. 3.

[3] [American] Edward W. Said. "Orientalism" [M]. Translated by Wang Yugen. Beijing: Life·Reading·New Knowledge Sanlian Bookstore, 1999: 2.

As introduced in Chap. 1, the initial encounter between the British and tea came from the fractions of information brought by the merchants and missionaries who traveled to China. For Europeans at that time, tea was a representation of Eastern civilization. As tea gradually shifted from luxuries to commonplace in the eighteenth century, we can see on their literatures how the British understood China through tea drinking, and how they constructed their imagination of the East through visual symbols on tea utensils. The British Romanticist writer Leigh Hunt once wrote:[4]

> "What then is a teacup?" cried the ostensible man; "it holds nothing but the tea." To you and your deficient head it may hold nothing but tea. We wish you a prosperity as insipid. But to the thoughtful tea-drinker it is -- what we know. It is the hieroglyphic of another epoch -- of a dynasty, whose subjects were clowns, and whose sovereigns were barbarians. It recalls the time when tea and Asia first became important.

Indeed, as Hunt stated, tea is a symbol of China's time-honored civilization, and a way of life and hospitality since ancient times. When Chinese people drink tea, they often use porcelain. When tea first entered England in the seventeenth century, there were no suitable vessels for hot tea. So people had to learn the Chinese way of drinking with porcelain. Although the history of porcelain in England is longer than that of tea, people's obsession with tea led to the further prevailing of porcelain. Chinese export porcelain also greatly increased after the prosperity of the tea trade. Therefore, from a certain perspective, the story of tea is also the story of porcelain, with these two products being intertwined in eighteenth-century England, as reflected in the literary works of the time.

In a poem from 1722, it was written: "The fairest works of mortal hands That e'er were fashioned, since the world began, Were candied cups and golden dishes span, For use in Temple, or for use at Court: But these were broken long ago; not one Remains to tell us where they went or came." Like tea, porcelain is a beautiful symbol of China as a land of civilization, a calling card of ancient China's cultural exchanges with the outside world. The decorations on the porcelain directly presented the aesthetics, customs, landscape, architecture, and other aspects of China: a concentrated form of Chinese culture. According to Henry Hobhouse in

[4] Leigh Hunt. The Seer: Or, Common-place Refreshed. London: Edward Moxon, 1840: 24.

his book *Seeds of Change*, from 1684 to 1791, on average more than 5 million pieces of porcelain were exported from China to Europe each year, and about 215 million pieces of Chinese porcelain were exported to Europe.[5] These artifacts, carrying the essence of Chinese culture, thought, art, and technology, were scattered throughout all classes, satisfying the needs for food, drink, and aesthetics of the British. They also enabled the British to construct their imagination and understanding of China and the Chinese people, starting with this "figuration."[6] The British Romantic poet Robert Southey believed that:

> Our knowledge of the Chinese, their manners, their arts in peace and war, their religion, policy, and literature, is almost entirely derived from their own accounts. If we had no other documents concerning this very extraordinary people, the series of drawings which they have executed would be of considerable interest. There is hardly any publication which gives so fair an idea of China as the richly ornamented works on porcelain.[7]

In the late eighteenth century, the female writer Joanna Baillie wrote a poem titled *Lines to a Teapot*, in which she imagined the distant China through her teapot. The depiction of small bridges, flowing water, pavilions, and towers in the poem easily reminds us of the willow pattern that became popular in the second half of the eighteenth century.

> On thy bright surface, gay visions rise, Of realms that to the inward eye appear; There beauty's fairy forms and features smile, And speak her strange and fascinating wiles. Maids with bright eyes, beneath their conies gay, To ev'ry passer by a smile bestow; Roses in rich profusion round them play, Steep'd in dews of the soft morning's glow. Meantime, hard by upon a rugged steep, Where rocks impetuous tumble to the plain, Gold-crested lion shakes his glittering mane, And lifts his ruddy sides to catch the beam. In pride of strength he rears his stately form, Then o'er the crags exulting dares to bound, And owns the sovereign sway of nature's storm, In elements which round his lair are pour'd. Far off, the grey and silent water flows, By rustling trees and shady hills embraced; A little boat along the surface goes, And dips, and rises as the billows chased. Beyond, a bridge its airy arch

[5] [British] Alan Macfarlane, et al. "Green Gold: The Tea Empire" [M]. Translated by Hu Xilin. Beijing: Social Sciences Academic Press, 2014: 117–118.

[6] Same as footnote 1, p. 95.

[7] Robert Southey. Letter from England, by Don Manuel Alvaraez Espriella.1 vols. New York: Published by David Longworth, 1808, pp. 186–187.

displays, Which gradual sinks till lost amid the trees; Whose deep embowering shades and twilight maze, No mortal eye can pierce with gazing ease. So fancy paints, so fancy views unfold, Each object hath a place, and nothing's real; Yet all the landscape round the teapot told, Is but the shadow of a tale ideal.[8]

Thomas Hood, in his prose "A Cup of Tea," narrates his imagination toward of China through the patterns on Chinese porcelain tea cups.

I like to see things old, and where they have been before—not brand new, just out of the shop. I like them even when they are a little chipped and worn. It gives them such a history; it makes me feel that they have lived.

Fancy is all one: give it a past, and it will make its own future. So with these cups—their shapes, their colors, their handles, their very chips and cracks tell of the centuries through which they have lived.

For what is there more magical than to sit by the fire on a wintry evening, with one's slippered feet in a comfortable chair, and one's soul in perfect comfort, and to hold in one's hands a cup whose sides are painted with garlands and faces, and whose bottom is round as the sun?[9]

These descriptions are filled with the authors' longing for the Eastern paradise. To the Westerners of that time, the East seemed to represent all that was good, elegant, peaceful, wealthy, prosperous, harmonious, and beautiful. Regarding this, J.J. Clark pointed out: "The East is the collective daydream of Europe, representing a sign of ennui that often haunts European culture."[10] Ad Reichweir summed it up: "In the subtle hues of the refined porcelain, in the floating luster of the trembling Chinese silk, the elegant European society of the eighteenth century saw a dream of a happy life, just as the optimistism that they had already dreamed of."[11] From this, we can see that the British, through tea and tea ware, used their imagination to construct an ideal China, a distant utopia. However, as French comparatist Professor D.H. Pageaux pointed out:

The "I" watches the other, and the image of the other also conveys a certain image of the "I" as the viewer, speaker, and writer. At the individual level (a

[8] Same as footnote 1, p. 62.

[9] Same as footnote 1, p. 104.

[10] J.J. Clark, Oriental Enlightment. The Encounter Between Eastern and Western Thought. Routledge, 1997: 19.

[11] [German] Lichten. "Cultural Contacts between 18th Century China and Europe" [M]. Translated by Zhu Jieqin. Beijing: Commercial Press, 1962: 21.

writer), the collective level (a society, nation, ethnicity), and the semi-collective level (a school of thought, opinion, literature), the image of the other inevitably appears as a negation of the other, complementing and extending the "I" and its space. This "I" wishes to speak of the other (most commonly for many urgent and complex reasons), but while speaking of the other, the "I" tends to negate the other, thus speaking of itself.[12]

In simple terms, through these literary works, the British fantasy of China was a perfect paradise. And tea, as an emblem of refinement, has also been imaginatively reconstructed by the British artistic circles, integrating tea into the elite culture of Europe, and reshaping it as a beverage associated with civilization, health, freedom, and even magical powers.

The British pastor John Ovington once traveled to India with the British East India Company and spent some time there. After returning to England, he published his first book on tea and its properties, *A Discourse of the Natural Properties and Quality of Tea*, which laureated him a tea expert. Although he had never been to China, he made several Chinese friends while living in India. In this book, he quoted, "Tea is sent from heaven to the races of the earth, an herb equal to its sacred name." The poet defined tea as a drink of immortals, imagining it as a social and spatial construct, thus consolidating the meaning system of tea in English culture.[13]

In fact, since the early eighteenth century, there emerged a surge of poems praising tea in Britain. These poems placed tea within the context of ancient Greece and Rome, elevating it to a divine status: a practice of neoclassicism, a complete cultural reorganization.[14] The forerunner of this trend was Nehemiah Tate, who was crowned poet laureate in 1693. His work *A Poem Upon Tea* was first published in 1701, in which he described the origins of tea and the state of tea trade in Britain by borrowing and creating complex theological analogies.

In the poem, the story of the first chapter takes place in ancient China. A tyrant named Qi reigned with excessive debauchery and incompetence, leading to a rebellion and the country fell into crisis. In the end, the

[12] Meng Hua. "Comparative Literary Image Studies" [M]. Beijing: Peking University Press, 2002: 150.

[13] [British] Markman Ellis, Richard Coulton, Matthew Maug. "Empire of Tea: The Asian Tree Leaves that Conquered the World" [M]. Translated by Gao Lingya, Xu Bo. Beijing: China Friendship Publishing Company, 2020: 96.

[14] Same as footnote 13, p. 103.

people went to the reclusive sage, Confucius, who introduced tea to them, which helped the whole country to peace down and recover. The prototype of the tyrant King Qi comes from the last monarch of the Xia dynasty, Jie.

Tate's knowledge of Chinese history came from *The Memoirs of the Chinese Empire* by the French missionary Li Ming (whose French name was Louise-Daniel Le Comte, Count Le Comte). In the second chapter of Tate, he imagined tea as a target of contention among the gods in Roman mythology, which is similar to the Judgment of Paris in Greek mythology. The gods gathered in Jupiter's palace on Mount Olympus, competing for the protector of tea. The goddesses each pleaded their own reasons, and at the end of the poem, Jupiter announced, "Tea has so many merits... only the god of all things is worthy." Similar to this poem was *A Poem in Praise of Tea* by Peter Mottew in 1704. In Mottew's poem, the gods debated the merits of wine versus tea. Mottew's tea brings health, freedom, and peace, and only the modern, civilized, and commercialized nations deserved it. These poets integrated tea into European mythology and cultural systems, which was essentially a re-contextualization and localization of tea in literature and ideology.

However, the British could not truly understand Chinese tea culture, and they were even less able to grasp the Oriental aesthetics and the spirit of Chinese art conveyed by the ceramic patterns. The decorations on Chinese export porcelain didn't follow the rules of perspective, appearing bizarre and absurd to Westerners. Charles Lamb, an English essayist who worked for the British East India Company, once said that in his youth he was very fond of "the random, azure-hued absurdity, unchained within certain concepts, and drifting in the world before the creation of perspective - that is, a Chinese teacup."[15]

But at the same time, he would also point out the peculiarities of these decorations: "A young, respectful official is presenting a cup to a noble lady - and they are standing several miles apart! ... The same lady, or perhaps another - as the features on the tea set are often quite similar - is poised to enter a pleasure boat, which is docked by the quiet stream in this secluded garden. But judging by the correct angle of her step (according to our Western principles of perspective), she can only be seen entering a romantic meadow of flowers - far beyond the distant bank of this strange

[15] [American] Robert Finlay. "The Story of Blue and White Porcelain" [M]. Translated by Zheng Mingxian. Haikou: Hainan Press, 2015: 320.

river!"[16] This also confirms the point raised at the beginning of this chapter—that Westerners would understand the East from their own perspectives, finding and building themselves through communication and interaction with the East.

2 Tea Spaces in Aristocratic Families and Their Oriental Aesthetics

Tea Table, Tea Manners, and Women Power

In the eighteenth century, the theme of "drinking tea" was also popular in painting. Although some scholars in art history believe that the symbolism in paintings outweighs their practicality, it is undeniable that paintings can show the figures, clothing, interior decorations, object forms and functions, as well as the social customs of the time in an intuitive way. In terms of the topic in this book, genre paintings themed by tea drinking or still-life featuring tea sets can help us understand the design and usage of tea utensils and tea spaces at the time, as well as the new etiquette that emerged around tea as a foreign commodity. From this, we can also trace the status of material cultural exchanges between China and England at that time.

Like the act of drinking tea, in the early days, genre paintings with tea-drinking themes or still-life paintings featuring tea sets were often to showcase the identities and status of the figures in the painting. After all, in the seventeenth century and the first half of the eighteenth century, it was a symbol of one's social status to be able to afford tea leaves, porcelain and silver tea sets, as well as tea furniture. Moreover, having a portrait painted while drinking tea further proved the wealth and status of an individual. Portraits with the theme of "drinking tea" became a trend in the 1720s, particularly among the royal family, nobility, gentry, and wealthy merchants. The typical scene would depict two or more family members or friends sitting around a tea table, drinking tea and chatting, with details of the tea set being intricately illustrated, reflecting real scenes.

In addition, we can also know about the fashion and interior decorations of the upper-class society at the time. Many tea paintings were named after "×× Family," such as *The Wollaston Family* painted in 1730, currently held in the Leicester Museum and Art Gallery; *The Western Family* painted

[16] [British] Charles Lamb. "Elia Essays" [M]. Translated by Liu Bing Shan. Beijing: Life·Reading·New Knowledge Sanlian Bookstore, 1987: 386.

in 1738, now housed in the National Gallery of Ireland; and *The Strode Family* painted in 1738 by William Hogarth, currently in the Tate Gallery in the UK. All these paintings depict the protagonists drinking tea, socializing, and chatting in a comfortable family setting.

William Verelst's work *The Gough Family*, created around 1741, depicts Harry Gough and his family drinking tea in the living room, and the tea furniture and silver and porcelain tea utensils. Among these exquisite utensils, there are three silver tea boxes placed in an intricately carved Chinoiserie ivory tea casket on the table (Fig. 7.1). Gough had served as the captain of the Streatham ship of the East India Company in 1705 and later became a prominent figure in the Company until his death in 1730. The ivory tea casket in the painting is recognized as being directly

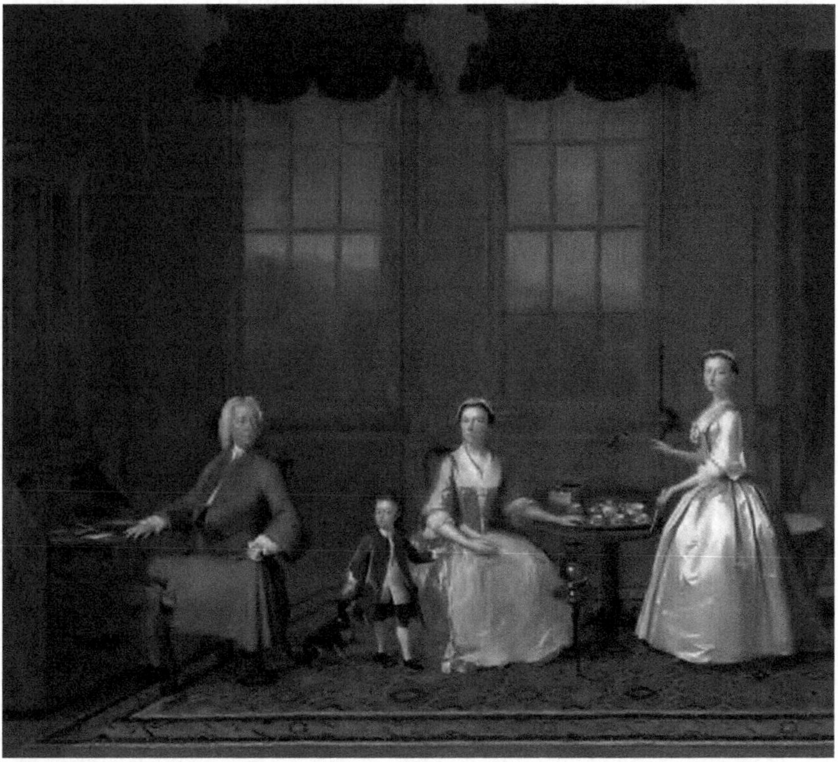

Fig. 7.1 William Verelst's work *The Gough Family*, created around 1741

purchased by Gough from China. Later, when Partridge Fine Art was selling a tea casket, a silver expert named Lucy Morton discovered that this casket was identical to the one in that painting. Thus, it was speculated that Gough, upon returning to England, designed the silver tea boxes to match the ivory tea casket, and even had a wooden box made to protect the valuable ivory. The tea casket in this painting not only highlights the status of tea but also reflects the trade and material and cultural exchanges between Britain and China, as well as the wealth of British merchants.

More paintings allow us to see how tea, after being introduced to England, was re-contextualized and localized in the domestic social contexts of upper class. "What is above form is called Tao (the Way); what is below form is called a utensil." During the eighteenth century, a series of English tea utensils were created according to the habits of natives, and the etiquette related to tea derived from British culinary and social culture were vividly displayed in these paintings.

In *The Strode Family*, a group of people sit around a tea table with a complete set of tea utensils, including a tea kettle, tray, milk jug, porcelain teapot, and teacups. A tea spoon used by one of the drinkers is standing in the teacup, indicating that they have just finished their tea. On one side of the painting, a servant is pouring hot water into the cups from a tea kettle. On the floor in front of the tea table, there is a typical rectangular mahogany tea caddy (Fig. 7.2). Another representative painting is *An English Family at Tea*, created in 1720 and currently housed in the Tate Gallery in the UK. In this painting, one person is measuring tea leaves with the lid of a tea caddy, another tea caddy is placed inside a tea chest at the front of the floor, and the black lacquered tea table in the middle is filled with precious tea wares—blue-and-white porcelain teacups, saucers, waste bowl, teapot stand, and a Yixing teapot. The hostess is about to pour the hot water from a silver tea kettle into the teapot. The painting unfolds a multi-layered narrative involving various aspects of an English tea party.

The genre painter Arthur Devis (1711–1787) also created a work with similar theme, titled *Mr. & Mrs Hill*, in 1750–1751 (Fig. 7.3). The focal point of the composition is the popular tea set of the time: seven teacups, seven saucers, a sugar bowl, a waste bowl, a silver milk jug, and a Yixing purple clay teapot, all placed on a mahogany tripod tea table. In the painting, Mr. and Mrs. Hill appear to be waiting for guests, with the husband's hand elegantly resting on his waistcoat and the wife gracefully holding a biscuit. Tea experts believe that their movements completely follow the guidance of contemporary British tea etiquette books, fully reflecting the manners at the time.

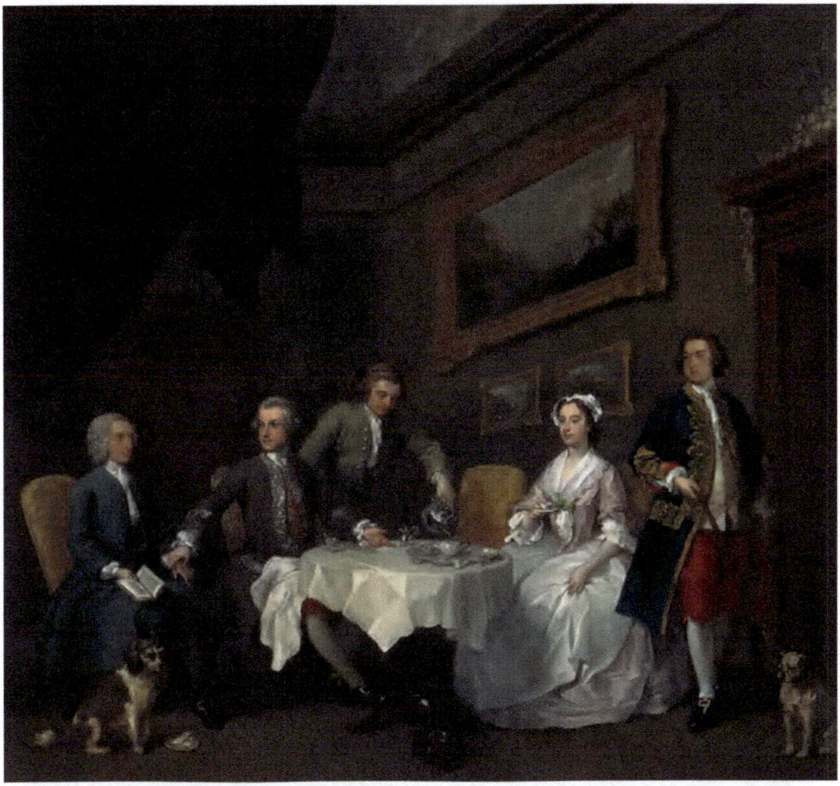

Fig. 7.2 Painted in 1738 and currently held in the collection of the Tate Britain, "The Strode Family" by William Hogarth

In Richard Collins's painting *A Family of Three at Tea*, except for blue and white porcelain cups and saucers, all the tea set is made of silver, including tea spoons, sugar tongs, a lidded sugar bowl, and saucers for placing spoons and sugar tongs (Fig. 7.4). The British often add sugar when drinking tea, thus generating the design of small accessories such as tea spoons and sugar tongs. Most of them were silver, among which the most typical one was the tea spoon used to stir the tea soup. When tea was expensive, teapot was usually large, and people drank tea in small sips even in the upper class. In that time, the capacity of the tea cup was limited, and the accompanying tea spoon was small and exquisite. From existing materials, we can see that tea spoons of various shapes had already appeared in the late seventeenth century. The newspaper *Political Briefing* mentions

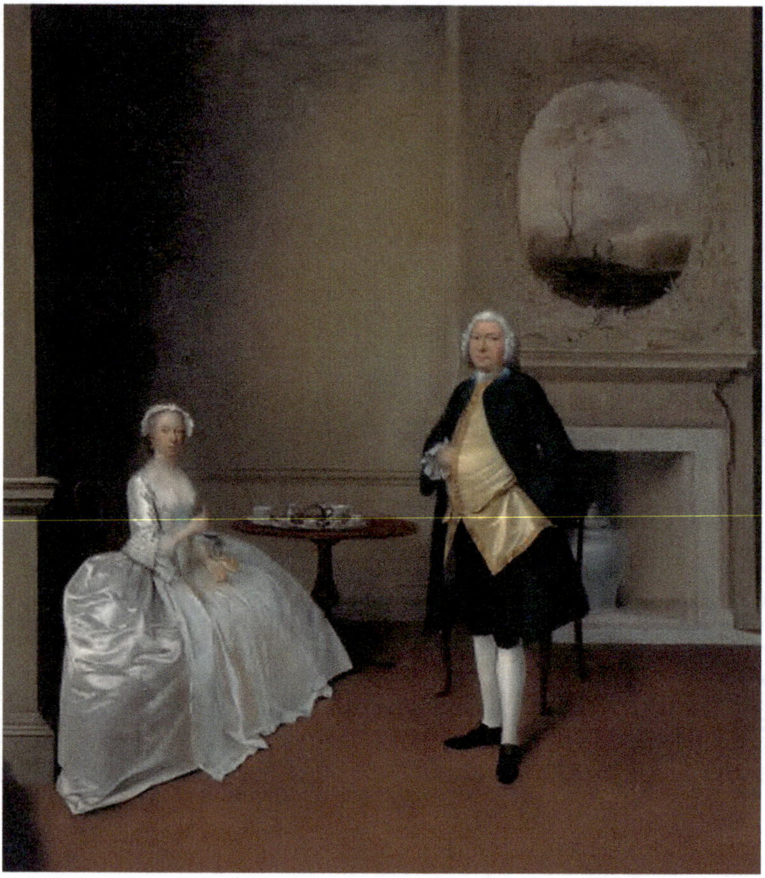

Fig. 7.3 Mr. and Mrs. Hill, themed tea drinking, created by The genre painter Arthur Devis

many cases of theft of silver tea spoons. From the descriptions in these cases, we can catch a glimpse of the rich variety of British tea spoon styles at that time, including forged small gold-inlaid spoons, spoons with wrapped handles, ball-shaped handle spoons, long spoons, and silver ball-shaped handle spoons.[17]

[17]Jane Pettigrew. Tea Design [M]. Translated by Shao Lirong. Jinan: Shandong Picture Book Press, 2013: 151.

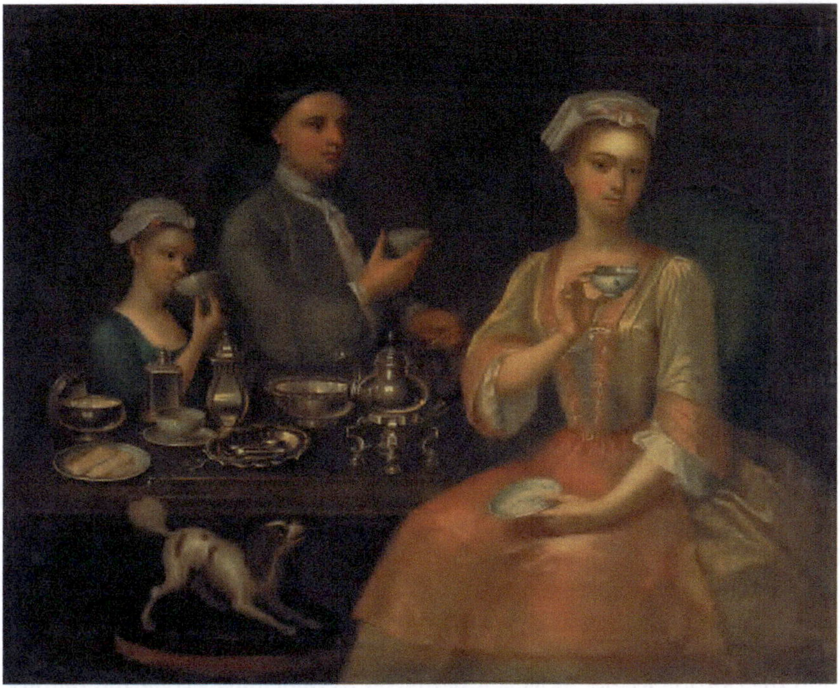

Fig. 7.4 Richard Collins's painting *A Family of Three at Tea*

Table manners at tea time have always been a point of emphasis for the British. When visiting someone's home, directly refusing to continue drinking would appear impolite. Therefore, the neat and accessible teaspoon has become an effective medium, playing a significant role in British tea etiquette. Some people place the teaspoon horizontally to indicate that they have finished, while others may place the teaspoon inside the tea cup or tap the cup gently with the teaspoon. Although these spoons are also used for hot chocolate and coffee, they are still referred to as "teaspoons." Additionally, the teaspoon has once "acted" as a measure for weighing tea leaves. Mrs. Beeton's *Book of Household Management*, published in the mid-nineteenth century, was a widely popular encyclopedia of domestic life in Britain at the time. Mrs. Beeton mentioned in the book that the appropriate amount of tea leaves was one teaspoon per person. The measuring function of the teaspoon has also extended to other areas. To this day, the "teaspoon" that originated from tea drinking has become the most common measuring tool in Western cuisine, and spreading to the rest of the world. This also illustrates, from another angle, the profound influence of tea culture on social life in the UK as well as the whole world.

Perhaps we can think of silver tea sets as a unique British cultural product created from their own needs and habits. The British-made silver tea sets complemented and cooperated with the Chinese-introduced ceramic tea sets, forming a complete British tea set system, and corresponding etiquette and norms were developed accordingly. Etiquette signifies cultural standardization, and thus culture can be passed down through behavior. Through these paintings, we can see that in eighteenth-century England, for the British who emphasized etiquette and social status, drinking tea was a chance to illustrate their identity. As tea was closely linked with affluence, elegant socializing, and conversation, it has become the core of the British tea culture.

In addition, since drinking tea often takes place in the relatively private family space, it has evolved into an important factor that influences modern family life.

All family members sit around the tea table in order, drinking and communicating, becoming closer to each other. Sometimes, a family also invite guests to participate, who would serve as the bridges between the family and the outside world, as well as witnesses to the family's style and dignity.

Women, as the leaders of family space, play a central role in tea drinking. Of course, this is also thanks to the tea's close relation to royal women in early introduction to England. So, the spread of tea drinking as a cultural phenomenon in England could trace to the promotion of upper-class women and is closely related to female culture. Therefore, we can say that tea table etiquette is an essential part of British tea culture, and the female host responsible for brewing tea is the core of the family. She determines all the procedures at the table, and her demeanor determines whether the atmosphere is harmonious and enjoyable.

In other words, taking charge of brewing tea is an honor, reflecting women's status in the family. This can be verified in the works of British female writers, such as Jane Austen. In *Pride and Prejudice*, the eldest daughter, Jane Bennet, is always responsible for brewing tea. And in *Mansfield Park*, Mr. Thomas always finds opportunities to have Fanny brew tea—he wants her to be his adopted daughter, endowing her the advantage of inheritance. The rituals at the tea table provide a way for people to identify the status and relationships among those present.

In William Congreve's *The Way of the World* (1700), the newlywed Millamant tells her husband Mirabel, "Without my consent, thou mayst not presume to approach (my tea table) of thine own accord." Mirabel agrees, stating, "I submit to the sovereignty of the tea table." Claiming the control over the tea table was one of the prerequisites for Millamant's agreeing to marry Mirabel.[18] In fact, it can be seen that in the UK at that time, the tea table was a unique space for women to exercise her power within the home.

Therefore, British women had to learn tea table etiquette from a young age at home, otherwise they are considered to be humble or lack breeding. Elizabeth Kowaleski-Wallace believes that "the habits of women sitting around the tea table are a record of the bodies of upper-class women and a sign of normal development."[19] In the clearly ranked social system of the UK, having good tea table etiquette is a necessary social skill for ladies, and also provides women from the middle and lower classes with opportunities to climb up through marriage. "Men can make the woman they marry noble, no matter what her background is; but for a woman, no matter how high her background is, a low marriage will lower her status to that of her man."[20]

Jane Austen opened the book *Pride and Prejudice* by expressing the view of women's marriage at that time: women without property needed to marry a wealthy husband, and at that time, the tea table was an ideal social occasion for choosing a spouse for both unmarried men and women. For example, in the work of Charles Shadwell, *The Sham Prince*, Mr. William agreed to have tea with the family of the shopkeeper Sevilles, and Mrs. Sevilles, who always hoped to enter high society, tried to flatter the "prince" and asked her daughter to participate in making tea. When her daughter made a small mistake, her mother and she argued, and the prince came to the rescue by inviting her to attend a social event hosted by the princess. Mrs. Sevilles immediately said that she would train her daughter to excel in the palace. Therefore, for women, being able to skillfully use tea tools was a necessary skill for entering high society. Having good tea

[18] Ma Xiaoli. A Study of British Tea Culture from a Multidimensional Perspective [M]. Hangzhou: Zhejiang University Press, 2010: 88.

[19] Same as footnote 18, p. 89.

[20] Richardson. Pemela or Virtue Rewarded. New York and London: W. W. Norton & Company. 1958.

table etiquette is not only women's self-requirements, but also one of their mother's key training points for daughters.

For the British, the tea table is more than just a tangible piece of furniture. In the early eighteenth century, the most influential journal in England, *The Spectator*, regarded the "tea table" as a social space, especially providing an ideal occasion for women to display fashion trends and gather for conversation. With tea as the medium, tea table became the place for speaking, listening, and discussion.

This magazine was co-founded by Joseph Addison (1672–1719) and Richard Steele (1672–1729). In this magazine, they re-evaluated social etiquette, satirized the corrupt customs in society, and engaged in debates on the behavior, morality, and of the people of the time. In Article 10 published on March 12, 1711, they proposed a new form of socializing:

> I heard that Socrates brought philosophy from heaven and offered it to all beings. I too dare to say this boldly - it is I who have brought philosophy from the closed rooms, libraries, and schools of various sizes to the tea tables of clubs or coffee shops where people gather.[21]

Addison believed that to make philosophy more accessible, it needed a transition both spatially and socially: it should be released from the confines of universities and libraries to new public spaces: assembly rooms, coffee houses, tea tables, and the like. In previous issues, he mentioned that these novel and unique social spaces in London in the early eighteenth century were indicative of humanity as a "social animal." He wrote in this article that he had found it very beneficial to link the magazine to the tea table for its promotion, as just this one topic could help the journal penetrate the women's market.

Therefore, I encourage those wealthy families to set aside one hour every morning to drink tea and eat bread with butter; in their best interest, I strongly recommend that they subscribe to this magazine in order to stay informed and become part of the tea-drinking circle.[22]

Addison hoped that this magazine would become a must-have for wealthy households for tea, like teacups, trays, teapots, sugar bowls, and teaspoons, becoming a kind of "tea set." Later, in many magazine articles, he expressed the desire that this periodical become an essential part of

[21] Same as footnote 13, p. 106.

[22] The Spectator, No.10(Bond edn), I, p. 44.

daily socializing and tea drinking. He hoped that people would discuss topics from the magazine while having tea, bread, and butter, and suggested that people read aloud to exchange views.

With the repeal of *the Printing Act* in 1695, the British press industry experienced significant growth in the eighteenth century. The political elite and the emerging middle class constituted the main readership of British newspapers. Jürgen Habermas believes that the public sphere with a political function first appeared in eighteenth-century Britain. Among these, newspapers with a rational critical spirit became a tool that submitted political decision-making to new public forums. People read and discussed newspapers in public spaces that sell coffee and tea. To make the content of the newspapers accessible to the illiterate, some coffee houses even provided a free service of reading newspapers aloud to customers, offering a space for free communication and discussion of political news. Similarly, the tea table in domestic spaces also served as a gathering place for people to discuss and express.

The "power of the tea table" signifies the beginning of a rise in the status and power of women and emphasizes the gentlewoman as a new social and cultural role. The tea table symbolizes the acceptance, demonstration, and exercise of power by women in the middle and upper classes of eighteenth-century family life. Tea parties provided a platform for women to display their cultivation and thoughts, engage in free conversation, and exchange with others, objectively promoting British feminism movement and involving women into the process of the nation's civilization.

The Imitating "Chinese Room"

In the late 1740s, the noblewoman Elizabeth Montagu (1718–1800) decorated the drawing room of her townhouse on Hill Street in London in a Chinese style. She established a salon in this "Chinese room." Traditionally, European salons only invited elites, requiring strict adherence to aristocratic social etiquette and decorum. However, Lady Montagu's salon shifted from elitism toward openness and inclusivity. She aimed to liberate women from mundane and closed domestic environments, allowing them to enter the public sphere to express their rational thoughts and concerns about society. She eventually created such a place in her private residence: this salon welcomed both men and women, with members including novelists, poets, painters, playwrights, historians, predominantly women but also men from diverse backgrounds. Gatherings were not for small talk, but rather for discussions on literature, philosophy, art, music, or current events.

It is said that once Lady Montagu invited the botanist and Latin translator Benjamin Stillingfleet. But the latter declined her invitation because he did not have the proper black stockings for a formal occasion. So, Lady Montagu comforted him that he could come in his regular attire and ordinary blue worsted socks. The salon thereafter became known as the "Bluestocking Society," and the term "bluestocking" in English has since been used to refer to women of intelligence and talent.

The naming of the Bluestocking Society further exemplifies its departure from traditional salon. Here, regardless of gender or social rank, everyone can communicate freely and equally. In eighteenth-century England, just as in China, women did not have the opportunity to receive a formal education, and the salon was one of the few informal settings where women could acquire knowledge and exchange ideas. The British writer Horace Walpole referred to the Bluestocking Society as "the first women's club in the world." Many scholars believe that the Bluestocking Society created opportunities for intellectuals to gather for tea and engage in conversations, exchange ideas, and participate in rational dialogue, allowing women to communicate on an equal footing with men and to join in various public affairs of society, thus laying the foundation for feminism that followed.

The rare Chinese porcelain and other "Oriental" objects decorating Lady Montagu's "Chinese Room" were all from her brother, Robert Robinson, who had served as a captain for the East India Company and had sailed to Guangzhou. As mentioned earlier, it was a privilege of the upper class to adorn their drawing rooms with Oriental items. Some criticized the rise of Chinoiserie, viewing it as extravagant but lacking in taste, driven by the selfish interests of merchants, lacking not only in faith but also in morals. Nevertheless, Lady Montagu found that, through "Chinese taste" she could not only create a gentle, feminine space, allowing her female friends to freely showcase their talents; but also accurately reflect her identity as a wealthy landowner and a "sociable creature."[23]

The French playwright Mary-Anne du Boccage (1710–1802) once spent a brief time in London in 1750, and upon visiting Lady Montagu's Chinese room, she described it as follows:

[23] Same as footnote 20, p. 194.

> Aujourd'hui, nous avons déjeuné chez Madame Montague. La salle à manger était en papier peint à la chinoise, le meubles étaient de chine prises dans leur essentiel: une table couverte d'une nappe de lin superieure, sur laquelle étaient servis mille tasses d'un opulence éblouissante, contenant du café, du chocolat, des biscuits, du beurre, de la crème, du pain grillé et un thé aristocratique. Tu dois croire que c'est à Londres que l'on trouve de si bon thé. La dame de la maison vaut même que les dieux l'aient fait l'hôte. Elle sert soi-même le thé,comme il se doit.[24]

There are few surviving examples that reflect the decoration and furnishings of the tea spaces of British noblewomen in the seventeenth and eighteenth centuries. One is Ham House, located in the west London suburb of Richmond, still retains one of the most historically significant English tea spaces. It has been recognized by the National Trust for Places of Historic Interest or Natural Beauty as of the finest preserved mansions in Europe that authentically represents the fashion and power scene of seventeenth-century England. Now this villa receives visitors from around the world who flock to experience the daily life of seventeenth-century British noble families.

In the late seventeenth to eighteenth centuries, there was a significant change in the living spaces of the British people, where there appeared a clear distinction between the public and private. Residences began to emphasize privacy, with different entrances, staircases, and corridors serving as spatial boundaries among servants, family members, and visitors. Production and living were completely separated, with distinct functional divisions in different rooms. People would place certain items in prominent positions to gain respect from visitors. Guest rooms replaced bedrooms in key locations, enabling family members to display elegant manners and gracious hospitality.[25] This trend has also been clearly presented in this villa.

Through the main hall, along the narrow corridor that was once used by servants, one can reach a secluded space not exceeding ten square meters. This is the private closet, located on the side of the mistress' bedroom. At that time, its main function was a study or a living room for entertaining close friends and relatives. It is widely believed in British

[24] Same as footnote 20, p. 195.

[25] Wu Guanzhong. The Origins of Modern Consumer Society: A Study of Consumer Issues in England in the 17th and 18th Centuries [D]. Nanjing: Nanjing University, 2014: 127.

academia that, in the early introduction of tea, it was private closets that served as tea spaces among the upper class. The Duchess of Lauderdale was a prominent figure in the British fashion world in the seventeenth century, and this closet is also believed to have entertained the "Tea Queen" Catherine. Therefore, we take it as a microcosm to analyze how expensive tea furniture from Asia decorated a noble's private closet (Fig. 7.5).

The centerpiece of the private closet is a tea table, equipped with a tea-pot and two tea cups all imported from China. The tea table is made of cedar wood, with a painted and gilded surface, and the top section looks like a rectangular rounded tray.

The tray is concave with a half circle border, black background with gold paint. The pattern on the tray is a scene of water with figures, pine trees, water grass, people riding elephants and horses, ducks swimming in the water, birds soaring in the sky, and pavilions built on the water filling the entire picture. Each of the six curved table legs has red background gilded relief carving. The lower half of the table legs have been modified and lengthened to accommodate the height of European chairs. The additional parts of the table legs are also six-footed, all in a serpentine winding shape, and the bottom of the table legs is spherical. This table was recorded in the Duchess's inventory in 1679.

Some people believe that this table was probably made in Java around 1650, which is still controversial. However, one thing can be sure that the carved plant and animal patterns on the surface and the high relief with a red background on the table legs were very common at that time in Java. There are some patterns on it that look like Chinese ones, while others are similar to patterns on Javanese textiles. Therefore, it is difficult to determine its origin only by patterns. Nevertheless, based on its height, we can infer that it was originally used in a culture where people are used to sitting on the floor. In the property inventory of the villa of Ham, such tables were referred to as "tea tables." A similar lacquered table with adjustable height but without English-style legs is now collected at Dyrham Park in England.[26]

Next to the tea table, there is a black lacquered chair with Chinese-style decorations, featuring gold floral and bird patterns as well as plant motifs. The seat is made of rattan, the back is hollowed out, with a Chinese-style elliptical shape and irregular arch-shaped structure at the top of the chair

[26] http://www.nationaltrustcollections.org.uk/object/1139867.8

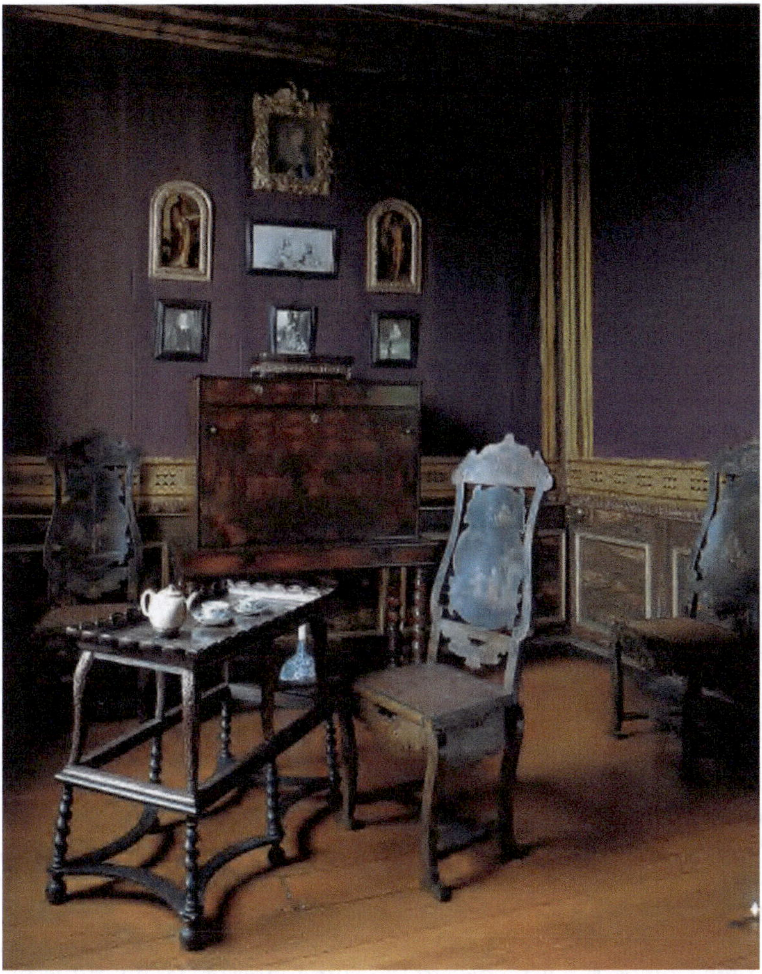

Fig. 7.5 Photo of the interior of Ham House in Richmond, where the Duchess of Lauderdale resided, drinking tea and entertaining guests. (Furniture dates back to around 1675, featuring an Indian tea table, a lacquered back chair with a rattan bottom. Furniture designs at the time were a mix of styles due to close trade relations between England and the Netherlands, with many tea tables being imported. Cabinets are made of West Indian satinwood, with spiral-shaped feet matching those of the tea table. Chairs were typically placed in the corners but moved to the center when tea was served)

back. There are four identical crossbars underneath the seat. The chair legs adopt a "Chinese-style" drum leg form, with small feet-like shapes at the end of the legs, and the four legs are connected by an H-shaped, curved edge frame. The unique layout of these chairs is likely to be originated from Italian low chairs.

The print *The Tea-Table*, created in London in the early eighteenth century, also showcases the tea space in an eighteenth-century aristocratic household. In the image, six women dressed in hand-loomed Indian silk skirts are sitting by a tea table, drinking. From this, we can see the trendiest decorative style and arrangement of the tea table in domestic space at the time: the living room walls were adorned with porcelain cabinets, paintings, mirrors, and Chinese silk curtains, while the floor was covered with an Indian woven carpet. On the tea table were all Chinese porcelain tea sets, including teapots, tea cups, sugar bowls, and milk jugs. All of them showcased the family's status and wealth, which is exactly what the host wished to present.

It can be seen that when tea first gained popularity in Britain, the British attempted to decorate the tea space with imported Chinese decorative artifacts or locally produced imitations of Chinese-style artifacts, in an effort to match the exotic charm in this Eastern beverage. Items such as porcelain, lac furniture, and paintings were commonly found in this period. Later, based on their understanding of Chinese art, the British created a style known as Chinoiserie. Chinoiserie is often characterized by elements such as black-based lacquerware, colorful silk, delicate wallpaper, and blue and white porcelain, which may not necessarily adhere to original Chinese conventions, but often incorporate the imagination and fabrication of Westerners instead. This style is considered by scholars to be a blend of Western interpretation of Chinese decorative art, fantastical visual effects, and the Rococo style.

Just as the boudoir of the Duchess of Lauderdale did, the British passion for Chinoseries extended to the entire interior design of the house, bringing a touch of exoticism to the property, particularly to the bedrooms, living rooms, dining rooms, and tea spaces. In the book *The Citizen of the World*, Oliver Goldsmith described a conversation with a Chinese art dealer: "Do you have any pretty Chinese goods, the sort that ordinary people do not know what to do with?... I have 20 things that only the Chinese know how to use. Look at these jars, genuine bean green... And these, although they may look good to you, are nothing to the Chinese. But they are useful utensils, so every household should have a set." This dialogue highlights the status of imported Chinese goods such as porcelain and lacquerware, which were deliberately displayed in a room with a Chinese style as part of the room's decoration.

In fact, this was indeed the case in the spatial configurations of eighteenth-century aristocratic households, where Chinese porcelain, wallpaper, and lacquerware furniture were often essential. Jessicaley, in her book *The Doll's House: How to Design and Create Miniatures for Doll's Houses*, described the composition of eighteenth-century English country estates. She believed that they typically included a Chinese Room, a Scottish Baronial Hall, a Print Room, a Yellow Drawing Room, and a Living Room. The Chinese Room was characterized by red walls adorned with black and gold lacquer-painted panels, gilded-frame mirrors, chairs wrapped in silk, and ceramics. The Chinese Room and its Chinoiserie decorative appointments were indispensable and even significant in eighteenth-century English history, culture, and daily life.[27]

Claydon House in Buckinghamshire is known for its Chinoiserie tea room, which is considered a classic case of the profound changes that tea brought to English social life and visual culture. This room was designed and completed by Luke Lightfoot in 1769. British art historian Hugh Honour described the room as follows:

> Each of the doors is in the form of a pagoda surmounted by a gilded fret and surrounded by a lattice of gilded rods. The pillars of the pagoda are figures of Chinese mandarins whose faces are surrounded by flowing scrolls in relief. Mysterious Oriental faces also peer out from among flowers and icicles on the carved overmantels. Yet the decoration of these doors and overmantels is as nothing compared to the cumulative exoticism of the Tea Room. Here gilded bells hang from the walls, here the surfaces are smothered in flowers and shells and frottage, and even the few plain walls are adorned with elegant Arabesque patterns drawn in tamarind brown... The overall effect of this extraordinary room, which looks not unlike the interior of a submarine, is to suggest a coral palace peopled by Neptune and his retinue, far down on the floor of the ocean.[28]

[27] Ma Liyun. Foreign Style and Domesticity - Reflections on Chinese Style in English Countryside Manors Through "Doll's House" [J]. Art Observation, 2020 (1): 59.

[28] Hugh Anner. China Style - Chinese Elements Lost in the West for 800 Years [M]. Translated by Liu Aiying, et al. Beijing: Peking University Press, 2017: 173.

Due to overdecoration, furniture is outshone by exotic elements. There is a long sofa chair and a niche for preparing tea, which enhance the overall tea-drinking experience. A delicately detailed painting on the wall indicates the purpose of the room: a scene of a Chinese family drinking tea, complete with a teapot, tea cups, saucers, teaspoons, and sugar bowl. All these elements undoubtedly create a novel atmosphere for those who engage in tea drinking, providing a unique aesthetic experience different from mundane lives. As for how many furniture items were original Chinese and how many were modified versions, it seems less important to those who present in the space.

3 Incorporation of Chinese Elements into British Public Tea Spaces

The British have always been fans of picnicking, whose history can be traced back to the Celts. With the popularity of tea, tea parties in gardens became a common leisure activity in summer. In the mid-to-late eighteenth century, London saw the emergence of Tea Gardens, also known as Pleasure Gardens. After the 1820s, coffee houses gradually faded, and people shifted their tea-drinking spaces to these open parks, including Vauxhall, Ranelagh, Marylebone, Cuper's, the White Conduit House, and Bermondsey Spa.[29] Among them, Vauxhall and Ranelagh are particularly famous.

Vauxhall Tea Gardens, located on the south bank of the River Thames, first opened in 1666 and was later transformed by Jonathan Tyers and reopened in 1732, experiencing an unprecedented surge in visitors. It was the first commercial garden in British history, and even in European history; it is open to everyone, no matter the royal family, the middle class, or the working class. The park had a Turkish pavilion, a Chinese pavilion, and regular performances. "It was so magnificent that most of the noblemen and upper-class living in and around London would frequently visit here during the three months of summer."[30] Here, visitors crowded the wide avenues, which were decorated with lights, and people gathered in "arbors" to enjoy tea, red wine, and light snacks while listening to outdoor concerts. Fashionably dressed ladies would come here to drink tea

[29] Same as footnote 5, p. 104.

[30] Roy Moxham. Tea: Habit, Exploration and Empire [M]. Translated by Hua Xiaoqing. Beijing: Sanlian Book Publishing House, 2015: 40.

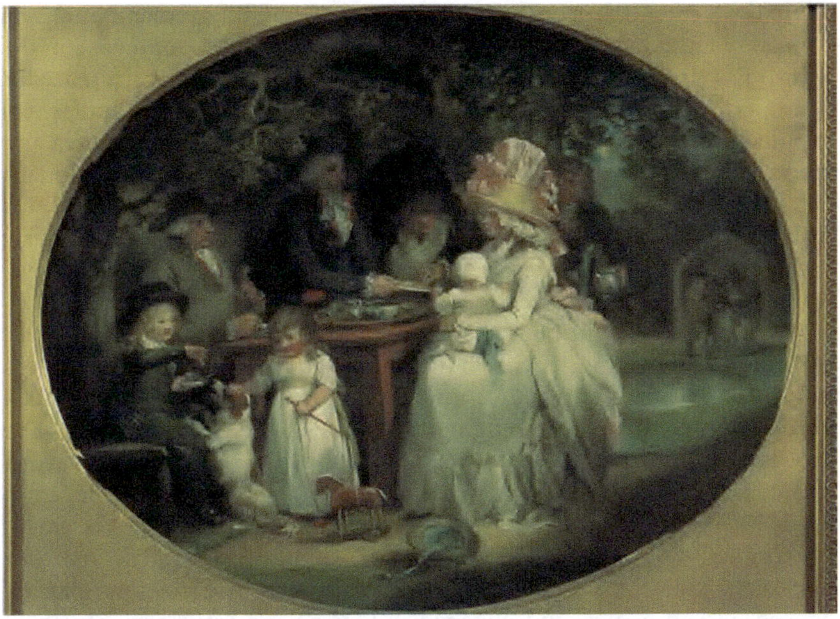

Fig. 7.6 *The Tea Garden* by George Morland from the 1790s, now housed in the Tate Gallery

and socialize. Of course, there were also servants from wealthy households who would come to the park on their days off, wearing the coats their mistresses no longer wore to enjoy the rare opportunity to participate in the latest fashion trends.

There is a widely circulated painting called *The Tea Garden* by George Morland from the 1790s, which is now housed in the Tate Gallery in Britain (Fig. 7.6). This painting depicts a scene of a middle-class family drinking tea in the garden in the afternoon. The family is leisurely enjoying tea under the shade of trees in the garden, with a tea table set up and various exquisite tea sets on the table. In the distance of the painting, we can faintly see the figures of other young men and women strolling in the garden. The background of this painting is the Ranelagh Tea Garden, located east of Chelsea Royal Park, and was once the residence of Lord Ranelagh in the late seventeenth century.

In the center of the garden is a circular building, resembling The Roman Pantheon. This building, constructed by the surveyor of the British East India Company, William Jones, features a fireplace, a space for band performances, a pipe organ, and 52 boxes for lighting candles distributed around the walls for people to gather around and enjoy tea and snacks. The park opened for business on April 22, 1742, and occasionally held concerts, providing breakfast to the public three days a week. Although it was once a crowd favorite shortly after opening, people quickly got bored. So, they had to add new features, including an artificial canal and a Chinoiserie house.[31]

The house was right next to the canal, with an overall style consistent with the trendy Chinoiserie architecture at the time. The building had a tower-like pointed roof, four corners that curved up, and scroll-shaped decorations. Bells were hanging below the eaves. The railings around the houses were all decorated with frets, which were widely used at the time and considered the signature of the "Chinese Chippendale" style, from inside the houses, such as bookcases, cupboards, chair backs, clocks, desks, chess tables, staircases, fireplace grates, and window sills, to structures outside such as pavilions and garden grids.[32] People held costume parties, danced, played games, and engaged in literary and artistic exchanges in this Tea Garden. Renowned guests included the poet Pope and English-born German composer Handel,[33] and young Mozart also performed here in 1764. A painting of Bagenal Wellesley Garden printed in 1778 depicts people sitting in small groups under the shade of trees by a stream, savoring the delightful tea while leisurely chatting. The garden was filled with the rich aroma of milky tea and the sound of pleasant murmurs.[34] British anthropologist Alan Macfarlane believed that in a sense, the Tea Garden was the "garden universities" of that time, where people were enchanted by the tea, architecture, and landscapes. These Tea Gardens "spurred the revolutionary change of British gardening, ultimately giving rise to 'Capability Brown' and his 'naturalistic' landscape gardening in the 18th century."[35]

[31] https://www.cityoflondon.gov.uk/things-to-do/history-and-heritage/london-metropolitan-archives/collections/ranelagh-gardens

[32] Same as footnote 28, p. 176.

[33] Same as footnote 5, p. 105.

[34] Same as footnote 30, p. 42.

[35] Same as footnote 5, pp. 105–106.

In *Chinoiserie: The Vision of Cathay*, completed in 1960 by the sinologist Hugh ONeill, it is pointed out that in the 1750s, parks were enclosed by Chinese fences in a cross shape, with delicate Chinese arches spanning the streams, and a multitude of exotic small temples sprouting amidst oaks and beeches.[36] Indeed, even in today's England, we still often encounter Chinese-style pavilions, fret grilles, and carved railings over small bridges in the parks. For example, the square Chinese pavilion at Shugborough Park in Staffordshire has a curved peak, a long eave, and a light green fret. Similar Chinoserie buildings can also be found in Stowe Garden in Buckinghamshire, Woburn Abbey in Bedfordshire, and Alton Garden in Shropshire, among other places.

One of the most iconic examples is undoubtedly the Chinese Pagoda designed by the architect William Chambers, located in Kew Gardens in the western suburbs of London. Chambers, in his youth, had traveled to China aboard a ship of the Swedish East India Company and briefly resided in Guangzhou. Keen on Chinese architecture, he had completed some sketches of temples and pagodas during his stay. Upon returning to Europe, he received formal architectural education in Paris and Rome. In 1755, he began his career as an architect in London, and in 1757, he published *Designs of Chinese Buildings, Furniture, Dresses, Machines, and Utensils*, which included the sketches mentioned above.

Unlike some Chinoiserie designers who would use whimsy and exaggeration to attract attention, Chippendale's furniture and architecture reflect his empiricism. However, the Chinese pagoda he built in the Qiu Garden does not conform to Chinese norms—the pagoda has ten levels, while Chinese pagodas typically have an odd number of levels. Nevertheless, since its completion, the pagoda has been a popular sight in the London suburbs. It's been featured in countless paintings and prints, and even printed cotton fabrics. The imitation of Chinese pagoda has been integrated into British life in various forms; for a British who has never been to China, pagoda would be the first image that comes to his mind when referring to Chinese. British sinologist Hugh Honor wrote in his work:

> When I was young, I had already formed a clear concept of what China was like. The white plates with blue willow pattern that we used for dining vividly depicted the Chinese landscape. Soon, I also learned the story of a pair

[36] Qin Gang. Blue and White Willow Pattern in Europe and Chinese Export Porcelain [J]. Literary Studies, 2011(4): 120.

of lovers who, pursued by an angry father, ran to a bridge strung with jade and turned into two birds flying in the clouds; they were depicted at the top of the plate. I was also familiar with the clothing of the Chinese people, as like other children, I occasionally went to costume parties dressed as a Qing dynasty official—a full set of embroidered silk clothing, a pair of straw sandals, a long braid hanging down from the back of my head, and a long mustache glued to my upper lip. The white plates with blue floral patterns, the colorful cloisonné dishes, and the lacquered wood panels that I saw in my home and others reminded me that these were products from this distant country. Visits to the Kew Gardens in London's western suburbs further exposed me to the style of Chinese architecture. All these items crystallized in my young mind a very clear image of China—a colorful country with somewhat delicate flowers, bizarre demons, and not-so-solid houses, where most of Europe's social norms were inverted. Even years later, when I discovered that many of the items I had seen were made in Europe, the original impression still lingered deep in my heart.[37]

In summary, in the second half of the eighteenth century, with the sprouting of amusement parks around London and other major cities, Tea Gardens became another public realm different from coffee houses, allowing ordinary women to join the trend, and promoting the further integration of tea culture into British social life. With a spirit of universality, tea can melt differences. It swept all classes of society in England as a fashionable novelty, at least to some extent erasing the long-lasting material differences that distinguished status.

The social critic Francis Place recalled his childhood, saying, "In the 1780s, when I was a child, my father used to go to public gardens to have tea on Sunday afternoons." According to the observation of Prussian Duc d'Archenholz at the time, "The English like to gather in public gardens in the center of the city to have tea, with an astonishing number of gardens near the capital. The order, regularity, and cleanliness, even their elegant posture, are truly admirable. At that time, fashionable celebrities rarely visited these places, but the middle class and lower classes often came and loved the pipe organ music played in nearby buildings."[38]

[37] Raymond Dawson. The Chinese Chameleon - An Analysis of the European View of Chinese Civilization [M]. Translated by Chang Shaomin and Ming Yi. Beijing: Zhonghua Book Company, 2006: 133–134.

[38] Same as footnote 18, p. 67.

Habermas believes that both civil society and the public sphere are forms of individual and collective activity in an independent state, leading to the ideal democracy. The tea, accessible to people of all classes, ages, and genders, has undoubtedly become such a democratic "zone." John Houghton, a member of the Royal Society in the UK, considers the café to be "a place for socializing for all sorts of people, where rich and poor, knowledgeable and ignorant, can talk and meet, promoting the development of the arts, commerce, and various kinds of knowledge, and, along with universities, fostering the growth of beneficial knowledge."[39] From the perspective of democracy and openness, the Tea Garden is similar and even more democratic: as cafes are mainly for men, while Tea Gardens also welcome female. It has got rid of the old formalities of class, status, and gender, achieving equality for all. This is precisely an embodiment of the core spirit of Chinese tea—tea embodies universal values. This consumer space built by imported goods like tea and coffee provides a free and equal platform for communication, gathers public opinion and ideal spirit, and becomes a battleground for public enlightenment and for spreading new ideas and concepts.

From the old pictures of the existing Vauxhall Park, we can see that one of the main architectures resembles a Chinese-style pavilion, with pointed corners and hanging bells all around, bearing a resemblance to the Porcelain Tower of Nanjing in the drawings of the Dutch envoy Niuhuo. And the resemblance to Vauxhall Tea Garden is Cremorne, built in the 1830s, features a main building in the shape of a Chinese pagoda. In the Victorian era, countless young people danced to the music of Strauss waltzes played by the band on this pagoda stage.[40] Yet, few people would inquire into or explore the stories behind the stage's form (see Fig. 7.7).

Original media theorist Marshall McLuhan proposed that the introduction of new technology and the resulting new technological environment would cause a massive reorganization of social experience. This point also explains this book, namely, the impact of tea on eighteenth-century British society. This impact not only brought about material transformations, foreign knowledge, economic shocks, and anxiety, triggering a reorganization of British social experience and a change in social and cultural psychology, but also disrupted traditional ways of life and influenced people's identity. These Chinese artifacts changed the artistic taste and

[39] Same as footnote 25, p. 91.

[40] Same as footnote 28, p. 246.

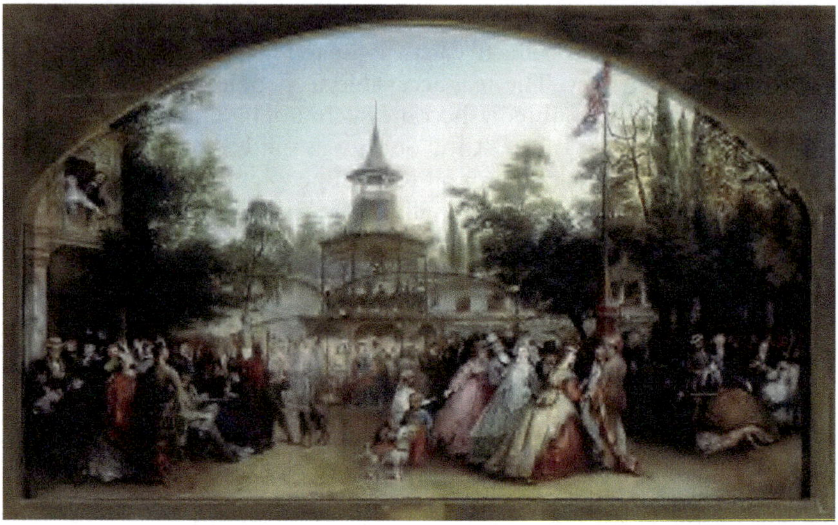

Fig. 7.7 The scene in Cremorne

aesthetic interests of eighteenth-century Britons, enriched the styles of home decoration, and contributed to the Industrial Revolution.

It can be said that in England, few artistic styles can compare to the impact of Chinoiseries developed from tea in the eighteenth century. To create an "authentic" tea-drinking environment, the British became addicted to Chinese objects and began to imitate all Chinese-style items, with the influence extending to both fine art and decorative art. A "Chinese craze" swept across the country, influencing the way of life. At the root of the "Chinese craze" is the imported tea, porcelain, silk, furniture, wallpaper, enamel, lacquer, etc. For these goods embody Eastern wisdom, inspiration, and lifestyle. Although sometimes the British cannot accurately understand them, Chinese aesthetics and culture have been instilled to various design fields, including interior and exterior design of houses, gardens, and decorations. Just like the Chinese pavilion in Cremorne where countless young people danced to Strauss waltzes, Chinese culture and design have integrated into the British way of life as a natural background.

Conclusion

> I have always been a man with one foot in the past and one in the present… For when you are studying the past and the present, it is not possible to be blind to the future.
>
> ——Arnold J. Toynbee

For a long period of time, design history has been lacking the study of the impact of modern Chinese industry, the Chinese economy, and Chinese design on Western countries such as the United States and Great Britain. In other words, there are few scholars who have explored how British design was influenced by the reverse impact during the trade with China. This complex, two-way influence relationship has been overlooked. However, being overlooked doesn't mean that it didn't exist; this history will eventually be discovered and highlighted.

This book takes this as its starting point and aims to conduct exploratory research on this issue. Of course, this perspective is relatively microscopic, and there has never been any relevant work to provide the necessary summary and organization, so it is very difficult to find ready-made conclusions as evidence. Many studies have to start from subtle and trivial historical details, which is exactly the value of this research.

During the research, the author has visited the UK three times to probe into various details of the early entry of tea into Western society, while paying attention to related research in other disciplines domestically and

C. Zhang, *Beyond the Teacup: 18th Century Sino-British Tea Trade and Design Cultural Exchange*,
https://doi.org/10.1007/978-981-97-7691-7

internationally. The exploration is conducted in a "jigsaw" manner within a vast historical scope. In fact, the scope of this study includes the design, designers, design processes, and design methods; but only an outline has been completed, and there remains a lot of space to fully reveal the details. There is still a long way to go. However, the work accomplished in this book will play a foundational role in connecting the dots.

Tea culture has a profound influence on the history of contemporary British design, which also reflects the depth of design culture and its close relationship with greater culture. While serving the mundane life, design has indeed produced stirring and memorable effects. Of course, there has left many issues that need to be further explored regarding the relationship between design and Sino-British cultural interactions, with tea as the medium.

"When the clock strikes four, all the world stops for tea." As celebrated in this English folk song, the British afternoon tea culture was officially established during the Victorian era, becoming an important social activity and leisure pastime for people in Britain, from the nobility to the commoners, encapsulating a strong and distinct aspect of British national character. The Victorian afternoon tea is believed to have originated from Anna Maria Stanhope, the wife of the seventh Duke of Bedford. She often had her maid prepare baked bread, cream, and tea, sharing a pleasant afternoon with her friends. This way of drinking tea spread among fair ladies, becoming the social mainstream among the British. Behind this is the freedom in finance and time of the British aristocracy, as well as an eager to showcase their tastes and manners. There are numerous etiquette-related books guiding people on how to participate or organize such afternoon tea events in the correct manner, even the royal family needs to specially learn how to partake in tea-tasting. In contrast, the working class developed "High Tea," a dinner gathering accompanied by tea, which both satisfied social needs and filled their stomachs.

The Cavendish Laboratory in the University of Cambridge has produced 25 Nobel Prize winners, making it the laboratory with the most Nobel Prize winners in the world. It has a tradition called "Afternoon Tea Chats." The purpose of these chats is to facilitate exchange from different academic backgrounds, where everyone is treated equally regardless of their position. Through this relaxed atmosphere, researchers spark insightful discussions, leading to the germination and progress of research. This kind of communication is referred to as the "Cambridge Spirit" or the "Spirit of Tea Cups and Teapots" within the University. Alec Broers, former Vice-Chancellor of the University of Cambridge, interpreted this spirit as "an active cultural openness and academic freedom." He believes that it is the free chat during afternoon tea time that promotes this spirited atmosphere.

Although the British successfully planted tea in India in the late nineteenth century and no longer needed to rely on China, Chinese tea has already become an inherent part of British life. Tea has brought together people of different genders, classes, races, and professions. British scholars often use the word "conquer" when writing about works related to "tea." They believe that the relationship between tea and Britain is profound—has tea conquered Britain, or the reverse? But for this book, one of the main points is that cultural exchange is actually a mutual process, so the word "conquer" may be too arbitrary.

Objectively, the British imported a large amount of tea from China, along with a wealth of tea-related items, which adorned the British tea space. But from the perspective of "tea," through the act of "drinking tea," tea has "tamed" the British, making them more gentle and healthy, strengthening the British East India Company, filling the British treasury, and laying the groundwork for the Industrial Revolution in terms of both manpower and financial resources. However, if we see from the point of Britain, it is a different story—China is just one of their tea suppliers. Whether to import tea from China is completely based on the needs of the British, and the whole process can be interpreted as the British transition from implicit colonization to explicit colonization. Nevertheless, if we see from the point of China, this process is more about China exporting tea to the UK, gained a trade surplus, with a large influx of silver. Afterward, the British did something bad to reverse the trade deficit, sold opium to China, and even started the Opium War. However, if we take a step back and look at this from a broader historical perspective, we will find that the conflict actually promoted the integration and exchange of the two cultures.

There are countless works related to tea and tea culture no matter in China or the UK, and the role of tea in the exchange of material culture between the East and the West has also been recognized in academic fields such as sociology, anthropology, and sinology. For example, British anthropologist Alan Macfarlane mainly discusses in his book *Green Gold: The Empire of Tea* how tea entered human society and spread to Europe, exerting a significant influence on the global political and economic landscape. Another example is the art historian Hugh Annerley, specialized in

Chinoiserie, calls the UK the "Land of Tea" in his book *Chinoiserie: China's Lost Century in the West*, suggesting that it was tea that brought China to the attention of Europe. However, due to the inherent biases of certain disciplines, these works do not fully address how tea combined multiple cultural elements in the exchange between the East and the West, thereby influencing people's lifestyles, aesthetic preferences, and ideological concepts. Nevertheless, this falls precisely within the scope of design research.

In the field of design, the Victoria and Albert Museum has also organized scholars to compile a book titled *Tea: East and West*, looking back at the influence of tea trade on European design. It is evident that this topic is not overlooked within the design community. Unfortunately, the book merely discusses the design related to tea that has developed in regions such as China, Western Europe, and Eastern Europe in separate chapters, without exploring the connections between these tea cultures and design. This is precisely the issue that this book aims to address.

Although tea as a drink may seem not closely related to design, history reveals that tea is deeply intertwined with design at every stage of its development in British society. It can even be argued that design has played a crucial role in the progression of tea culture. By studying the role of design in British tea culture, we come to realize that every stage is connected in some way to Chinese culture. It can even be said that the germination and growth of tea culture in the UK reflects the British perception, views, and attitudes toward China and Chinese culture.

When tea first entered England, it coincided with the rise of the Consumer Revolution. The British invented some marketing strategies, including advertising design, packaging design, and store design. All of these were applied to this exotic Oriental product. For the British, the consumption of tea was a new subject that required understanding and differentiating; while familiar drinks like beer and wine did not require advertising or marketing, just like what tea is to Chinese. One of the key contributions of tea being accepted by the British was the promotion by the British East India Company and domestic merchants, embodying the British curiosity and admiration for Chinese culture. These aspects were also reflected in the advertising, packaging, and store design of tea at the time—Chinese elements were inevitable, no matter how superficially appeared. This was necessary to convey that these were "authentic" teas imported from China, so as to better attract customers.

Another important reason for the popularity of tea is the inherent "upward" tendency of British culture, that is, the entire society is eager to imitate the aristocracy. As the middle class and working class emulated the upper classes by drinking tea, tea became the "national drink" of Britain, forming a trend where "everyone drinks tea and every household has teaware." Simply importing tea ware from China could no longer meet the demand, providing an impetus for the British ceramics industry, the most prominent manufacturing industry of the Industrial Revolution.

Through imitating the shapes and patterns of Chinese export porcelain, the British ceramic industry gained initial momentum. What is worth mentioning is that Wedgwood conducted industrial innovation by learning from the organization in Jingdezhen, advancing the factory-based production organization closer to modern factory management, while introducing modern marketing and machinery. This pushed forward the entire ceramic industry, making it the latest pillar of the Industrial Revolution. Meanwhile, Wedgwood's ceramic became a representation of British art and technology.

The climate in Britain is not suitable for growing tea. To secure the free trade with China and ensure tea supply, in 1793, the British government sent George Macartney to China under the pretext of honoring Emperor Qianlong's 83rd birthday. Macartney presented Wedgwood's porcelain as a gift to Qianlong. The special attention paid by the Qing court to these ceramic products seemed to indicate that the British ceramics industry had surpassed China's. Unfortunately, Qing implemented isolationism at that time, refused to Macartney's requests. So the British resorted to more wicked methods—firstly, they flooded China with opium, leading to the Opium Wars in 1840 and pushing China into semi-feudal, semi-colonial abyss; secondly, they "stole" tea plants from China, successfully cultivating them in India. As a result, the long-lasting and massive Sino-British tea trade came to an end. The economic strength and international status of China and Britain switched during this trade process.

Although the tea trade is no longer as prominent, the daily lives of the British people still reveals that Chinese culture has infiltrated various aspects of British lifestyle, ideologies, and aesthetic preferences. The traditional alcoholic breakfast beverages have been replaced by tea, and affluent households often have dedicated spaces for tea, while average families may possess a few simple pieces of tea ware. Women, who were previously excluded from public spaces of alcohol and coffee, gained the access to public social gatherings through tea. Tea rooms and tea gardens have flourished in central cities like London, providing entertainment for the entire population. Tea has brought the British together, transcending class, gender, and age. To enjoy tea in a more "authentic" setting, the aristocracy decorated their tea spaces with various Chinese imports. As the concept of the tea space spread throughout society, this decorative style became a fixed mode of decoration and aesthetics for tea spaces. As a result, Chinese decorative arts entered British homes and public spaces.

The above paragraphs are close to what art historians and sinologists refer to as "Chinoiserie." When people talk about the influence of Chinese art on Europe in the eighteenth century, they often say it is "Chinoiserie." Some people believe that Chinoiserie is a crude imitation of Chinese art, while others argue that it is a European style that expresses the perspectives of Western artists and craftsmen on the East. Regardless of how it is defined, it has only remained on the visual level. So, what lies beneath? As stated by Mr. Zhang Guangdu, a reference in the previous text, "One of the best ways to reach the core of a culture is through its guts." Viewing the cultural encounters between China and England in the eighteenth century from the perspective of tea, we can see that China's influence is not only in art design, but also in ideology, industrial development, and lifestyle. And tea, as the most characteristic embodiment of Chinese culture, is undoubtedly the best medium.

It needs to be mentioned here the research of export porcelain. Undeniably, Chinese export porcelain also played a significant role in the cultural encounter. In fact, porcelain exchange is more complex, and better reflects the impact each culture has on the other, which is particularly true for custom-made porcelain. British consumers submitted their desired patterns and shapes to the East India Company, which then entrusted Chinese merchants to place orders in Jingdezhen. Chinese artisans then processed the porcelain according to the samples provided. The export porcelain orders, characterized by "the novelty of designs, with no fixed patterns from year to year," and in large quantities, posed challenges to China's ceramic industry. The ceramic workers in Jingdezhen successfully faced this challenge with their own flexible production model, gaining fame both at home and abroad. Due to the Qing government's "one-port policy" at the time, Guangzhou became the center of foreign trade.

To facilitate more efficient and accurate completion of orders, the decoration process in Jingdezhen shifted to Guangzhou, giving rise to Canton enamel. After its introduction to Britain, it had a profound impact on the British porcelain production. There have been numerous research on export porcelain both domestically and internationally; however, from the perspective of this book, ceramic is the top choice of tea for Chinese people; and when introduced to Britain, it also became essential for tea among the British. So it can be said that tea contributed to the prosperity of the British ceramics industry. Although in Europe, porcelain was introduced earlier than tea, the British East India Company did not intend to buy porcelain in large scale; instead it only existed as ballast for tea. It was not until the fashion for drinking tea arose that the demand led the Company to expand porcelain trade. Moreover, for the ceramic orders introduced to China, a significant proportion of them were sets of tea ware. Additionally, porcelain is often used as decoration in the tea spaces of the British. Therefore, this book narrows down the research scope of export porcelain to ceramic tea ware and explores the ceramic exchanges between China and Britain from the perspective of tea.

During the Victorian era, the British Empire had numerous colonies, through which British tea culture gained global influence. When British tea culture was later reintroduced to China, it influenced Chinese tea culture in reverse. There are Chinese modern tea brands such as Wuyutai and Zhang Yiyuan, which bear some resemblance to British Twinings; Chinese get to know brands like Wedgwood; and Chinese white-collar workers in the twenty-first century are fashionably enjoying "English afternoon tea." Belgian sinologist Victor Segalen proposed a fourth theory in his work *The Methods of Cultural Encounter: Taking the Cultural Encounter between Central Europe and China in the 17th Century as an Example*. This theory suggests that discussions of cultural encounters should consider the impacts on each culture individually. But unfortunately, due to limitations in time and space, this book primarily discusses the influence of China on Britain, with only brief mention of the impact of Britain on China, mostly focusing on the effects of ceramic orders on the Chinese porcelain industry. This also sets the direction for my future efforts.

References

1. Books

1. 中国硅酸盐学会 . 中国陶瓷史[M]. 北京:文物出版社，1982 年 .
2. 冈夫 . 茶文化[M]. 北京:中国经济出版社，1995 年 .
3. 陆羽、陆廷灿 . 茶经[M]. 北京:中国友谊出版社，2005 年 .
4. 孙机 . 中国圣火——中国古文物与东西方交流中的若干问题[M]，沈阳:辽宁教育出版社，1996 年 .
5. 陈椽 . 茶叶通史[M]. 北京:中国农业出版社，1982 年 .
6. 朱雍 . 不愿打开的中国大门——乾隆时期的中英关系[M]. 南昌:江西人民出版社，1989 年 .
7. 余春明 . 中国名片——明清外销瓷探源与收藏[M]. 北京:生活·读书·新知三联出版社，2011 年 .
8. 彭兆荣 . 饮食人类学[M]. 北京:北京大学出版社，2013 年 .
9. 刘昭瑞 . 中国古代饮茶艺术[M]. 西安:陕西人民出版社，2002 年 .
10. 项翔 . 近代西欧印刷媒介研究——从古滕堡到启蒙运动[M]. 上海:华东师范大学出版社，2001 年 .
11. 马晓俐 . 多维视角下的英国茶文化研究[M]. 杭州:浙江大学出版社，2010 年 .
12. 袁宣萍 .17 至 18 世纪欧洲的中国风设计[M]. 北京:文物出版社，2006 年 .
13. 袁熙旸 . 非典型设计史[M]. 北京:北京大学出版社，2015 年 .
14. 胡巧利 . 广东方志与十三行—十三行资料辑要[M]. 广州:广东人民出版社，2014 年 .
15. 梁嘉彬 . 广东十三行考[M]. 广州:广东人民出版社，1999 年 .
16. 徐德志 . 广东对外经济贸易史[M]. 广州:广东人民出版社，1994 年 .

C. Zhang, *Beyond the Teacup: 18th Century Sino-British Tea Trade and Design Cultural Exchange*,
https://doi.org/10.1007/978-981-97-7691-7

17. 严中平 . 中国近代经济史统计资料选辑[M]. 北京:中国社会科学出版社，2012 年 .
18. 方李莉 . 景德镇民窑[M]. 北京:人民美术出版社，2002 年 .
19. 傅振伦 . 景德镇陶录详注[M]. 北京:北京书目文献出版社，1999 年 .
20. 朱培初 . 明清外销瓷和世界文化的交流[M]. 北京:轻工业出版社，1984 年 .
21. 吕章申 . 瓷之韵——大英博物馆、维多利亚与艾尔伯特博物馆藏瓷器精品[M]. 北京:中华书局，2012 年 .
22. 黄启臣 . 广东商帮[M]. 合肥:黄山书社，2007 年 .
23. 广东民间工艺博物馆 . 世纪嬗变——19 世纪以来的省港澳广彩[M]. 广州:岭南美术出版社，2008 年 .
24. 广州市文化局编 . 海上丝绸之路——广州文化遗产:文献辑要卷[M]. 北京:北京文物出版社，2008 年 .
25. 赵国垣 . 赵国垣广彩论稿[M]. 广州:岭南美术出版社，2008 年 .
26. 许之衡 . 饮流斋说瓷[M]// 中国陶瓷名著汇编 . 北京:中国书店出版社，1991 年 .
27. 钱乘旦 . 英国通史(第四卷)——转型时期:18 世纪的英国[M]. 南京:江苏人民出版社，2015 年 .
28. 孟华主编 . 比较文学形象学[M]. 北京:北京大学出版社，2002 年 .
29. (清)朱琰 .《陶说》译注[M]. 傅振伦，译注 . 北京:轻工业出版社，1984 年 .
30. (清)曾衍东 . 小豆棚[M]. 济南:齐鲁书社，2004 年 .
31. (清)蓝浦 . 景德镇陶录[M]. 济南:山东画报出版社，2004 年 .
32. [英]彭妮·斯帕克 . 设计与文化导论[M]. 钱凤根等译，南京:译林出版社，2012 年.
33. [英]马克曼·埃利斯，理查德·库尔顿，马修·莫格 . 茶叶帝国:征服世界的亚洲树叶[M]. 高领亚，徐波，译 . 北京:中国友谊出版公司，2020:44.
34. [英]休·昂纳 . 中国风——遗失在西方 800 年的中国元素[M]. 刘爱英等，译 . 北京:北京大学出版社，2017 年 .
35. [英]威廉·乌克斯 . 茶叶全书[M]. 依佳，刘涛，姜海蒂，译 . 上海:东方出版社，2001 年 .
36. [英]罗伊·莫克塞姆 . 茶:嗜好、开拓与帝国[M]. 毕小青，译 . 北京:生活·读书·新知三联书店，2015:18.
37. [英]简·佩蒂格鲁 . 茶设计[M]. 邵立荣，译 . 济南:山东画报出版社，2013:20.
38. [英]雷蒙·道森 . 中国变色龙——对于欧洲中国文明观的分析[M]. 常绍民，明毅，译 . 北京:中华书局，2006 年 .
39. [英]福蒂 . 欲求之物:1750 年以来的设计与社会[M]. 苟娴煦，译 . 南京:译林出版社，2014 年 .
40. [英]艾伦·麦克法兰，等 . 绿色黄金:茶叶帝国[M]. 扈喜林，译 . 北京:社会科学文献出版社，2016 年 .
41. [英]埃德蒙·德瓦尔 . 白瓷之路[M]. 梁卿，苟娴煦，译 . 桂林:广西师范大学出版社，2017 年 .

42. [英]乔治·马戛尔尼，约翰·巴罗 . 马戛尔尼使团使华观感[M]. 何高济，何毓宁，译 . 北京:商务印书馆，2013 年 .
43. [英]马克辛·伯格 . 奢侈与逸乐:18 世纪英国的物质世界[M]. 孙超，译 . 北京:中国工人出版社，2019 年 .
44. [英]塔尼娅·M，布克瑞·珀斯 . 茶味英伦——视觉艺术中的饮茶文化与社会生活[M]. 张弛，等，译 . 北京:北京大学出版社，2021 年 .
45. [法]皮埃尔·布尔迪厄 . 区分:判断力的社会批判[M]. 刘晖，译 . 北京:商务印书馆，2015 年 .
46. [英]乔治·伦纳德·斯当东 . 英使谒见乾隆纪实[M]. 叶笃义，译 . 北京:群言出版社，2014 年 .
47. [英]乔治·马戛尔尼 .1793 年乾隆英使觐见记[M]. 刘半农，译 . 天津:天津人民出版社，2006 年 .
48. [英]约翰·巴罗 . 我看乾隆盛世[M]. 李国庆，等，译 . 北京:北京图书馆出版社，2007 年 .
49. [英]查尔斯·兰姆 . 伊利亚随笔[M]. 刘炳善，译 . 北京:生活·读书·新知三联书店，1987 年 .
50. [英]菲利帕·梅里曼 . 银子:一部生活史[M]. 安静，译 . 北京:北京大学出版社，2016 年 .
51. [美]马士 . 东印度公司对华贸易编年史[M]. 区宗华，译 . 林树惠，校 . 广州:中山大学出版社，1991 年 .
52. [美]彭慕兰 . 大分流:欧洲、中国及现代世界经济的发展[M]. 史建云，译 . 南京:江苏人民出版社，2004 年 .
53. [美]菲利普·查德威克·福斯特·史密斯 . 中国皇后号[M]. 广州日报国际新闻部法律室，译 . 广州:广州出版社，2007 年 .
54. [美]汤姆·斯丹迪奇 . 上帝之饮——六个瓶子里的历史[M]. 吴平，等，译 . 北京: 中信出版社，2017 年 .
55. [美]爱德华·W. 萨义德 . 东方学[M]. 王宇根，译 . 北京:生活·读书·新知三联书店，1999 年 .
56. [美]罗伯特·芬雷 . 青花瓷的故事[M]. 郑明萱，译 . 海口:海南出版社，2015 年 .
57. [德]雷德侯 . 万物——中国艺术中的模件化和规模化生产[M]. 张总，译 . 北京:生活·读书·新知三联书店，2012 年 .
58. [德]利奇温 .18 世纪中国与欧洲文化的接触[M]. 朱杰勤，译 . 北京:商务印刷馆，1962 年 .
59. [法]杜赫德编 . 耶稣会士中国书简集·中国回忆录第二卷[M]. 郑德弟，朱静，等，译 . 郑州:大象出版社，2001 年 .
60. [法]费尔南·布罗代尔 .15 至 18 世纪的物质文明、经济和资本主义[M]. 顾良，施康强，译 . 北京:生活·读书·新知三联出版社，1996 年 .
61. [法]帕特里斯·万福莱 . 销往欧洲的宜兴茶壶[M]. 施云乔，译 . 杭州:西泠印社出版社，2015 年 .
62. [西班牙]门多萨 . 中华大帝国史[M]. 何高济，译 . 北京:中华书局，1998 年 .

63. [意]利玛窦，金尼阁．利玛窦中国札记[M]. 何高济，等，译．北京:中华书局，1983 年．
64. [日]浅田实．东印度公司:巨额商业资本之兴衰[M]. 顾姗姗，译．北京:社会科学文献出版社，2016.
65. [日]矶渊猛．一杯红茶的世界史[M]. 朝颜，译. 上海:东方出版社，2014:11.
66. [美]凡勃伦．有闲阶级论[M]. 蔡受百，译．北京:商务印书馆，1914.

2. Thesis

67. 秦刚．欧洲青花柳树对纹样与中国外销瓷[J]. 文艺研究，2011 年(4).
68. 李竹雨 .18 至 19 世纪欧洲茶叶盒略谈[J]. 农业考古，2018 年(2).
69. 李金明 ．明清时期中国陶瓷文化在世界的传播与影响[J]. 中国社会经济史研究，1999 年(2).
70. 吴冠中 ．现代消费社会的起源——17、18 世纪英国消费问题研究[D]. 南京：南京大学，2014.
71. 牟晓琳 ． 海外需求对明清景德镇瓷器的影响[D]. 北京:中国艺术研究院，2014.
72. 刘章才 .18 世纪中英茶贸易及对英国社会的影响[D]. 北京:首都师范大学，2008.
73. 侯铁军 ．他者之物与自我之物——18 世纪英国文学中的瓷器研究[D]. 武汉:武汉大学，2015 年．
74. 黄圣芝．广彩外销瓷研究[D]. 中国台北:台北艺术大学，2012.
75. 赖芊晔．从中国外销瓷看英格兰贵族的消费文化(1688—1730)[D]. 中国台北:台湾政治大学，2012.
76. 杨静萍 .17—18 世纪中国茶在英国[D]. 杭州:浙江师范大学，2006:45.
77. 张应龙．中国茶叶外销史研究[D]，广州:广东暨南大学，1994.
78. 刘丽娴，等．韦奇伍德的设计管理思想与商业实践[J]. 装饰，2020(1).
79. 陶德臣 ．印度茶业的崛起及对中国茶业的影响与打击——19 世纪末至 20 世纪上半叶[J]. 中国农史，2007(1).
80. 马丽云 ．异域风尚与本土——从“玩偶之家”思考英国乡村庄园里的中国风[J]. 美术观察，2020 年(1).
81. 汪敬虞 ． 中国近代茶叶的对外贸易和茶业的现代化问题[J]. 近代史研究，1987年(6).
82. 李砚祖．设计的文化身份[J]. 南京艺术学院学报，2007 年(3).
83. 江凌 ．清代景德镇纹章瓷装饰工序产地转移与社会变迁的关系[J]. 中国陶瓷，2010年(5).
84. [比利时]钟鸣旦．文化相遇的方法论:以 17 世纪中欧文化相遇为例[J]. 刘贤译，清史研究，2006 年(4).
85. [美] Shirley Maloney Mueller. 想象与多元:17 世纪中国的茶壶贸易[J]. 王倩，译．美成在久，2016(4):58–61.

3. References in English

86. Gladys Scott Thomson. Life in a Noble Household 1641–1770. Ann Arbor: University of Michigan Press, 1959:168–170.
87. Rose Kerr, Luisa Mengoni. Chinese Export Ceramics. London: Victoria & Albert Museum, 2011:39.
88. Ian Woodward. Understanding Material Culture. Sage Publishing Ltd., 2007.
89. Margaret Jourdain, R.Soame Jenyns. Chinese Export Art in the Eighteenth Century. New York:Charles Scribner's Sons, 1950.
90. Lornia Weatherill. Consumer Behaviour and Material Culture in Britain, 1660–1760, Routledge, 1996.
91. Stephen H.Twining. Twinings, Two Hundred and Fifty Years of Tea and Coffee, R.Twining & Co.LTD, 1956.
92. Claire Walsh. Shop Design and the Display of Goods in Eighteenth-Century London, Journal of Design History. Vol 8, 1995.
93. Stobart Hann. Site of Consumption: the display of goods in provincial shops in eighteenth century England, in Cultural and Social History, 2005.
94. Beatric Hohenegger. The Story of Tea From the West to East, ST. Martin's Press, New York, 2006.
95. Neil McKendrick, John Brewer, J.H.Plumb. The Birth of a Consumer Society. The Commercialization of Eighteen-century England. Cambridge: Cambridge University Press, 2009.
96. William Harrison. Description of Elizabethan England 1577, Whitefish: Kessinger Publishing, 2004.
97. Samuel Pepys. Diary of Samuel, 2:88, (April 24, 1661), Berkeley: University of California Press, 1970.
98. Jane Pettigrew. A Social History of Tea. London: National Trust. 2001.
99. Woodruff D. Smith. Consumption and the Making of Respectability, 1600–1800, Routledge, 2002.
100. John Goldsmith Phillips. China-Trade Porcelain, Harvard: Harvard University Press, 1956.
101. S. Wells Williams. A Chinese Commercial Guide. 4th ed. Canton. The Office of the Chinese Repository, 1856.
102. David Howard, John Ayers. Masterpieces of Chinese Export Porcelain form the Mottahedeh Collection in the Virginia Museum, Sotheby Parke Bernet, 1981.
103. Rose Kerr, Nigel Wood. Ceramic Technology. Science and Civilization in China. Ed. Joseph Needham. Cambridge University Press, 2004.
104. Alan Macfarlane, Iris Macfarlane. The Empire of Tea: The Remarkable History of Plant Took Over The World, New York: Over Look Press, 2004.
105. Anthony Farrington, Tradiny Places. The East India Company and Asia 1600–1834, London: The British Library, 2002.

106. William Henry Hall. The New Royal Encyclopaedia 3 vols, London, 1788.
107. Reka Fisher. English Tea Caddy, Bulletin (St. Louis Art Museum), Vol.15, No.2 (April–June 1979).
108. Recent Accessions. The Metropolitan Museum of Art Bulletin, Vol.11, No.9, May 1953.
109. A. Hepplewhite and Co.,Cabinet-Makers. The Cabinet-Maker and Upholsterer's Guide, Published By I.and J. Taylor, London the Architecture Library.
110. Hepplewhite and Co. The Cabinet-Maker and Upholsterer's Guide T.Sheraton, The Cabinet-Maker and Upholsterer's Drawing-Book, London: T, Bensley, 3rd edition, (1802).
111. Thomas Chippendale. The Gentleman and Cabinet-Maker's Director, London: T.Osborne, 1754.
112. P. Thornton, Authentic Decor. The Domestic Interior 1620–1920, Weidenfeld & Nicolson, 2000.
113. Jeffrey Meikle. Twentieth Century Limited, Philadelphia, 1979.
114. Roger Lonsdale, ed. The New Oxford Book of Eighteenth-Century Verse, Oxford: Oxford University Press, 2009.
115. George Leonard Staunton. An Authentic Account of an Embassy from the King of Great Britain to the Emperor of China, vol.2, London: Printed by W. Bulmer and Co., 1797.
116. John Barrow. Some Account of the Public Life and a Selection from the Unpublished Writings of the Earls of MaCartney, vol. 2, London, Printed for T. Cadell and W. Paries in the Strand, 1807.
117. Ulrike Hillemann. Asian Empire and British Knowledge: China and the Networks of British Imperial Expansion, New York: Palgrave Macmillan, 2009.
118. Leigh Hunt. The Seer:Or, Common-place Refreshed. London:Edward Moxon, 1840 Robert Southey. Letter from England, by Don Manuel Alvaraez Espriella. 1 vols. New York: Published by David Longworth, 1808.
119. J. J. Clark. Oriental Enlightment. The Encounter Between Eastern and Western Thought. Routledge, 1997.
120. Richardson. Pemela or Virtue Rewarded. New York and London: W. W. Norton & Company. 1958.

Index

C. Zhang, *Beyond the Teacup: 18th Century Sino-British Tea Trade and Design Cultural Exchange*,
https://doi.org/10.1007/978-981-97-7691-7

GPSR Compliance

The European Union's (EU) General Product Safety Regulation (GPSR) is a set of rules that requires consumer products to be safe and our obligations to ensure this.

If you have any concerns about our products, you can contact us on ProductSafety@springernature.com

In case Publisher is established outside the EU, the EU authorized representative is:

Springer Nature Customer Service Center GmbH
Europaplatz 3
69115 Heidelberg, Germany

Batch number: 10725851

Printed by Printforce, the Netherlands